Swimming Upstream

Swimming Upstream

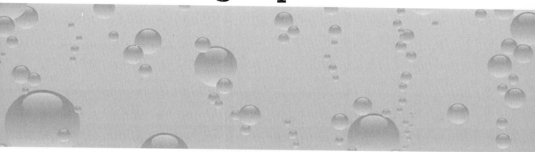

A Lifesaving Guide to Short Film Distribution

Sharon Badal

ELSEVIER

AMSTERDAM • BOSTON • HEIDELBERG • LONDON
NEW YORK • OXFORD • PARIS • SAN DIEGO
SAN FRANCISCO • SINGAPORE • SYDNEY • TOKYO
Focal Press is an imprint of Elsevier

Publisher: Elinor Actipis
Publishing Services Manager: George Morrison
Senior Project Manager: Dawnmarie Simpson
Assistant Editor: Robin Weston
Marketing Manager: Marcel Koppes, Becky Pease
Cover Design: Dennis Schaefer
Interior Design: Joanne Blank

Focal Press is an imprint of Elsevier
30 Corporate Drive, Suite 400, Burlington, MA 01803, USA
Linacre House, Jordan Hill, Oxford OX2 8DP, UK

Recognizing the importance of preserving what has been written, Elsevier prints
its books on acid-free paper whenever possible.

Library of Congress Cataloging-in-Publication Data
Swimming upstream: a lifesaving guide to short film distribution/
[edited by] Sharon Badal.
    p. cm.
Includes index.
ISBN-13: 978-0-240-80955-7 (pbk.: alk. paper)
    1. Motion pictures—Marketing.   2. Motion pictures—Distribution.
    3. Short films.   I. Badal, Sharon.
PN1995.9.M29S95 2008
384'.80688—dc22

                                                                  2007032517

British Library Cataloguing-in-Publication Data
A catalogue record for this book is available from the British Library.

ISBN: 978-0-240-80955-7

For information on all Focal Press publications
visit our website at www.books.elsevier.com

08 09 10 11   5 4 3 2 1

Printed in the United States of America

Working together to grow libraries in developing countries

www.elsevier.com | www.bookaid.org | www.sabre.org

ELSEVIER   **BOOK AID International**   **Sabre Foundation**

Contents

For My "Sweet Pea" Noelle Capri —
You are the brightest star in my night sky

Acknowledgments

First and foremost, this book would not exist without the participation of this amazing group of 47 essay contributors and interview subjects. I am extraordinarily grateful to each of you for trusting in me and the idea behind this book. Thank you so much for sharing your experience and advice.

Thank you to Elinor Actipis, Cara Anderson, and everyone at Focal Press. You championed my rather untraditional approach every step of the way. Thanks for fighting the good fight.

Thank you to Peggy Gormley, David Irving, Cathrine Kellison, Jack Lechner, Roz Lichter, Jon Patricof, Paula Silver, and Jason Squire for your advice, encouragement, and feedback.

Thank you to Sargina Tamimi Silvani and Dennis Ivan for the initial book cover concepts that sparked my imagination and to Tom Drysdale for one of the only photos ever taken of me that I actually like.

Thank you to everyone at Tribeca, especially,

Bob, Jane, and Craig—That very first festival will always hold a special place in my heart.

Peter, Nancy, and David—Thank you for the opportunity of a lifetime.

Maggie—You are the perfect programming partner and a great friend.

Thank you to my NYU colleagues and my students. You inspire me.

Thank you to my friends at the Leary Firefighters Foundation for keeping me "off the streets" between festivals and including me in a cause that means so much to me.

Thank you to all my dear friends, especially Barbara, Brian & Carol, Donna, Grela, Karen, Kathy, Stacey, Teddy, and Wayne. Thanks for sitting next to me on the roller coaster of life, screaming and laughing all the way.

Most of all, thank you to my family—my Mom, Aunt Jeanne, and Greg for supporting all of my crazy dreams, no matter what, and my Dad and my sister Linda, who I am certain have been cheering me on from above. And to my niece Noelle Capri, this book is for you.

Finally, to all those people too numerous to mention who have crossed my path, leaving their fingerprints on my heart and words of wisdom in my soul—I thank you.

Preface

When I was 14 years old my father opened a small movie theater in suburban New Jersey. It was the land of McDonald's and Dairy Queens. My mom sold the tickets, some neighborhood boys were the doormen, and I was the usher/candy counter girl. As I leaned against the wall in the theater auditorium, eating one too many bags of Peanut M&Ms and watching the stories unfold on the big screen, I confess: I got hooked.

There was no question in my mind that I wanted to work "in the movies." And so I did. From theatrical distribution to live events to film festivals to teaching, I have gleefully embraced this wonderful energy vortex. I have cried when some projects ended, and cried during some projects when they seemed to go on forever. Perhaps the biggest lesson I've learned is that every aspect of the film industry is collaborative. It is no surprise, then, that this book is truly a collaborative effort. It is not simply my voice, but many voices, and together my contributors and I have created something that I hope you will find unique.

Both of my jobs have helped to inspire this book. As a member of the faculty of New York University, Tisch School of the Arts, Kanbar Institute of Film and Television, I have the privilege of nurturing hopeful student filmmakers and helping them find their path in this crazy industry. As a programmer of the Tribeca Film Festival, I spend months each year swimming through a tidal wave of short film submissions, looking for great stories, great characters, and new talent. I know that by selecting their films I can help these filmmakers launch their careers, and I take that responsibility very seriously.

I have watched technology change, from heavy ¾-inch tapes that I could use as a doorstop to 100 DVDs that I can now carry home in my bag. In part, it is the new technology that makes this book possible. The accessibility of technology has given birth to a new breed of beginning filmmaker. Suddenly it seems as if everyone is making a short film, and I couldn't be more thrilled.

When people asked me during this process what it was like writing a book, my response has been that it seemed a bit surreal. As the vision became a reality, and all these incredible professionals agreed to be part of my "book family," the book seemed to take on a life of its own, just like every film does. I hold my breath now as I gently push my baby out of the nest, hoping it will fly, or, in this case, swim.

It has been a wonderful experience writing this book, and I loved *almost* every minute of it. Now, so many years and a lifetime later from those nights in my father's movie theater, I realize that deep inside I am still that 14-year-old girl enamored with "the movies."

Love what you do. The rest will take care of itself, eventually.

Introduction

Nearly every motivational book by business leaders, cultural visionaries, and other pundits stresses that to be successful you have to have to take a risk and let go of your fear. That's much easier in theory, and much more difficult in the "real world," if such a place even exists. Whenever you create something, there is some element of fear. Fear of rejection. Fear of criticism. Fear of failure. Filmmaking in particular is prone to the manifestations of these fears because it is such a personal and visually vulnerable endeavor.

A filmmaker spends an enormous amount of time and energy creating a short film. For many, it is their first foray into the industry. For others, it is the end product of educational training, be it in a traditional film school environment or in an intensive workshop or course. For still others, it's a way of simply trying to tell a story, period. Regardless of their starting point, thousands of filmmakers complete short films each year and then sit stymied, wondering what to do next. If you are reading this, then perhaps you made a film and you are, indeed, sitting stymied; or you're thinking about it and want to read everything you can before you begin. Once you understand the short film distribution environment, you will not only be aware of the available options, but you will also have a much better idea of where your project fits in. A little knowledge is not a dangerous thing. It helps you to be fearless.

The approach of *Swimming Upstream* is to cover the terrain of short film distribution using a combination of conversations and guest essays and to employ a workbook methodology to help the filmmaker with his/her own projects.

The book begins with an overview of theatrical film distribution by professionals actively working in that part of the industry. The book then covers buyers, exploring all options, thinking globally, the Internet and new technology, and film festivals. The chapter called *How I Learned to Swim* contains survival stories from the filmmakers themselves. In this industry particularly, if you ask 10 people the same question, you might get 10 different answers. You might get a consensus. That's why this book is not simply one person's opinion. It's your job to take all this information, accept some, reject some, and in the end, come to your own conclusion. Each of the contributors has valuable information to share. What you take away from it is up to you.

That's why the final chapter in the book contains a workbook with a series of exercises to help you analyze your film and strategize festivals and distribution. It gives you the opportunity to digest what has come before and apply that information specifically to your film ideas. By the end of the book you should be asking yourself questions about your own ideas and answering them honestly. Don't worry, no one can hear you. This book will prompt you to look at your project wearing a different pair of glasses. These glasses won't always be rose-colored, but they should give you 20/20 vision regarding your short film.

One thing I know for sure is that no matter how much advice you give to filmmakers, they are probably going to make their film anyway. No matter what. That's the nature of the beast. Writers, painters, and filmmakers are all artists, rooted by that creative spark and the passion that must accompany it. There are many books on the production of the short film, so my perspective is that you've already read those other books and you may have made your short film, anyway. Your way.

It is my hope that this book will help you to understand how to get that short film out into the world and that it will be both inspiring and informative.

Filmmakers have unbelievable tenacity, even when the odds are stacked against them. That's why I called it *Swimming Upstream*. Consider this book your floatation device.

So go ahead, swim.

Testing the Waters:
The Indie Landscape

What does "independent" mean?

Regardless of its context, be it politically or culturally based, the word "independent" almost automatically bestows a badge of courage upon whomever it is being ascribed to. Its connotations are positive, its attributes admirable. To be "independent" means to be beholden to no one. To be "independent" means one has the strength and fortitude to stand up against the tidal wave of tyranny, the winds of oppression. To be "independent" means you are free. In fact, the oft-used phrase "fiercely independent" furthers the nearly superhuman characteristics and emotional ability to stand firm.

So what does being an "independent" filmmaker mean?

For some it means not being part of the studio system and being able to maintain the integrity of a project without someone else's thumb in the creative pie. Keep dreaming, my brave filmmaker friends, and take off the superhero cape for just a moment.

It's pretty lonely on that self-imposed pedestal, and no one works alone in this business, not if you want your work to be seen by others, that is. There are so many "independent" producer/director/ writer/editors that it seems at times as if the filmmaking world is composed entirely of one-person bands. That's great, really, that you have such a finger on the pulse of your project that you are the only person in the universe who can bring your vision to fruition. But (and it's a big "but") what happens when you're done with that film? After you pat yourself on the back and receive bouquets of praise from friends and family, don't you, deep down inside (c'mon, admit it), want your film to reach an audience?

In order for your film to do that, you have to understand what's happening in the industry and where "independent filmmaking" sits in the grand scheme of the distribution universe.

Distribution is getting the film into the theaters and marketing is getting the bodies into the seats. Now, however, those "theaters" and "seats" go well beyond the multiplex. Films reach their audience through a variety of different portals, be it the traditional movie theater, television, or newer electronic media such as the Internet, iPod, or cell phone. Projects segue seamlessly from one distribution platform to another, sometimes simultaneously. Distribution has changed, but the core philosophy remains the same. How do we make that film available to an audience and how do we attract the audience to it?

In the heyday of Hollywood, studios were firmly identified by the use of the company logo (perhaps the original form of branding), whether it was the sky-sweeping klieg lights of Twentieth Century Fox or the lion's roar of MGM. The phrase "The Dream Factory" was aptly coined to describe not only the escapism of the films itself, but the constant output of features by the studios, swept into grand movie palaces like the Fox Atlanta or the Roxy, where thousands of people sat in rapt attention as the stories unfolded on the screen.

In the fifties life in America changed and so did the movies. A combination of the exodus to suburbia, the popularity of the automobile, and the advent of television caused the movie palaces for the most part to become obsolete. This new lifestyle led to the emergence of the drive-in as well as eventually to the twin cinema, the birth mother of today's megaplex. Theatrical distribution in the fifties and sixties found it difficult to maintain a constant moviegoing population with the novelty and increasing appeal of television, and it was a tough period for the industry.

And on the seventh day, God created the videocassette player. As people became more accustomed to watching film in the comfort of their living room, studios focused on large-scale blockbuster-type films to lure them off their couches. Consequently, it appears as if now nearly every film is geared to the 18–24 demographic, and that's because this group wants to leave the house and "go to the movies." For the older demographics, it's much easier to say "let's watch a movie," rather than "let's go to the movies."

Most recently, the traditional theatrical distribution model has been pummeled with the knockout combination punch of digital technology, advances in home theater systems, and rising theatrical admission prices. Many would say this foretells the death knell for the traditional distribution model where a film moves through the pipeline from theatrical to non-theatrical to home video to broadcast distribution, with each revenue stream being fairly exhausted before the film reaches its final resting place on television. What used to be a large "window" between theatrical and home video has been slammed shut. The pipeline is no longer a straight one, but a combination of platforms that can be made available to the viewer when, and how, that viewer wants to watch the product.

We have the Internet and mobile technology, and an entire generation of young people who spend more time on the computer or with their iPods than they do in front of a television. Regardless of the alphabet letter this generation is assigned (and perhaps it should be "Generation W" for "web"), they experience entertainment without regard to viewing environment or screen size. They want their entertainment to be immediate and accessible.

There are a lot of branches of the entertainment industry in tears. The music industry is crying because CDs are becoming obsolete.

The film industry is sobbing because it is more difficult for a feature film to find its audience. The television industry is weeping because TiVo and digital video recorders have meant they have to rethink the whole advertising model. When the major television networks provide episodes of their most popular series in full for viewing on their web sites, clearly things have changed.

These changes directly affect how and where films are distributed, especially films that we consider "independent." If we agree that the primary characteristics of an "independent film" are that the film was produced and financed outside of the studio system, has a relatively low budget in comparison to the Hollywood product, and, in most cases, is of a specialized nature, then we have to look at distribution in a new way.

Even with all these changes one thing has remained constant: independent filmmakers continue to raise the money, make their films, and seek a distributor. "Indie" film has gone through its own roller coaster ride of sorts, rising and falling in popularity as the cultural zeitgeist changes. Each calendar year seems to bring forth one or two breakout independent films, such as *Napoleon Dynamite* or *Little Miss Sunshine*. Films like these have bucked the odds, finding both a distributor and an audience, and become widely popular and successful. Technology has fostered the ease with which independent filmmakers can create their projects, be it in less expensive shooting formats or the ability to edit on the computer, but the challenge still lies in finding a distributor willing to take on the risk of releasing the film.

Even though large umbrella corporations represent many smaller entertainment companies that cross media platforms and appeal to different audiences, independent film is still difficult to market in the theatrical realm; in fact, it has become even more difficult to obtain distribution. Independent film does not inherently appeal to a large audience immediately. These films must be nurtured carefully to theatrical fruition, and the marketing and distribution plans are critical to the film's ultimate success. Even with a stellar strategy, many independent films will never exceed their initial specialized audience appeal.

Many filmmakers of short films aspire to make a feature one day. Short film is a good way to test the waters with your talent and your ability, and it's important to understand what you're up against before you begin the journey.

This book therefore begins with essays and interviews about the current film distribution environment by the people who are the decision makers. This industry overview from some very prominent professionals will help you to understand the distribution landscape as you embark on your filmmaking journey.

JACK FOLEY is President of Distribution for Focus Features and has shepherded the distribution of many critically acclaimed and successful films there, including *Eternal Sunshine of the Spotless Mind, 21 Grams, Lost in Translation, Motorcycle Diaries,* and *Brokeback Mountain.* He began with October Films and worked through the USA Films and Focus transitional periods in which he handled films such as *Topsy-Turvy, Being John Malkovich,* and *Traffic.*

Mr. Foley has had a lengthy and illustrious career in theatrical distribution, starting out in 1975 with Columbia Pictures in Sales, in which he worked for ten years in that company's Boston, Des Moines, Kansas City, and Dallas branch offices and then segued to DEG Entertainment in Southern Sales.

He was President of Distribution for MGM from 1987 to 1993, during which his releases included *A Fish Called Wanda, Moonstruck, Rainman,* and *Thelma and Louise.*

From 1994 to 1996 he was President of Distribution for Miramax, during what many consider to be one of the peak periods for that studio, and as such he distributed *Pulp Fiction, Il Postino, The Crow, Emma, Trainspotting, The English Patient,* and *Scream.*

He also worked in exhibition as Film Buyer for City Cinemas for several years.

Mr. Foley works in New York City and lives in New Jersey, happily in both cases!

Gore, Penguins, and the Cultural Zeitgeist of Distribution

By Jack Foley

I've worked in theatrical distribution for 30 years. My career has been spent making critical decisions that impact a film's life always in distribution. Over these years, the distribution business has radically changed. The business has grown more competitive and expensive. The decisions that you have to make regarding how to position a film's opening, from release to release pattern, every weekend has become increasingly difficult, sometimes seemingly impossible. Today, there is a glut of product competing for the same dollar. The glut imposes severe demands on studio heads to carefully scrutinize the competition: minimize competition for exactly the same demographic target; evaluate the competition each weekend, prior to and thereafter, gauging how long the target demo will sustain its attention for a film. The opening weekend box office is absolutely the essence to a film's success in the long run. Distribution plays a huge role in contributing to that success from opening throughout its life. It's not an easy job since so many people, and the time they gave of their lives to their films, rely upon distribution.

The truth about grosses

Opening weekend is a big view into the ultimate box office life of a film. You can usually judge the ultimate gross by the opening weekend by using 2½–3 times multiple: a $30 million weekend indicates a $90 million dollar ultimate box office. Evaluating the ultimate box office result relative to the normal trend is insightful. The ultimate box office trend a film develops speaks about its breadth of appeal or lack thereof. The deviation from the normal weekend trend, or any of the many industry grossing trends, demands understanding since it reveals specific demographic results that arose beyond the normal. The trend could be anomalous or indicative of a new commercial development in the business. That information could come be useful when distributing similar films in the future. God is in trends and God is nuanced.

God lives in popular culture. Gross trends manifest cultural consciousness in the marketplace, generally and specifically. Trends define consumer desire and values. The greater the gross a film generates, the greater the measure of value popular culture reflects for a film or genre. Commercial and high-end/art filmmakers should live by that creed. Hollywood thrives on this format of filmmaking: give them what they want. Art films do too: Jane Austen is a product. Money measures cultural value for a movie; it is not, however, a measure of art.

Clearly, today, comedies are king in value to popular culture. The most successful films in the market recently are comedy. America wants or needs to laugh. Many of these comedies are wholesome and are particularly targeted at the family. Family films, which are generally comedies, are live-action or animated and the type of movie that plays to all ages without segmentation. They are the most expensive films for families to patronize; yet families patronize them copiously. Ticket purchases for the whole family are expensive. Concessions purchases aggravate the cost for a family. I will leave out transportation, parking, or any other costs. Yet, families are undaunted by these costs, apparently regardless of income, since these films perform consistently well nationally. Consider the events *Pirates of the Caribbean, Harry*

Potter, or any of the animated blockbusters, like *Shrek.* The penguin world of *Happy Feet* with over $200 million at the box office reflects America's love affair with penguins: they certainly marched with happy feet to the box office again for these creatures.

Family films reveal that family values are critical to popular culture, they are popular culture. Every studio realizes they have to be in the family business now, that they have to exploit this cultural gold mine while it is hot. Every studio, beyond Disney's branded hold on family entertainment, knows there is too much money at stake, too much to lose by neglecting these values. Now recognize that the weekend gross is not an announcement about success alone, but is also heralding the measures of society's cultural values.

Jane Austen, the queen of the art film story, reflects the cultural values society has in a limited way for high-end movies. *Pride and Prejudice,* popularized by Kiera Knightley's starring role, found success in smart upper income and middle income theaters throughout the nation when it was released. It actually played beyond the art circuit level due to the commercial appeal Ms. Knightley brought to the film. It is one of the biggest grossing period films in history at $30+ million U.S. box office. Americans love Jane Austen. Her stories, told and retold, grow bigger in value with each new version in popular culture.

Brokeback Mountain defied industry wisdom by grossing $83 million U.S. It also defied the idea that Red states and Blue states are separate and do not share the same values. The massive success of *Brokeback Mountain* denied thoughtless, if not arrogant, industry wisdom as it deviated from expected trend results among industry watchers. *Brokeback Mountain,* a so-called gay cowboy movie when it opened, clearly demonstrated that America thinks for itself, beyond the rhetoric of pundits. The nation embraced the film, a great film, and went to see it throughout the country, Red, Blue, all 50 states. *Brokeback* denied the thought that the conservative right has a hold on the minds, hearts, and moral values of the nation. The film's success, its deviation from jeremiadic trendsetters, reveals the importance of understanding why trends and departures from them are important. An honest distributor must interpret the language of grosses, recognize what the trends say about cultural values, and proceed with his plans for each release strategy, film by film.

Movies as business

Theatrical distribution persists as the engine for the entire movie business from the beginning to the end point of all the ancillary markets. A theatrical release is the consummation of the marketing campaign.

A theatrical release brings down to the ground the message that's been put out on the airwaves via television, radio, even newspapers. Seeing a movie in a theater is the final marketing experience for a film, leaving the viewer with the power of their message, which they broadcast, by word-of-mouth to others. Word-of-mouth is critically powerful in its ability to validate or destroy a film's importance in popular culture by declaring the viewer's satisfaction based on artistic merit. The will may be in the nation to see a movie, but the experience has to be satisfying. The most blessed phrase arising from word-of-mouth is: you have got to see this movie. That phrase consummates a great release strategy. Word-of-mouth can create a powerful historical moment for a movie that will embed it in current popular culture and perhaps enable it to endure for future years: *Blazing Saddles, Back to the Future, The Godfather*, or even *Casablanca, The Wizard of Oz*, or *Gone with the Wind*. Obviously, word-of-mouth influences not only the theatrical window but also the DVD sales and all other aftermarkets.

There are two kinds of movies. There's the movie that comes crashing in and imposes itself on you like ready-made culture. Examples of ready-made culture are movies like *Spiderman, Pirates of the Caribbean* or *Lord of the Rings*. The juggernauts create, nurture and sustain their own popular cultural value to society. These films are embraced by everyone and must be distributed everywhere, accompanied with massive marketing campaigns. They are scorched earth campaign movies: they appear satisfactorily at theaters everywhere for everyone of the entire desiring public to see and they leave no money behind in the 6–10 weeks they might possess the marketplace. Big movies are supposed to consume the public's attention, that's the idea. The process of these commercial event releases leaves behind deeply imbedded values and long term identification with these stories, which become part of our national myths and deeper psychic culture. Hollywood films often create history and new deeper attributes of our national spiritual culture. These capabilities should always be in the mind of distributors. Distributors should be sensitive to the potential and actual zeitgeists: *Ghostbusters, Risky Business, Pulp Fiction, My Big Fat Greek Wedding*, and *Borat*.

The other kind of movie, the art film or smart film, like *Brokeback Mountain*, is a more challenging kind of film to release. It demands a process that is more grass-roots positioning, a specifically detailed theatrical strategy that all converges to literally create a popular cultural impact. As opposed to dropping huge advertising dollars, art film distributors have to be budget sensitive and spend in ways that tend to be out of the box. In fact, distributing art films is best done originally and out of the box.

Brokeback Mountain was first a great movie, and that was critical to its success. As a result of the viewers' experience of the film, *Brokeback* broke all the bounds that first constricted it as a "gay film." By accessing the broader market in a calculated release strategy that successfully moved the nation the film achieved a gross of $80+ million in the US and Canada. It did so because it was able to blow away the cultural restrictions that exist in our society.

The distribution and marketing processes worked to manage the development and growth of the awareness and respect for the film, which transformed it into a popular cultural event. Everybody was talking about it. First of all, it defied its image as a "gay cowboy movie" because it was more than a gay cowboy film. By bringing *Brokeback* down to the ground, putting it in specific theaters in markets from the start to gain it validity, market by market the first advocates urged the masses to see this film. That first important word-of-mouth validation grew the film as it entered into new markets accompanied by great anticipation from real voices on the ground, no longer from the media pundits. *Brokeback* was no longer a gay cowboy movie; it was *Brokeback Mountain*—an important movie depicting a tragic family condition and lost love.

Breaking down *Brokeback*'s cultural barriers through a distribution marketing strategy is an act of cultural infiltration. Hollywood films exploit massive budgets and conduct scorched earth campaigns: they buy their audience, hopefully. Art films and smart films win them by careful planning and through the advocacy of apostles who mandate: you have to see this film. That is the magic, precious phrase to an art film.

Growing taste

The last 10+ years have grown the art film niche radically. Now more than ever, more people are willing to see art/smart films, whether fictional narratives or documentaries. In effect, these niche companies have grown cinematic taste and receptivity among the commercial moviegoers who ordinarily would not have attended these kinds of movies. These companies have expanded high-end film culture. That is a remarkable accomplishment. It is essentially the result of a process of education through marketing and distribution strategic release successes. The turning point for this growth arose around 1995, where smart films began to break out into new levels of success. Two high-water films were *Pulp Fiction*, $107 million box office, and *The English*

Patient, $80 million box office. Other subsequent contributors to the growth phenomenon were *Shakespeare in Love, Traffic,* and *My Big Fat Greek Wedding*. Going to art films was becoming like sinning, once you have done it, you'll more willingly do it again! Commercial ticket buyers are a tough group and are still quite resistant to being ready patrons to smart films, but they will go. *Pan's Labyrinth* most recently proved that fact. The mandate for art/smart film distributors is to continue momentum that dynamically captures the imagination of our society, to subvert old ways of thinking about movies and create inviting successes with their films in theaters that sustain the commercial world's interests. By expanding popular culture's sensibilities, these companies expand their commercial potential. These art films are businesses essentially, no one can afford to run museums and maintain elitist supercilious notions that any movie is too good for all but a few. That attitude will put anyone out of business. Growing culture is better than shrinking it.

Due to the successes of the art market, there is a greater capability and a will to finance and make smart movies, more than ever before. Every major studio has a specialized division and is also promoting new talent found in the specialized films into bigger projects with big budgets. This is a healthy growth process where new, creative, and imaginatively original blood is gaining access to Hollywood. The art film condition is improving movies for everyone. Everyone gains.

Blurring the lines
Blurring the lines between art and elitism and commercial patronage, or growing culture, has always been a goal of mine. Ten or 12 years ago, and prior to that, art films had to open with Landmark Theaters (premiere art house chain) and the venerable Lincoln Plaza, New York, in order to launch an art film successfully. One religiously began opening a film in NY and/or then LA. Then the process of release would continue. The art niche acted hegemonically in the market by validating a film and perhaps but rarely creating the possibility for commercial breakout. Commercial houses were taboo theaters to exploit since popular culture's perception of them seemed to deny their entry into the rarified art world. Art films were elite and remained cloistered to a specific group of highly educated, moneyed, and fairly urbane people who lived in certain places throughout the country. Pushing an art film beyond this core was difficult and generally considered not possible due to Hollywood's conditioning of the masses' taste for film. Therefore, an art film was niched to a small group along with its gross possibilities. This model did not satisfy me. Art film needed to be

seen by more people. The behavioral model had to be modified. More money had to be made by developing a greater smart movie culture. The only way to adjust the consciousness was to introduce certain houses that would appeal to the smart set and also attract a curious viewer who would attribute a theater's programming as validation for the film. Therefore, an art film had the possibility of being perceived as more commercial. The introduction of new people to smart movies could change habits of perception, mind, and action. The art market needed to be shaken up, the line blurred.

Topsy-Turvy, a very arty Mike Leigh film about Gilbert and Sullivan, opened the Paris Cinema exclusively in New York City. That theatrical setting was the perfect market milieu for this film, the diamond in the perfect theatrical setting. The Paris speaks to a devoted urbane, validating word-of-mouth by the New York art film patron. The Paris is the theatrical equivalent culturally as the Lincoln Center for Opera, Carnegie Hall for concert, the most elite validating, risk-mitigating theater in the country: a perfect environment for *Topsy*. *Topsy-Turvy's* exclusive U.S. opening at the Paris was supremely successful and made a strong commercial impression on art film buyers across the country. Step 1 accomplished: this is a hardcore art film and they are buying tickets.

Step 2. Two weeks later *Topsy* opened in Loews Village 7, a very commercial mainstream theater in Greenwich Village. Some of my art film distribution peers questioned the decision to play the film there and offered advice: "It's the wrong theater. You should be in the Angelika (a NYC bastion for art film)." Playing the Angelika would have been conforming to the Pavlovian format of preaching to the choir and deliberately shunning commercial and cultural growth opportunities. I wanted *Topsy* to be perceived by the smart down-town set as the smart, more commercial movie that they should see and the Village 7 would send that message to them blurring the art–commercial lines nicely. The Village 7 outgrossed the Paris on its first weekend, much to the shock of the critics of the theater choice. The point: the theater selection opened the film's audience potential to the smart set, well beyond the elite art set. There were now two market segments buying tickets to *Topsy* and the film was grossing more than it would remaining strictly in the art niche. This art/smart hybrid approach was carried out throughout the rest of the release. It remains a practice in distribution, which I continue to pursue to broaden the smart film culture, break down barriers, and grow new patrons for upscale film. All of which increases the box office value for these movies and nurtures the growing popular cultural value for them.

TESTING THE WATERS: THE INDIE LANDSCAPE

The process

A good deal of thought and experience goes into my release planning process. I will read the script. I consider the story and characters and the tone and vision. I like to see the film a number of times in rough cut, mostly in front of people at research screenings. I take research screenings seriously, but selectively relative to the results in the scores versus the film's cultural capabilities as I see them. In other words, I do not always agree with the research, but it is good to know. I consider the audience a film will appeal to as I begin considering the release strategy:

Where does the core audience for this film live?

How old are they?

What sex are they?

How deeply appealing is this film to whoever those people are?

How many people make up the audience for this movie?

What is in this film that mitigates the risk in attracting the core audience?

How aggressive should the presence of the film be in markets and theaters?

How fast can you release this film?

How will the critics treat this film?

Will the audience like the film?

What will make the audience like the film?

What are the best markets and theaters to exploit the audience to gain word-of-mouth and when throughout the release process?

What date is best?

What film competes with this film in the market at that time?

What is the most exploitable strength of the film to use in the release process?

How valuable is that strength, a.k.a., actor, director, story/author, etc.?

Every time I distribute a film it is my intention to make this film commercially reliant upon a patronage that is greater than its core group of devotees. It's always a desire to break it out commercially, to make more money with it, to push cultural barriers if not break them down. For example, when I released the Jim Jarmusch film *Broken Flowers*, first I looked at all of his films specifically assessing each film's grosses by market and theater. I discovered most distributors modestly released his past films and perhaps randomly. I found, however, that a deliberately calculated release that attempted to create national momentum for his films (perhaps a reason that his past films grossed modestly) didn't matter: Jim Jarmusch films constantly performed half decently in certain smart markets like NY, LA, Chicago, Washington, Boston (the same thing with Pedro Almodovar). His people were going to see his movie no matter when you released it in their markets.

As I thought about the fact that my job was useless based on the they-will-come-no-matter-how-smart-or-stupid-you-are-as-a-distributor, I was struck with an epiphany. What if all of the best Jim Jarmusch markets opened altogether, something never done before: 18 markets, 30+ theaters? This idea represents results at opening that some distributors realized totally on some Jarmusch films after months in release. If you could depend upon the core Jarmusch patron showing up on the first weekend, then word-of-mouth would be strong throughout the nation arising out of those 18 markets. *Broken Flowers* would be exploiting its key strength: Jarmusch fans. They would push the box office and create momentum . . . and this idea is not even considering what Bill Murray fans would do to the grosses. This plan created an art film event and the film opened to one of the biggest results for that number of theaters in history. Furthermore, *Broken Flowers* went on to gross more than the total gross of all of Jim Jarmusch's previous films. Clearly, word-of-mouth was good, the business momentum sustained through the late summer, the hungry smart marketplace totally exploited the film, core fans enjoyed the movie in nearly 400 theaters: the plan worked.

The big picture and the big screen

Another telling change in the marketplace worth noting about our popular culture is how slasher/horror films have become consistent, big business in the last 5 years. Violence has replaced sex as a pleasure for popular culture. The *Saw* franchise, with all its aggressive daring marketing, absolutely confirms the trend. Joining that trend is, also, *Texas Chainsaw* returning successfully, a lighter horror franchise *The Grudge*, among others. People love gore and pain, they are stimulated by it. That is what the grosses on these franchises and films measure. They are very lucrative franchises and they defy the general opinion of conservatism of our times. When hard R-rated violent, gore-filled movies gross $70M, $80M, $90M, $100M, society is being told mass culture is embracing these films regardless of what the rhetorical jeremiads from churches to Congress might say. They are all ill informed or simply disingenuous about recognizing the real values of popular culture. Added to these financial results is that women are attending horror/slasher films as much as men. Perhaps these films fulfill the public's need for stimulation that excites them out of ennui. Whatever the reason, these films are filling an aggressive need in the culture for satisfying entertainment. Ironically, gore is as important to contemporary culture as marching penguins with happy feet! F. Scott Fitzgerald would be impressed by this culture that can hold two opposing ideas in their minds at the same time.

People love gore. People love violence. People love penguins. America possesses a fascinating popular culture. It demands that distributors appreciate it. If they do not heed culture's dynamics, they will fail.

JASON KLIOT cofounded Open City Films with his partner Joana Vicente in 1995. He is also Co-President, with Vicente, of HDNet Films, Mark Cuban and Todd Wagner's high-definition production company. Among the many films Mr. Kliot has produced are such eclectic films as Tony Bui's Sundance Film Festival Grand Jury Prize and Audience Award Winner *Three Seasons*, Jim Jarmusch's *Coffee and Cigarettes*, and Niels Mueller's *The Assassination of Richard Nixon*. He was nominated for an Academy Award for his film *Enron: The Smartest Guy in the Room*.

Prior to HDNet Films, Kliot and Vicente ran their own digital production company, Blow Up Pictures. Their run of successful low-budget digital features includes *Lovely and Amazing*, directed by Nicole Holofcener; Miguel Arteta's *Chuck & Buck*; Dan Minahan's *Series 7*, *Love in the Time of Money*; and *The Guys*, directed by Jim Simpson.

Mr. Kliot is an award-winning director of short films, music videos, and public service announcements, including *Late Fall*, which premiered at the Sundance Film Festival in 1994, and *Site*, which premiered at Sundance in 2002; was an official selection of the Berlin International Film Festival, New Directors, New Films; and was exhibited at the International Center of Photography. It is part of the permanent collection of the Museum of Modern Art.

Mr. Kliot is a *summa cum laude* graduate of Amherst College and was a fellow at the École Normale Supérieure in Paris. He is one of the original founders of City Harvest, the world's oldest and New York's only food rescue program, and serves on its board.

The Producer's Perspective

By Jason Kliot

Having been a part of the midnineties boom in digital filmmaking, which saw many DV companies emerge, among them Peter Broderick's Next Wave, Gary Winick and John Sloss' InDigEnt, and our own DV shingle, Blow Up Pictures, I have watched as, with few exceptions, the explosion behind this digital revolution has burst— somewhat like the dot-com bubble. The vast majority of companies have disappeared, unable to reach the audiences these films deserve amid the bigger budgeted, bigger cast, and more widely advertised mini-major output. Many notable movies emerged from this wave of digital filmmaking, but were largely reliant on the festival circuit to secure distribution, which didn't necessarily make for the most consistent business model.

With the advent of affordable consumer and pro-sumer-grade digital video cameras, now including HD models, we continue to see more and more smaller, truly independent films being made, with or without the support of such financiers. Unfortunately the distribution landscape for such movies has remained pretty bleak. We've reached the first phase of the digital revolution, where production has become democratized, but until a similar transition takes place in distribution and exhibition, this surge of digital filmmaking will result in a glut of product, making it tough for everyone to reach screens through traditional means.

This, in tandem with the emergence of the studio specialty division with their immense marketing muscle, makes it difficult to get noticed without spending three quarters of a million dollars on advertising to get your film in the public consciousness. Change, it seems, may finally be on the horizon, but the economics remain untested.

Given the expense inherent in releasing a film, it's also encouraging to see companies like Netflix taking on a more curatorial function, in the vein of small independent and art house theaters in the seventies and eighties. Smaller, truly independent films are likely to become targeted to niche audiences, capitalizing on the ability of such sites and programs to home in on their customers' interests. Because a person has rated Richard Linklater and Hal Hartley highly on their queue, similar films can be target marketed based on related interests and tastes. Similarly, sites like YouTube contain a social aspect that facilitates the sharing and recommendation of short content. Such approaches will provide new opportunities for films at a lower cost, but unfortunately only to a relatively narrow audience. Digital distribution flexibility might lead more theaters to start showing films once a day, as they do at some theaters in Paris, allowing more films to make it to the marketplace. Or, with the advent of products like Apple's AppleTV, you may see consumers downloading more movies to their television.

Theatrical releases will remain important, as they have with the advent of VHS and DVD. Both were of course viewed as threatening to exhibitors, but what is clear is that they are no longer the sole means by which the public chooses to view movies. Exploiting other venues is key to the continued vitality of independent film.

What we're hoping to do with HDNet Films, our high-definition production company that my partner Joana Vicente and I began with Mark Cuban and Todd Wagner, is to step into the middle ground between the studio specialty division and the microbudgeted independent. We've adopted a strategy that allows us to reach out and find broader audiences than a traditional, staggered means of distribution allows, exploiting the benefits of a theatrical release while capitalizing on the short window of awareness that smaller films have in this crowded marketplace by allowing audiences access to the DVD and broadcast of films concurrent with the theatrical release. In partnership with fellow Wagner/Cuban companies Magnolia Pictures, Magnolia Home Entertainment, the Landmark Theatres chain, and HDNet Movies, we're privileged to have a theatrical and video distributor, exhibitor, and broadcaster uniquely suited to serve the type of films we make. We're shooting our movies entirely in high def and releasing them in theaters on Landmark's digital screens, bringing out the movies on Blu-ray, HD-DVD, and standard DVD, and showing them on the high-def cable network HDNet all on the same day, permitting audiences to consume our films in any way they choose, all within the same window, and all on the native format.

If I'm going on a date that night and I remember hearing about an interesting movie, I may want to go to see it at a Landmark theater that evening. If I've just had a baby and can't get out of the house, but I have an HD system and have subscribed to the standard HD cable package, I might see it that night at home. If I'm somewhere outside of a major metropolitan market and don't have a Landmark or any indie theater at all, but heard about that same movie in the national press, I could buy the film at Best Buy or get onto Netflix and add it to my queue. The idea is that when people are aware of a movie immediately, they can view it the way they want. That's our strategy.

At the budgets we work at, up to $5 million, it's madness to commit nearly a million dollars to a film for marketing only to have to re-up three months later for the DVD launch. No matter how much we spend, we're a drop in the bucket compared to a Disney or Universal, so it's important to make the best use of our resources and cast a wide net. We're limiting our risk to allow new emerging filmmakers and established auteurs alike the freedom to capture their visions.

While it's our hope that this pioneering strategy allows the filmmakers we work with to reach the audiences they deserve, we by no means intend to rest on our laurels and set our model in stone. The industry as a whole should be more open and adaptable to new technologies and to new means of doing business. As hinted at earlier, I'm thrilled to see new venues and markets for filmmakers emerging on the web and on mobile devices. Initiatives like Sundance's Global Short Films Project, where a half-dozen filmmakers have been tapped to make movies specifically for cell phones, are indicative that there are going to be mobile platforms where short films can be distributed. There will be more of an underground currency to short films than ever before because of all these different ways of seeing them and sharing them with others. While not a viable forum for commercial features, shorts will begin to find larger and larger audiences. Which is great news for the filmmaking community as a whole, as it will introduce new and innovative voices to the world. I'm seeing more shorts than I've ever seen before because of this Internet explosion.

While we're an established company, which managers, agents, and producers approach as a known source of financing, we also find many of our projects through scouting features and shorts at festivals. I'm a great believer in the short form, which has been an effective proving ground for emerging directors. The lower cost of production can make digital filmmaking quite liberating, but too often new directors have taken this freedom and leapt too far into the deep end of a first feature. It's a rare case that a director is truly ready until having shot footage and confronted one's own images in an editing room, whether it's a short or a feature. It almost goes without saying, but I can't stress enough how the successful completion of a short can act as a calling card, particularly when it reflects the content of a prospective feature film.

A good example from our own stable of films is *Three Seasons* director Tony Bui. Tony was 24 years old when he made a short in Vietnam called *Yellow Lotus*. He convinced a group of his loyal classmates to fly to Vietnam and sleep on his grandmother's floor for the duration of the shoot. It was an incredibly difficult production, but the result is a really beautiful short film that had some elements of the feature script he brought to Joana and me to finance.

Joana and I read the script and loved it, but it was only when we saw his short that we actually believed it was feasible to make *Three Seasons*. Tony had proven that one could make a beautiful film in Vietnam for little money. He showed that he had a lyrical style that was very strong and that he could effectively convey a narrative within that style. He proved that he could make an entertaining film that was in Vietnamese that a Western audience would appreciate.

At this time, no one had ever made an American feature in Vietnam, ever, in the history of the two countries. The embargo made it such that it was even questionable if one could even finance a movie if it was shot in Vietnam. No completion bond company had ever bonded a film in Vietnam, and the movie was in Vietnamese and only had one English-speaking role for about 15–20 minutes in the film. Basically, Tony's short definitely helped *Three Seasons* get financed under the most difficult conditions possible.

He proved all of that through the short. Without *Yellow Lotus*, I don't think it would have been possible to concretize his dreams and our dreams as producers to make this feature. Given the gradual democratization of production, and with a similar forthcoming trend in the way audiences can view films, I'm hopeful that we'll see many more such promising filmmakers emerge, equipped for a new revolution in digital features.

ANDREW HERWITZ is president of The Film Sales Company, the New York-based domestic sales agent/producer's rep. The Company specializes in securing domestic and international distribution for English and foreign language finished films as well as financing for English language packaged projects. Recent completed fiction films sold include 2007 Sundance Film Festival sensation *Waitress* (Fox Searchlight) and *Dirty Laundry* (CodeBlack/Fox).

The Company has had particular success in financing and selling documentary films. Among the more notable documentary films the Company has sold are *Iraq in Fragments* (2007 Academy Award Nominee), *Born into Brothels* (2005 Academy Award Winner, Best Documentary), *Fahrenheit 9/11* (highest grossing documentary film of all time), and *My Architect* (2004 Academy Award Nominee). Documentary films released in 2007 included *Crazy Love* (Magnolia Films released in June 2007) and *War Dance* (winner of the Best Director award at the 2007 Sundance Film Festival; ThinkFilm released in November 2007).

Prior to establishing this company, Mr. Herwitz was at Miramax for six years, where he served as cohead of the film acquisitions department. Before that he practiced entertainment law at Paul, Weiss, Rifkind, Wharton and Garrison in New York City. Mr. Herwitz is a graduate of Harvard College, Columbia Business School, and Harvard Law School.

Conversation with Andrew Herwitz

SB: You worked in acquisitions with Miramax for years and now represent films directly to distributors with The Film Sales Company. How did that transition work and what strategy did you take with you to the other side of the table?

AH: I think the skill set is quite similar. In both capacities the question is not only "Do I like this film?" or "Do I think it's a good film?" but also "Is this a commercial film?" That translates to the questions of "How can you get people into the theater to see the film?" and "How can you market the film?"

One common problem filmmakers find difficult to fathom is that although when people who see the film may really like it, it may still be very hard for them to get the movie distributed. The answer lies in the fact that economic realities of the marketplace are such that positive word-of-mouth is not sufficient, a film needs some hook or element that gives the distributor the ability to market the film on day 1. In other words, a distributor may have no doubt that audiences would like a film *if* they saw it. The trick is how do you get the audience to see it.

To get people into the theaters there's usually some element that you can use to publicize the film before it's released. That's the way you'll get people to come to the box office on the first weekend. That could be a documentary with a specific topic that is of interest to people, or there is a known cast member, or there's some unlikely storyline which captures public imagination, or it is based on a book that has some recognition. I was making those evaluations when I was at Miramax and I'm still making those evaluations in determining the films that would be a good fit for our company to take on and represent.

SB: I particularly notice with independent films and even shorts over the past few years, the importance of casting recognition. Is this more important now for a filmmaker to think about?

AH: It's always been important for filmmakers to think about. There are still independent films that break out in one way or another that don't have any known or recognizable cast in them, but then they probably have some other element that brings the film some attention. Just the fact that the film is an audience pleaser is rarely enough in this marketplace to get a following, because, as I said, there is not enough time for word-of-mouth to build.

SB: What is the difference between a sales agent and a producer's rep? Are they one and the same?

AH: There are people who occupy those functions who do a variety of work in the same realm and who choose to identify themselves differently, but I don't think there is a clear distinction between the functions of the sales agent and the functions of a producer's rep.

SB: When you evaluate a film, presuming all rights are available, are you primarily thinking of it in terms these days of domestic theatrical release? How are you evaluating a film with all these different arenas in play now?

AH: It depends on the movie and the expectations of the filmmaker. Generally speaking, most filmmakers want their films to be theatrically released, and the most successful films in terms of the amount of money made are generally those that are theatrically released. There are all sorts of exceptions to that like the recent Disney *High School Musical*, which has been wildly successful. That's an example of a really successful movie that has never been in movie theaters.

A smaller budget movie relative to its cost with a rather modest success at the box office (or even just on DVD or on television) may be very successful in terms of what sort of return the filmmaker has made on his/her investment, without reaching a significant box-office level because the cost of the film has been so low. There are cases where the distributor has spent so much in marketing the film that it may have done a sizable number at the box office, but the amount spent to get that number at the box office has far outstripped what the box office was. What do I look at? It depends on the movie. There are a variety of ways to gauge the commercial success of a movie.

SB: Are there particular genres that work better than others?

AH: Assuming a consistent level of quality, yes, I'd say horror really works. Urban films with some recognizable cast I've found recently work extraordinarily well. Gay-themed films usually sell to someone but often not for a great deal of money.

SB: Is it common these days that when you encounter a film, the filmmaker has presold certain rights in order to raise the money to make the film?

AH: Often I get involved with preselling rights on behalf of the film-maker. It is rare that I encounter a film where the filmmaker has sold rights him- or herself. And if there is somebody else who has sold the rights, then that somebody else probably controls the rights yet to be sold.

SB: What is the primary way that you encounter films and filmmakers?

AH: I'd say references from filmmakers I've worked with or other people I know who refer me. We very aggressively track films in the office from filmmakers we know or from films in production or from other industry people who, in one way or another, bring our attention to a film. Usually by the time the film is in a significant market or festival like Sundance or Toronto or Berlin or Cannes, it's generally too late for us to bring any value because generally the distributors to whom we might pitch the film have probably already seen it. Once they've seen it either they want it or they don't, and if they've determined that they don't, it's much harder to turn a "no" to a "yes" than an "I don't know" to a "yes."

SB: When you take on a project, how does the agreement work?

AH: Every deal is different. Sometimes we are paid a retainer to represent the rights to the film. Sometimes there is no retainer. We always earn a commission based on what's earned from the license of the movie in terms of an advance, and then if there are overages.

SB: What advice would you give to a filmmaker coming out of the gate with a short film?

AH: Try to get the short into prestigious film festivals. If the filmmaker's goal is to write and direct his own material, the short is a way to give a financier comfort that he has talent and skill. If the short is a way for him to get a directing job, then he needs to bring the short to the attention of a talent agent who can set him up with a directing job at a studio or a production company.

SB: What if it's a case where the filmmaker wants their short to be expanded into a feature and they have a feature script; would they come to someone like you?

AH: We certainly look at a lot of scripts and shorts. If it's a first-time director, and there are no attachments other than the first-time director,

I think it's hard to generate any market interest in the project. And by market interest I mean presales or equity financing from people who don't know the filmmaker personally.

SB: If they had a recognizable cast member, would that improve those chances?

AH: Yes, it improves them dramatically because it gives market validation to the project that this known cast member wants to do it, and it also gives any potential sources of financing the safety net, that if the film doesn't work out as well as hoped, there's still some value. You can still sell a film with Brad Pitt in it even if it's not as polished as might have been hoped.

SB: Speaking of polished, how does shooting format come into play today, with all the different formats available?

AH: I don't think so much. If there's no budget to blow it up to 35 mm, or if the distribution advance does not cover blowing it up to 35 mm, then you've just limited, in this day and age, how widely the film can be released. Otherwise, I think filmmakers try to pick a medium appropriate to the story they're telling.

SB: What do you advise somebody that wants to make an independent feature these days?

AH: They probably should do it, because there's no experience probably that doesn't have some value. It may not be the result you had hoped for but hopefully something else—the life experience or relationships or people you've worked with that you never had the chance to work with before—has occurred. You have to have a healthy balance between believing in your project and being mindful of what the market is telling you. If people continue to tell you that your story is uninteresting, or it's confusing, or seven hours is too long for a film, you need to at least listen. It may not affect your fundamental belief in the strength of what you've created, but you need to try to synthesize the information and the response you're getting from those that have seen the movie.

I think it's increasingly hard for independent films with low budgets and unrecognizable casts to get any distribution, let alone to get into a movie theater. There are always films that seem to break through in one way or another, which is encouraging, and wonderful, but most films don't.

Don't start shooting until you're comfortable with the script. And don't start sending out the film to film festivals until you feel really good about your finished product, because you only get one chance.

WILLIAM R. THOMPSON is Senior Vice President and Co-General Sales Manager for Picturehouse, the distributor of *A Prairie Home Companion, Pan's Labyrinth, La Vie en Rose,* and many others. As Head of Distribution at Newmarket Films, he worked on *Whale Rider, Monster, The Passion of the Christ, The Woodsman,* and *Downfall.* He has previously held executive distribution positions with Lot 47 Films, USA Films, Gramercy Pictures, and Miramax Films. He has also worked as a film buyer for several theater circuits based in New York, such as City Cinemas, Cineplex Odeon, Walter Reade, and Cinema 5 Theatres. A longtime member and past president of the Motion Picture Club in New York, Mr. Thompson is also a member of the Motion Picture Pioneers. For the past 16 years, he has taught a popular course on the motion picture business at New York University.

Strategizing Specialized Film

By William R. Thompson

"Specialized film" is the general term for the type of film that requires careful nurturing due to the fact that a large audience does not initially exist for it. Most independent films produced and financed outside of the studio system fall into this realm.

We have an unusual situation at Picturehouse in that we are a joint venture between HBO and New Line, so if HBO has produced a film that they want to release theatrically, that will be our responsibility. Picturehouse also produces one or two films a year. However, the majority of our films are independently produced, which we acquire from outside producers. Once that is done, either at Sundance, Cannes, Toronto or through some other means, then we will go through a regular process of getting a film ready to distribute.

For each film, there are two major decisions that we have to make at that point:

Number 1—What kind of release plan or pattern are we going to use in selling the film? Is it going to be an exclusive or limited release, or a wider, more commercial release?

Number 2—When are we going to release the film? Picking out a release date is not simple. Generally, from the time the film is acquired that release date is usually six months down the line in order for us to give plenty of time to our marketing department to create a campaign and to the publicity department to create awareness on the film.

Who is the target audience and where do we find them?

We start with a realistic appraisal of the film's appeal. If we think that it has a very specialized, limited appeal (which is the majority of our films), then we will generally open it in New York and Los Angeles in one or two runs, a week or two later open up the next 8 or 10 cities, and the week after that the next 20 or 25 cities. Whether we go wider than that is predicated on the box-office performance of the initial runs. Ideally, if it's a case like *Pan's Labyrinth*, it opened with just New York, Los Angeles, San Francisco, and Chicago in a dozen runs, but then it did such great business that we kept adding more and more runs every week. However, we have also had a number of other pictures, much less successful, that have opened limited and have remained limited. They never expanded very much because the box-office results of the initial runs did not warrant it.

That's the danger of a limited release plan because at any point along its life the brakes get put on and that's the end of it. It's the danger and it's also the reasoning behind it. If it opens and doesn't perform well you can cut your losses at that point, whereas if you open it wide and spend a lot of money to support it wide and it doesn't work, you've already spent all this money and the potential losses are that much greater.

When we released wide on a picture like A *Prairie Home Companion* it was because Garrison Keillor's radio program had a huge national audience and it had Meryl Streep, Lily Tomlin, and many other names in it. From that point it seemed to be a safer bet to go with a fairly wide release on this Robert Altman film, although that's not always the case with his films. Some started smaller, but this one had the elements so we felt it was safe to open on a wider basis.

Over the past couple of decades, the biggest change in both exhibition and distribution has been continuing consolidation on both sides. When I started at Fox there were 31 branches around the country; now they are down to New York and Los Angeles, which is what most major companies have. A couple of them still have a Boston or Dallas branch but for the most part they are concentrated on the two coasts.

Concurrent with the change in distribution is the consolidation in exhibition. The larger circuits are buying up the smaller circuits, and they continue to get bigger and bigger. The great majority of new theaters are being built by the major circuits so their domination of the marketplace is increasing. Now you can seemingly book a film nationally by making a dozen phone calls to key film buyers around the country and get the great majority of theaters you need with just a small number of phone calls.

The whole moviegoing pattern in New York and Los Angeles has changed a great deal as well. For example, in Manhattan the Ziegfeld, Cinema 1, Paris, and many other theaters used to play exclusive of all other theaters in Manhattan, and they now often play with several other runs. Not that long ago, the only thing that mattered to many producers and filmmakers was where their film played on the Upper East Side of Manhattan and in Westwood in Los Angeles. Now, neither zone really matters all that much—a lot of our films never play in either zone. Now the booking that matters the most is Lincoln Plaza or Lincoln Square in New York and the Arc Light, The Grove, or Century City in Los Angeles. This reflects not only changing moviegoer demographics in both those cities but also changing release plans on the part of the distributors.

Surely one of the biggest changes is that now a lot of theaters have no local overview of what's going on in those local markets. For instance, in the Washington DC market, where I started, there's almost no local ownership of theaters there and no local distributors. These theaters are booked by, and sold to, people in other cities, and that's often the case in many other cities around the country. Whether that's necessarily good or bad of course is a matter of debate, but it's certainly a significant change.

For the more specialized films, there are still some locally owned "art theaters" around the country. Many art-house theaters are individually owned or individually booked. For the commercial venues, if I'm going to book a film in the Washington DC market, I call AMC in Kansas City and Regal in Knoxville and Redstone in Boston. The great majority of the first-run theaters are handled by a film buyer at a circuit in some other city, so it's a strange development.

Computerization has allowed fewer people to do more work. Even though the dollar volume has grown, there are fewer people involved in the buying and selling of these films. You can accomplish a lot more and that translates into fewer people being involved in our end of the business.

The existence of the mega-complexes can help open up the opportunity of booking specialized film. If the picture is a strong one, or at the very least if the perception of the potential of the picture is fairly strong, there are more locations available. If the perception is that the picture is not going to do much business, then you're going to have a hard time selling it anyway. As soon as somebody smells money on a particular picture they come out of the woodwork looking for it. Certainly with more screens that are out there, there's more potential for a picture to expand quickly but it's all predicated on how much business it does initially.

If your film is doing a lot of business, then all sorts of opportunities may open up to you. You can expand quickly, spend more money, and get the most out of your film. But if you have mediocre grosses then it may ultimately depend on how crowded the marketplace is. If it's very crowded exhibitors are not going to take off something that's doing business to open a new picture if they don't perceive it has a chance of working. If it's not that crowded then they may have screens to fill anyway and will take a chance. That's why picking out the release date itself can be a tricky proposition. You need to see what other similar-type films are in the marketplace around the time that you want to release that film, and these dates change frequently so they can affect your release date.

There is no doubt that with a more specialized film, particularly one that does not have major names or a hook with it, to a certain extent, the public may be influenced by where it's playing. In New York, if it's playing at the Lincoln Plaza or the Sunshine or the Angelika they may perceive it as being a more important film than if it was playing at another theater. If it comes down to choosing between the Angelika and the Sunshine or theaters like that, there I hesitate to really believe the public is going to see the film at one theater but refuse to see it at another. Now, whether they would be more likely to see a film at one of those specialized theaters as opposed to seeing it at a Loews Village or Regal Union Square is debatable.

There's only one chance to release a film. You can't go back and do it over again and try opening in a different theater to see if it works better there. To me it's more a question of perception. Simply by the fact that it's playing in one theater the public may rightly or wrongly perceive certain things about the film simply because of where it's playing.

The type of film and the subject matter also impact our release strategy. For example, with our recent Sundance acquisition of *King of Kong*, from our point of view we recognize that it's a documentary and for much of this country that is almost a dirty word. It's something that people will not necessarily want to spend money on. Particularly people who are only going to one movie on a Saturday night; are they going to spend their 8 or 10 or 11 dollars on a documentary? Even in the case of *King of Kong* where it's a fairly light entertaining subject matter (it's about guys who are still playing Donkey Kong 25 years later) we recognize the difficulty of playing documentaries so we factor that in when we're talking about both the release plan and the marketing budget. We know that it's very difficult to get a good return on those films.

Overall release strategy is impacted by the other revenue streams. Films do not have to play off more quickly during their theatrical life or to have a shorter theatrical run, but there is a desire to have the video availability much closer to theatrical in order to more quickly gain the revenue from the home video side. Home video revenue often is greater than the theatrical revenue.

Our company has always been opposed to the idea of going "day-and-date" with home video/cable and theatrical, but there's no doubt that for every company those windows are getting smaller, particularly for films that are not successful. I don't think that hurts movie theaters as long as there is still a window. When you get a lot closer or when the public has a choice between seeing it at home or in a theater, then there may be a tendency for a number of them to simply avoid theaters altogether. From our point of view, that's not a good thing, so we're still avoiding making it available too soon to the home market.

No doubt with a film like *Pan's Labyrinth*, it's going to be a huge success on home video, but we're still betting on the fact that a lot of people enjoy the experience of seeing a film communally in a theater, and there is still a dating audience that likes to go to movie theaters. Not everybody has a great home theater system. So we count on those things, and even though we know that New Line Home Video will probably have a great success with the film when it comes out on home video, we're hoping to have a long theatrical life on this film before that.

We have an interesting situation with HBO, and it varies from film to film, but certainly playing on HBO is an option with a number of films. In a lot of cases it depends on what rights we acquire on a film. In some cases we buy worldwide rights, in some cases it's just domestic theatrical, and in other cases it's a variation in between for some territories and media as to which ones we are acquiring. That's something that both sides are keenly aware of:

What exactly have we bought and for what period of time and for what media?

Almost all of our films have been challenging; I'm not sure any of ours have been ordinary to any extent. In our earlier incarnation as Newmarket Films, and now as Picturehouse, we've handled a lot of unusual films from *Whale Rider* to *Monster* to *Passion of the Christ*. Each film has had its own challenges.

Pan's Labyrinth has been one of our most satisfying efforts. When we got involved over a year and a half ago, none of us had any conception that it was going to be as big a film as it has turned out to be. At that point it was a Spanish language film about the Spanish Civil War with some fantasy aspects to it. We never would have dreamed that it would become the largest grossing Spanish language film ever released in this country.

LAWRENCE MATTIS gave up his career as an attorney to become the founder of Circle of Confusion, a New York-based management company representing writers and directors in the film industry.

Among Circle's clients are Larry and Andy Wachowski (creators of *The Matrix Trilogy*), Simon Kinberg (*Mr. & Mrs. Smith*, X-Men 3), James McTeigue (director of *V for Vendetta*), Gregg Chabot and Kevin Peterka (*Reign of Fire*), Iris Yamashita (*Letter from Iwo Jima*), and emerging young filmmakers such as Jed Weintrob (*Online*) and J. T. Petty (*S&Man*), both of whom premiered their films at Sundance. Circle also represents video game creators and comic book authors, most notably the Eisner Award-winning creator of *Powers*, Brian Michael Bendis (also writer of *Ultimate Spiderman*, *X-Men*, *Daredevil*, and *Fantastic Four* for Marvel).

In 2002, Mr. Mattis expanded the operations of Circle of Confusion to include a Los Angeles office and a more active production agenda. Circle has set up two dozen projects and is producing a slate of independent films, including the supernatural thriller *Reaper* with Media 8 and *St. John of Las Vegas* with executive producer Spike Lee. In television production, Circle has a two-year first-look deal with Paramount, with a dozen projects in development. In 2005, Circle entered a strategic partnership with Foundation 9, the largest independent video game developer in the world, to create original IP franchises across multiple media platforms.

Management Matters

By Lawrence Mattis

You did what!?!?

Made a short film. Well, that's interesting. Why the heck did you do that?

Okay, so you made a short film and you're interested in talking to me, a literary manager. What can we assume? You must want to make a movie. A feature length movie. You want a green light. And maybe you want more than one. Maybe you want a career as a filmmaker. Okay. Let's look into this.

So assuming you want a green light—and possibly a career as a filmmaker—how do you get one of those and how can a literary manager help?

Well the formula for a green light (and by extension to a large degree for a career in the film industry) is:

MATERIAL + RELATIONSHIPS + MONEY = GREEN LIGHT.

Your manager works to develop all three of these crucial elements.

29

Material

If you are a director, there are two sources for material, internal and external. Either you self-generate material as a writer–director, which in some ways makes things easier, or you don't write, in which case you need to go find some material that you can direct.

I represent both kinds of directors. On a good day, I can provide service of some value to both varieties. Most well known, I represent the Wachowski Brothers. They have directed four movies (*Bound* and *The Matrix Trilogy*) and are about to direct their fifth (*Speed Racer*). They write all their own movies. Well, that's easy, or maybe not always. In the case of Larry and Andy Wachowski, they happen to be truly exceptional in their ability to create worlds and narratives that are new, visually compelling, and viscerally amazing. I have some other less-known writer–director clients who can go off into their basements and return two months later with a script that is close to ready for the cameras.

But there are other writer–director clients who need guidance. They need help choosing in what arena to set their new script, what kind of story they should frame, and how big—or small—the movie they are about to map out is going to be. Those are the kinds of decisions that a manager can help resolve. A manager's advice in this regard should be specific to those creative issues, but also address the business matter of what movie will most likely lead this specific client to succeed. For example, what genre will this director execute most artfully? What size movie will the market most likely support for this director? For example, if the goal is to create the client's first feature, they probably shouldn't be writing *Independence Day*.

Then there are directors who are just directors. And hey, it's hard enough to do any one creatively demanding job. Those writer–directors are just show-offs. Most directors are "just" directors. Some you may have heard of are Steven Spielberg, Martin Scorsese, Ridley Scott, Gore Vrabinski, and David Fincher. So how do they find their movies? When you are one of the five aforementioned directors, it is easy. Every studio and agency in town sends you every script that's ever been written and yet to be made into a motion picture (and a bunch that have already been made into a motion picture, or two). Even then, or maybe especially then, a director can use a good filter. Managers help do triage on incoming scripts to winnow out the ones that are most likely to fit the director's general sensibilities (e.g., dark thrillers, family comedies) and specific goals (a big-star Oscar vehicle, something the director can shoot in LA to be near home, a movie about singing antelopes—you never know).

Even for directors who are not megastars, a manager can be very helpful in sifting submissions. I represent a few emerging genre directors. They get almost every horror script around sent their way. Some of those scripts are pretty interesting, but many are tired retreads, or even simply bad. A manager's job is to cherry pick the good ones to give the client some choices that are all worth consideration.

Conversely, a manager has to help a director go out and find material. For most directors, every script in town doesn't simply appear at their doorstep. A manager needs to keep an eye out at every studio, agency, and production company to see what projects might be nearing production that fit the mandate of a specific client. More proactively, a manager must also constantly be planting the seeds of a client's identity and profile at those studios, agencies, and production companies. Every director is a brand. A manager is, among other things, a traveling advertisement, going from place to place and person to person in the film business to educate people on the existence and properties of that brand. "Hey, Mr. Studio Executive, do you know the Wachowski Brothers? They are great with sci-fi, special effects, and big smart movies. Ever see *The Matrix?* Let me send you a DVD. . . ." Or in your case, "Hey, Mr. Studio Executive, do you know Novice Film Maker Jones? She is great with visuals and character—and very deft with comedy. Let me send you her short. . . ."

And this brings us to:

Relationships (and money)

What a manager probably has in spades more than a beginning filmmaker with a short or two under their arm is relationships. As the age-old adage goes, it's not what you know, but who you know. And managers build a Rolodex of "who"s to know. Relationships are also inextricably connected to the third ingredient to green lights—money. Because the sad truth is, the reason we build relationships in the business is because we think they lead to money. Either this is directly (the person we are relating to has money or works for a person or entity that has money) or indirectly (the person we are relating to activates or controls someone who activates money). When I started my company in New York, everyone told me I should move to LA because the movie business was in Los Angeles. Well I stayed in New York and it worked out okay. Everyone will also tell you that to make a movie, you need money. Well . . . they're right.

A short aside on that. I represent writers and directors. In the film business for the most part you want to be a director. They get paid more than writers and people listen to them way more than they listen to writers (even when the writers are really smart and have come up with brilliant characters, stories, and set pieces from whole cloth and all the director has done is shoot Coke commercials with pretty bubbles). The one humungous advantage writers have over directors is that it doesn't cost anything to write. You can go to your basement or local Starbucks and write. And you are always 120 cost-free pages away from an Oscar, or at least a spec sale for some pocket change.

But if you are a director and you want to/need to direct a movie, well that costs money. You need equipment. You often even have to pay people to show up and work, or act, or whatever. It's all about the benjamins.

That's where the relationships come back into play. Managers know people who connect to money. The direct connection—people who have, or work for those who have, money—applies to studio executives and independent distributors and financiers. Studios are the big sugar daddy or money out there and everyone wants some of that sugar. Mostly it goes to the established big boys of directing (aforementioned Spielberg, Scorsese, Fincher, . . .). This is especially true because the studios are very risk averse and feel that giving $100 million to a director who has done this sort of thing before—even if only in a mediocre way—is safer and smarter than giving that kind of bank to some kid with a 15-minute short (no matter how much their manager says it is brilliant).

That said, for studio movies that are less expensive, there are occasional opportunities. For example, low-budget comedies are a good proving ground for a young director—even one with just a great short. Comedy shorts are, for that reason, sometimes a better stepping stone to a directing career, more so than other genres. *Luke Greenfield.*

George Lucas in Love. There may be a new trend though because of low-budget horror and thrillers. *Nine.*

For many younger directors, their first feature won't be at a studio but financed by an indie, which could be a small distributor, like Samuel Goldwyn, or an independent fund, like Michael London's Groundswell. The budget of these movies is significantly smaller than studio budgets, so there is less risk being placed on a newer director. Because the chain of command is shorter, there is more likelihood of a person at the top who will get excited about a project and "roll the dice" on the director of that snappy short. The top of the pyramid at Warner Brothers or Paramount is hidden in the clouds of a corporate board room. And those guys don't roll the dice.

A good manager will help expose a young director—by way of their short film—to both studio execs and indie financiers. Managers will also help introduce their clients to producers, who may not themselves have money but as they run around town with projects will eventually run into a studio or indie who wants to fund their movie. Then that producer will need a director. . . .

The indirect connections that I referenced earlier relate to mainly actors. Actors, at least the right actors, will trigger studios and indie finance companies to green-light movies. A director's manager can reach out to talent managers and agents to educate them about his client. (By the way, note that "talent" refers to actors. Actors have the "talent" in the movie business. Writers and directors are "lit.") This can be especially helpful for young directors about make their first feature who need that one "name actor" to get their dream project rolling, but a manager can also be very helpful later in a career, connecting more established directing clients with bigger stars to help build projects.

Putting all these things together, staying on them, and working them day in and day out takes stamina and inhuman (and some days inexplicable and rationally indefensible) optimism. That's another job of the manager. Cheerleader. The road to a green light isn't a road. It's a roller coaster—a nasty up-and-down all-around roller coaster. The manager has to help keep the train on the tracks and keep the client as safe and upbeat as possible—especially through the long harrowing slides downward (and don't even start me on the stops).

One of the truly exciting parts of managing for me is the fact that I sign clients because I have a real connection to what they are trying to do creatively. I am excited by the creative process in general, and by my clients' creativity in particular. So when things are not going that well—and there will be those times for everyone in our industry—part of what a manager does is simply remind the client why they signed them in the first place. They are talented. They have great potential and they can't give up!

Oh yeah. There is another element vital to success in the movie trade. Luck. Sad to say, but serendipity plays a fantastically powerful role in this business. It's being in the right place at the right time, happening to hear of the right opportunity and being able to take advantage of it. But then you realize that luck isn't all luck. It's being ready to take advantage of opportunity, and making your own luck. As you can see, a manager keeps his or her finger on the pulse of the town, be it LA, New York, or some film-subsidy-pushing outer province of Canada. A manager keeps a focus on the client's goals and needs. Putting the knowledge of external conditions and internal needs together increases the odds that "luck" is going to land in your client's lap. It may take a while, but if you stick to it long enough and have a good team in place, you can leap from that short film to a feature-directing career.

And that brings me to my final point. This business is a marathon, not a sprint. It is a long-term game, where you build relationships and store up resources for the long haul. A manager has to take the long view and help the client stay the course. Sometime there will certainly be opportunities for short-term gain that are useful and well worth scooping up. More often than not it is about preparing and executing the long play that will get a director that coveted green light, and even that career in the film business.

So be prepared to persevere. Work hard. Don't take no for and answer. And good luck!

Swimming Lesson #2

Learning to Float:
The Buyers

Call them film buyers, call them acquisitions executives, or call them programmers. Whatever their title, these are the people responsible for selecting the short films for their particular distribution outlet. They are the gatekeepers. One thing I can assure you is that each person who does this job loves short film. They have to in order to be able to objectively review hundreds, sometimes thousands, of shorts and make a decision on each and every one of them.

I think that's the first lesson to be learned when dealing with buyers—their own personal opinion of the film is not as important as their overall determination if that short is right for their distribution platform and their audience. It always comes down to the audience. Will they like it? Will they walk away amazed after viewing the short? That's why no matter how good your short is, it may be rejected by a buyer simply because it doesn't "fit" with their audience. Any good buyer knows who their audience is and keeps them in mind during the viewing process.

A frequent question that is asked of buyers is "Do you watch the whole short?" The answer is usually "No," followed by a despondent look on the part of the filmmaker. You may think this is unfair. You may have a really great twist toward the end of the short, but we're never going to get to that unless the first couple of minutes engages us. Those first few minutes are integral to the buyer—and if the buyer does their job well, they know in the first few minutes if the short works for their distribution outlet. Those first few minutes give a true sense of the story, characters, and production values/directorial control. The clock is ticking, folks, so get it out there from the start. Show us what you've got! If we're interested, we'll keep watching, and if not, the shorts are lined up like jets at JFK during rush hour—there is simply not enough time to watch a short once you've made a decision on it. The truth is, those first few minutes do tell the tale, so the advice is to get it going. One of the most frustrating trends in short filmmaking is feature-length main credits. Credit everyone in the end credits, but make your main credits short and sweet. There is absolutely no reason in the world a 10-minute short should have a 1-minute main credit sequence.

A second important aspect of being a buyer is to truly understand your marketplace and the competition. I liken it to the "needle in the haystack" philosophy. Each buyer sifts through shorts hoping to find that next great one, or that next great filmmaker. Each buyer would love to say "I discovered so-and-so" and is always on the hunt for new and unexposed short films. We want to find you and we want to find your film. Our jobs depend on our programming and selection skills, so we're always looking. That's why it is particularly

36

important for a new filmmaker to investigate the marketplace and ascertain which distributors and which platforms are the right ones for their films. Elements that make a film right for online distribution are not necessarily the same criteria as for one right for broadcast. Each platform has its own requirements.

Don't make a decision based on desperation simply because someone offers to distribute your film or because a sales agent asks to represent it. Before you sign those papers, make sure that you are confident that they are the right distributor for your film. You can retain that control.

The third lesson I'd like to share with you is the phrase "nothing personal." Believe it or not, buyers are human, and there's nothing harder than rejecting a film from a filmmaker that you know and like. Knowing the buyers helps you to reach out to them with a project, but it's not going to help in that final decision. That's based on your film and your film alone. We have to be objective. That being said, word-of-mouth in this industry, particularly the short industry, is very compelling. If your short comes through the pipeline recommended by someone in the industry, that little seal of approval is going to help get it watched more quickly and probably by one of the programmers rather than one of the screeners. The end result is the same. If you get rejected, move on. I have been screamed at, been sent nasty letters, even had filmmakers beg me to reconsider my decision. It's "nothing personal," and you need to develop a tough skin in this business; remember, it is a business when it comes to distribution.

Filmmakers will also ask for feedback. They'll say, "Why did you reject my film?" That's a tough question to answer, since it's not a good vs bad decision. Many elements come into play, and many of these are out of your control entirely. For example, let's say a film buyer has already bought a comedic short about a road trip, and you have a comedic short about a road trip too. That makes it less likely they will accept your short because most buyers are looking for variety, and that subject has already been covered. There's no way for you to know this. Similarly, let's say a film buyer is now concentrating on acquiring more international shorts and yours is a domestic short. That short may be rejected because they are looking for something else; again, not in your control. You should make your short based on the project you want to create, not design it for "optimum viewing." Every single buyer, when discussing their selection criteria, will always go back to the root of the film: Does it have a good story? Are there compelling characters? Without a good story you've got little to work with, so don't try to "design" a short that is going to be palatable to distributors. That rarely works, because the passion for it isn't there, it's motivated by an agenda. Instead, make the short you want to make, being sure to spend the time in the script stage to make it the best story and characters possible.

Each film buyer has their own criteria, and running time is one of these aspects. Some platforms, like the Internet, may look for shorter, crisper pieces, while others, such as a compilation DVD, may look for longer length shorts. It's important for you to investigate the distributors so that you don't waste your time, energy, or money submitting films that don't meet the criteria. In terms of feedback, you should look to get that in the rough-cut stage, not after the short is locked and loaded. If acquisitions executives were to write the equivalent of coverage for every short film, they would never have the time to watch anything. Get feedback from the beginning so you still have time to rework things.

This chapter contains essays written by film buyers to offer you their advice, tell you where they look for short films, and give their tips from the trenches. You will be inundated with the words "rights," "clearances," and "deliverables." Pay attention. These are issues that come forward time and again. After being hammered by these warnings, perhaps you won't make the same errors in judgment. These essays are written by the people who have the power to select your film, and they answer many of the questions that you might pose to them in "real life."

IAN BRICKE is Director, Acquisitions & Programming, for the Sundance Channel. Before joining the channel, he worked at Killer Films on projects including *Storytelling* and *Hedwig and the Angry Inch* and at the Independent Feature Project on three consecutive Independent Feature Film Markets. He also worked in development for Open City Films and Pipedream Productions.

Mr. Bricke has appeared on panels at South By Southwest, the Sundance Film Festival, the IFP Market, the Atlanta Film Festival, the Clermont-Ferrand International Short Film Festival, and the Sithengi Film & TV Market. He has also served on juries at the Edinburgh International Film Festival, the New York Exposition of Short Film and Video, the Gen Art Film Festival, the Austin Film Festival, the Florida Film Festival, and New York University's Wasserman Awards. Mr. Bricke has served on the Advisory Committee of IFP/New York's Project Involve program and is currently a member of the Advisory Board of the Film Festival Collection, a nonprofit short film distributor. A graduate of Swarthmore College, he is a native of Kansas.

Who Is This For, Anyway?

By Ian Bricke

So, why are you making this short in the first place? No, seriously. Who is this *for*?

As someone who has spent a great deal of time over the last many years at the business end of the world's accumulated short film production, it's the first question I'd ask you, the filmmaker, to ask yourself. Don't worry, there's no wrong answer.

Is it for your accountant? In other words, do you actually think you're going to get rich off a short film? Put down the crack pipe and we'll talk. Yes, it *is* possible to make money on a short, *if* you win an Academy Award *and* you license the film to iTunes *and* a couple home video distributors *and* you sell it to television in pretty much every country in the world. It's possible to make money even if you don't nail the hat trick, but not a lot of money.

In the United States, the handful of broadcasters (IFC, Sundance Channel, Logo, your local PBS affiliate) that acquire shorts pay somewhere between $500 and $3000 (and expect delivery of a fully cleared, maybe even closed-captioned, digibeta broadcast master with all the trimmings). Elsewhere, in Canada and Europe and Japan, license fees are a little better, but to get those deals you're probably going to need a sales agent, which means handing over 40–50% on each sale (check out the attendee lists for the annual Clermont-Ferrand and Toronto Worldwide Short Film Festivals to get a sense of who's buying shorts out there in the world, and who's selling them to them). Home video deals for shorts are thin on the ground, generally geared toward niche audiences (e.g., Strand, Picture This!, and Wolfe Video's successful gay and lesbian short film compilations), and usually conspicuously lacking in an advance (the money's not great, but if you have a festival hit on your hands it's worth checking out alternative home video distributors like the nonprofit Film Festival Collection and McSweeney's Wholphin). Internet sales can make you some money, if you're lucky enough to have the right film at the right moment (ask the JibJab guys).

And don't forget about the hidden costs—duplication and closed-captioning and music clearances. In other words, no matter what anyone tells you, short films are not a commercial proposition. They're wonderful things, for all kinds of reasons, but they're not going to make the down payment on that condo. Plan to lose money (that's where those tax breaks come in) or, if you're feeling optimistic, plan to break even. But don't make a short film to make money.

OK, so there *is* a wrong answer. But it's the only one, I promise.

Is it for your resume? There's a stigma attached to the so-called "calling card" short but, you know what, if it gets the job done... Short filmmaking is the proving ground of aspiring feature filmmakers. If you can show that you can tell a story in 10 or 15 minutes (10, please, it's the rare short that's short enough), then your feature pitch is that much stronger. It's brutally hard to get your first feature off the ground, pretty much impossible if you haven't made a short. So make your calling card short, by all means, but think about how you want to go about it. If absolutely necessary, go ahead and make that 30-minute short with three acts (not a terrible idea, if you want to prove to potential producers or financers that you can sustain a feature-length story), but know that it's going to have a tough time on the festival circuit (no one wants to sit through a 30-minute short before a feature, which means that your epic gets confined to the comparatively underattended short-film sidebar) and a tough time in the "marketplace" (see above).

Maybe there's a chunk of your cherished feature script that you could shoot as a short film. Just make sure that the short works on its own terms. Ryan Fleck and Anna Boden's Sundance Film Festival-winning short *Gowanus, Brooklyn* is a terrific example of a beautifully made, self-contained short that did double duty as a dry run for its makers' first feature, indie sensation *Half Nelson*. Unlike 99% of calling-card shorts, *Gowanus* worked as a short *film*, not just as a showreel. And you never know—sometimes it's the least pragmatic choices that get the job done. Look at the careers of ex-drummer Michel Gondry and skate videographer Spike Jonze.

Is it for the gatekeepers? By gatekeepers, I mean film festival programmers, distributors, acquisition execs, jaded types who decide what makes the cut and what goes where. More or less by definition, filmmaking is about bringing your vision to an audience, whether that audience is your roommate and your roommate's girlfriend or a packed Sundance Film Festival screening. In the best of all possible worlds, the gatekeepers are a means to an end, the crucial bridge between your film and an eager worldwide audience. In the real world, they're cranky, overworked, overscreened, and maybe a little bit dismissive (*you* try watching 1000 short films a year). How do you win them over?

The obvious answer is the most important. Make a *good* film. Make a film that hasn't been seen before—a new story told in a new way, or at the very least, an old story told in a new way. Give 'em something to chew on, something that makes 'em pay attention. Make sure that your film opens with a bang, 'cause most shorts get ejected after two minutes. Get your hooks in early. What else?

Don't bother with a fancy press kit, but *do* bother with a nice-looking DVD label, one that includes your contact info, right there on the DVD. If you're burning DVD-Rs, and you probably are, send two for every submission and test them on a couple different players before sending them out. Think about where you're submitting your work. Does it make sense in context? Your slick *X-Men* homage may be the perfect Hollywood calling card, but it's not going to go far on the festival circuit. Figure out how many film festivals you want to, or can afford to, submit to, and strategize a bit. Do your homework. Then call to follow up, or better yet, email. If you don't hear back, email again. But don't be a psycho—you want these people to watch this film *and* the next one *and* the one after that.

Is it for the audience? Which audience? I'm not talking about focus groups and demographics here, but if the point of making a film is to communicate with an audience, it's worth thinking about how you're saying what you have to say, and to whom. Industry types— the gatekeepers and producers and whatnot above—are part of your audience. But so are the hundreds or thousands or even millions (well, more likely hundreds or thousands) of people who might see your short film at a film festival or a micro-cinema screening or online or on DVD or on TV.

Is your storytelling lean and effective? Is your film straightforward where it needs to be, and mysterious where it can be? Does it have the visual scope to fill a darkened movie theater? Or is it small in scale, better suited to a browser window than a giant screen? Form and function are pretty much the same thing when it comes to filmmaking, so think about how and where you want people to experience your film, and make the film that delivers that experience. At the same time, don't spend too much time worrying about the hypothetical audience (and that goes for the gatekeeper, too). If you make the best film you can, the film that speaks truly and clearly in your own voice, people will see it, and when they see it, they'll get it.

So that brings us back to you, the filmmaker. Is this for you? Is this filmmaking as self-expression? If so, more power to you, as long as you don't blow through too much of other people's money doing it (if you do, at least get 'em a tax break... more than likely you'll be going back to that same well, and you're going to want to do everything you can to keep the goodwill coming). Too many filmmakers take too few chances making shorts. It's not like you have 20 studio bean counters, five executive producers, two producers, and your lead actor's manager breathing down your neck, making sure that you bring your short in on budget and ready to be focus grouped. With limited resources and no real commercial prospects comes freedom. Use it well, take chances, figure out what you have to say and how you want to say it.

If you're pursuing a filmmaking career, you'll never again have the same freedom you had as a short filmmaker. If you're not pursuing a filmmaking career, what do you have to lose? There's nothing worse than a bland, derivative, packaged, *safe* short film. What's the point? If you're going to make *a* short film, make *your* short film. The rest will take care of itself.

ANNA DARRAH began as Director of Acquisitions for The Spiritual Cinema Circle in November 2003, originating the position with the SCC and helping to launch the company five months later. She has signed more than 50 films each year since that time, as the SCC continues to grow and expand.

In addition to her position as Director of Acquisitions for The Spiritual Cinema Circle, Ms. Darrah also helps to source films for The Spiritual Cinema Network, an alternative-release church network, and Gaiam, currently the fifth largest distributor of DVDs in the United States.

Ms. Darrah was the director of events and development for the Santa Fe Film Festival and the Screenwriting Conference in Santa Fe prior to joining The Spiritual Cinema Circle. She has produced two documentaries that have aired on the Sundance Channel. Anna earned a B.A. in theater from Guilford College, Greensboro, North Carolina, with an emphasis in Shakespearean drama. She lives in Santa Fe, New Mexico, with her 10-year-old daughter.

Swimming with Dolphins: Shorts Distribution 101

By Anna Darrah

In the realm of distribution, the most fun you can have as a buyer is with short films. They are little gems that you can get very excited about as a buyer, but you can still keep your wits about you. You won't be competing with Harvey Weinstein for a short. You won't be staying up till four in the morning at Sundance in a bidding war with Paramount. With shorts it's just fun deal-making all the way around and everyone involved can come out happy. It's unlikely in the world of shorts that you will ever feel like you are swimming with sharks. It actually feels more like swimming with dolphins.

I'm a buyer, which means that I license films directly for the consumer. My title is Director of Acquisitions for The Spiritual Cinema Circle. We're a DVD club that mails out a new volume of films every month to our members all over the world, for them to keep. Each volume contains two shorts, a feature film, and a documentary. I'm classified as a buyer because I'm buying films directly for my members (direct to consumer) and I don't sublicense any rights to anyone else along the way. I look for uplifting, inspiring, transformational films that are entertaining, well crafted, and in some way spiritually themed (though totally nondenominational). I license about 50 films a year, which keeps me pretty busy.

Clearances and rights

When you have completed your film and all of the music, stills, and clips are cleared; you've done your title search and your copyright registration; then you are ready to sell your film. For details on how to accomplish all of these ugly little details, go to Google or your local library—there are lots of great books that can tell you how to clear your film correctly, point you to a good title search company, and show you how to register your film with the copyright office. And you must do these things to be able to sell your film.

Anything in your film that you yourself did not create must be cleared. This simply means that you must get permission to use any intellectual property within your film that you did not create totally by yourself. The process goes a little something like this:

"Hi, can I use this (clip, still, music, painting, diagram, etc.) for 30 seconds in my film?"

"Sure, can you pay us ___ for it?"

"Oye—can I actually pay you ____ instead?"

"Let's split the difference. Send us ___ and we're done."

"Okay, you got a deal. Here's your money."

"Great, here's your paperwork proving that ___ is cleared for festival, broadcast, Internet, and DVD rights for 7 years."

"Oh thank God." (It's really not all that difficult, but you will be ready for a drink when it's over.)

Important note: Music rights are a notorious pain in the butt. Just because you know the band, or the lead singer handed you the CD and said "Dude, use this in your film," does not permission make. You still have to clear two sets of rights for every piece of music you use. This is because once the band has a CD of their music, they no longer own it (unless they made the CD in their garage—but I'm talking about commercial music here).

Handling your music rights is like a producer's rite of passage; it's traumatic—but afterwards, you can call yourself a producer.

The two sets of rights you have to clear are publishing rights (the lyrics themselves) and master sync rights (the original recording of the piece). These rights will be owned by two different companies. Not only do you have to find those two different companies (read the back of the DVD cover, then Google) but then you have to write, fax, grovel, beg, and sometimes cry in order to get the deal made. These companies are HUGE and they just really don't care about the tiny little amount of money (your life savings) that they are going to get from you for 10 seconds of U2 in your short film. But you can't sell your film until they give you permission to use the music or until you replace the music with something that's free and clear, like your sister screwing around on her keyboard. This option becomes more and more attractive the more you work with music rights.

Once you figure out who owns which rights and how to contact them, you will need to present them with a complete music cue sheet that states exactly what music plays, for what duration, with the time code of each music clip within the film. You will be asked what kind of rights you'd like to clear your music for (festival rights, educational rights, DVD rights, broadcast rights, etc.) and the answer is "all commercial rights" if you want to be able to sell the heck out of your film without worrying that you might need to go back and clear more rights later. It is of course cheaper to only clear festival rights (giving you the right to play your film at festivals) but then you'll have to go back and renegotiate when you want to sell your film later. All buyers and distributors will ask you to prove that you have your music rights cleared before they license your film, and you do not want to have to clear your music more than once if you can help it. Alternatively, you could use only original music and recordings in your film, enabling you to skip this entire, traumatic music rights clearing experience, which I highly recommend.

So let's say your film is now totally clear and you are the rights holder. (Ahh, another detail—it's important to know who the rights holder is, you, or a company name (like if you made your film under an LLC), or an investor who you made the film through, etc., and some companies will want to see a Chain of Title that documents ownership from the beginning of the project.) Okay, so let's say your film is cleared and ready to meet the world. Like you, your film was born with many rights.

There are so many possible rights to sell, there's an incredible smorgasbord of ways to get your film seen. New rights get created every day, as new applications for seeing your film get invented. To name a few obvious ones, you have theatrical rights (the rights to play your film in a theater), broadcast rights (the rights to play your film on a channel), DVD or home video rights (the rights to sell your film on DVD), Internet rights, cell phone rights, non-theatrical rights (churches, clubs, hospitals), educational rights (schools, universities), catalog rights, and more, believe it or not.

Once you are clear that you own your film and you understand the rights that your baby was born with, you get to decide how you'd like to send it out into the world.

Buyer vs distributor

There are two ways to go with a short: (1) you can give your film to a distributor who will sell your film for you, or (2) you can represent your film yourself, and look for buyers who will license specific rights from you directly.

The difference between distributors and buyers is that distributors want you to give them all the rights to your film, so that they can sell them off in as many ways as possible, giving you a cut of those deals. Whereas buyers want to get very specific rights to your film (say, exclusive broadcast rights for one year), will pay you up front, will ask you for the elements (master, stills, transcript, bio, awards sheet), and will be done with you once they have what they need. Some buyers will only buy directly from distributors because they don't want to take the time to walk filmmakers through the licensing process each time they buy a film.

It's a great idea to work with a distributor if you want someone else to figure out who to sell your film to, how the deals should go, and where and when to send the elements, etc., while you go off and make your next masterpiece.

As a filmmaker, if you can get a distributor to take your film and sell it for you, that's a very good thing for your filmmaking career. To the rest of the world it means that you have a sellable film (they wouldn't take it otherwise) and for you it means that on your *next* film, you have a relationship already in place with a distributor, which can sometimes help you to convince investors that you will be able to sell your next film. Also while you may be able get one major deal on your film by yourself, it's very tough to maximize all possible sales, selling further territories and secondary windows on your own.

Distributors can save you a lot of hard knocks and confusion and can make receiving money for your hard work very simple and easy. But be prepared; they will sell your film in as many ways as they possibly can, because that's how they make their money. So don't be surprised when you see your film on three different Internet sites, and a friend sends you a cell phone link for it as well. If you go with a distributor and you have a hot little film, it's gonna happen. And that's great if you're off making your next movie anyway.

I'm always amazed by the errant email I get from a filmmaker saying, "I saw my film on one of your volumes, but I don't remember ever licensing my film to you. What's going on?" Since I'm not actually allowed to respond to them directly (because I licensed their film from a distributor, and most distributor agreements have nondisclosure clauses), I have to send their emails on to the distributor who I licensed their film from, asking them to please let their filmmaker know that they have sublicensed their film to us and it's all legal and good.

Selling your film

If you have a great short—the kind of short that has every festival drooling over it—if you are getting into every festival you apply to and you'll be hitting the biggest festivals of the year, then you could consider representing your own film because the buyers will find you on their own if your film is going to be that widely played. But be warned, if you decide to represent your own film, you're going to learn a lot very quickly and you're going to spend a pretty penny doing it. It's Distribution 101 if you take the DIY (do it yourself) approach. At the end of it all you won't have a producer's certificate from grad school, but you will have spent almost as much as if you had gone back to school, and you will probably know enough to be on an equal playing field with those who did.

Let's say you have a really good short film and it's going to be seen at lots of festivals where lots of buyers will get to see it directly, and you have decided to skip the distributor route and sell your film yourself. This means that it's your responsibility to find the buyers who might want your film, and your responsibility to close the deals with these buyers. This can be tricky, and I have some advice for you if this is the way you are going to go.

To buy or not to buy

I have only ever been a buyer for The Spiritual Cinema Circle, so I don't claim to know what the buyer's life is like in any other company, but I can tell you what my experience has been. Being a buyer is great fun. Festivals love buyers, so do filmmakers. It's nice to be loved. But the job isn't all rosy all the time. Buyers have to watch an incredible number of films each year and are tireless in their search for great product. There are certain things that filmmakers can do to increase their chances of being bought by hungry buyers.

First of all, if you are at a festival looking to sell your film, have lots of DVDs of the film with you to hand to buyers. We don't want huge press kits, but you could include a well-designed postcard that has all of your pertinent info on it. Each DVD should have your info on the DVD face and on the case so that if they separate, we can still find you. Make sure that you have watched every DVD before you hand them out to be sure that they will all play correctly. It's so frustrating to play a film that doesn't work or is filled with dropouts and glitches. I have a lot of patience, but a bad copy of a five-minute short makes me crazy. It's not hard to QC (quality check) a five-minute short to be sure it plays well—it's definitely worth your time not to piss off your prospective buyer!

The deal

There is an art to the deal with shorts: it's called nonexclusivity. My advice to filmmakers selling their own film is to do everything you possibly can do with your film; take every sale that comes your way, and do it all *nonexclusively*. I have some distributor friends who would have my head for putting that in print, but they'll forgive me next month when I buy three more shorts from them. The only exception is with broadcast. If a very reputable company wants your film for broadcast on a channel that will give you great exposure, then you should agree to the exclusive deal in a certain territory for an agreed-upon term.

For instance let's say a buyer for a well-known comedy channel is looking for films under five minutes that make you laugh out loud, and you have that film. They want exclusive broadcast rights for a one-year term in the territory of North America. They will pay pretty well for this because of the exclusive part (maybe a couple of hundred dollars per minute, maybe more—could be as much as $5000 for a five-minute piece). (1) You are getting paid well. (2) You get to say that your film played on that channel. If you ever want to make another film, this can be really helpful. It's only exclusive for broadcast in North America for a year. That means you can still sell broadcast rights outside of North America, and you still have all of your other rights to sell as well.

When you are selling your film yourself, the first question to ask when dealing with a buyer is "How reputable is this company?" If it's a well-known company, a company that's been in business for a few years, if you can talk to other filmmakers who have worked with them and have been paid, then you can trust that the agreement they send to you is going to be fairly basic and utilitarian. If it's a reputable company, you don't need to sweat over the legalese.

Tip of the Day: Don't sit around negotiating for weeks over normal, boring legal parts of the licensing agreements. Make sure that the deal points work for you and *just sign the damn paperwork!* Indemnities are not interesting. They are in every agreement you will sign. Pay them no mind. Watch the big stuff: term, territory, format, fee. What rights are they asking for, in what territory, for how long, and for how much? If those pieces make sense and you are willing to give them what they are asking for, for the money they are offering, then they have a deal. Sign the paperwork, send the master, and move on with your life!

You can definitely negotiate the major deal points. Ask for what you want, they can only say no—and you might be surprised by a yes here and there. But don't be a *prima donna*. Keep in mind that you have made a short film; this is not going to be the next *Spiderman* franchise, no matter how you spin it. Yes, you want to take care of yourself and get the best deal you can get, but don't get intense over the details. If you are dealing with a reputable company, the legal stuff is just a normal part of the licensing process.

Disclaimer: Don't get me wrong—it's important for you to understand what you are agreeing to. I'm not advocating blindly selling off rights because you are so happy that someone wants your film. My lawyer friend is going to make me put this part in: You might want to run the long-form contracts past a lawyer, especially the first few times you sign a contract, just to be sure that you clearly understand what you are getting into. I would recommend at the very least getting a few books out of the library about film deals so that you can become familiar with the language and purpose of each section of a licensing agreement and can feel confident about signing on the dotted line.

Selling your film can be the most fun you've ever had if you're the producer type who likes this sort of detailed puzzle work involved in plotting out and executing a distribution plan for your film. If all of this makes you want to run screaming back to the comfort of your warm bed, then find someone you trust who can do this for you. And then get out there and make your next movie!

DAVID RUSSELL began his career in theater and film production, spanning over 25 years as an actor, writer, director, and producer. His work as the production manager for Robert Altman's first foray into theater (*Two by South*) led further into behind-the-scenes work and eventually to the film world. His experience as a production coordinator on feature films at 20th Century Fox, Vestron, Nelson Entertainment, Interscope, Orion Pictures, and New Regency laid the foundation for his own independent production company, Adobe Pictures, with which he produced an independent feature (*Wanna Be in Pictures*).

Big Film Shorts was formed in 1996 to help serve the short-form filmmakers and the perceived need for their content in the expanding worldwide marketplace. A pioneer in the sales and marketing of short films, BFS was the first Internet company to represent and sell short films worldwide to all markets. In 2003 Mr. Russell and his partners formed Nano Network, Inc., to package, program, and exhibit short films for the traditional markets and the emerging new technologies. In 2006 they launched Nano, their own video-on-demand channel, on Comcast—the first television channel in the United States devoted exclusively to short films. Similar channels are also available on broadband and cellular mobile outlets.

Who's Gonna Rescue Me if I Start to Drown?

By David Russell

So, you want to make a movie? Why don't you get a cell phone camera and shoot some people lighting matches to their farts, send it to MySpace, then email all your friends to check it out? If that takes care of your fantasy to make a movie, then great, you're done.

But if you really want to make a movie, not just an indulgence, then there are some other things to consider. First, you're either not too bright or you're brilliant. One thing's clear: you're not very realistic. What are the chances of you getting millions of dollars to make your dream? Who's going to trust you to do what you say you're going to do? Who's gonna care?

But, maybe you have a passion that no one can see yet; visions of a herd of elephants falling off a cliff, fires eating whole cities, oceans sucking up continents. Or, just a car driving across the desert. Even with all the new technologies your visions can be expensive.

Without a passion, without a vision, you're sunk. Now, you just have to figure out how to pay for it.

This is where the short film comes in. You've got to prove to a lot of people that you're a storyteller and you've got something worth saying. Let's assume farts on fire don't quite cut it for you (if they did, you probably can't read and this book isn't really aimed at you anyway). So, start with a short. It's just logical. Maybe even realistic.

Okay, you're going to make a short film. Now what?

There are two options. One is to make a calling card film, just for the experience, and try to get it into festivals. Maybe someone will see it and want to see what else you've got. The other is to make a legal film that can work as a calling card but can also be sold in the short film markets. This option requires more work.

As distributors of short films, our company, Big Film Shorts, has seen and considered thousands of shorts over the last 10 years in both categories. I'm not even talking about the other thousands of films that cause the clichéd "What were they thinking?" response.

Generally the calling card film and the legal film are easy to differentiate. The calling card can be very good and very watchable but usually starts out with music that would be impossible to afford the rights to. It often has the use of logos and trademarks that are either abused or clearly unaffordable. Therefore it's assumed the filmmaker, 90% of the time, probably didn't get signed releases from actors or composers of original music. In other words the film just can't be sold because you didn't get all the permissions required to prove that you own your film. Oh, you might get it into festivals. Most festival programmers don't have to care about your due diligence for cleared rights. And you might be able to get an agent or producer to check it out (don't quit your day job). What if people do like your film and they'd like to buy it or sell it for you? You think you can go back to all those people and get them to give you signed releases after the fact? You've already stolen from them once so even if they'll cooperate and give you permission now you'll be shocked by how much they'll want you to pay them.

Making a legal film that you have all the rights to and can control its destiny is the best option. Any salable film will also be a calling card you can use within the industry. Let making your short film be your film school. Learn everything you can about what it takes to create a story on film. This involves more than just the creative vision, the passion. You'll have to learn about the business of making a movie. And who knows, someone might even pay you some money for it.

Wouldn't it be satisfying to be able to start paying back the Bank of Mom and Dad?

From the distributor's point of view you'll need to have about 39,000 things in order before a buyer will pay you money for your work. Okay, maybe it's only about 35,000 things. But there's a lot of stuff to think about besides the fun parts.

Before you put pen to paper or buy someone's story, check out the markets. Television, broadband Internet, mobile/cell phones, DVDs, maybe even schools, libraries, and hotels. Any place where shorts are being exhibited. Find out who's showing the kinds of films you'd like to make or plan to make. These markets are changing and growing. It's essential that you make the film you have a passion to make so it will be very helpful, even inspiring, to know if there's an audience somewhere for it. If your research shows there isn't an apparent audience, just wait a week; there may be a new one popping up. We get constant inquiries for content to fit a specific niche.

Once you've determined what project you're going to proceed with take the time and make the effort to get your ducks in a row. In other words get the rights to every frame of sound and picture as you go through preproduction, principal photography, and postproduction. It starts with the script or story. Spend some time on this, the most crucial aspect of any project. Because, believe me, you can't "fix it in post."

I once worked on a feature film that had not yet received permission from a federal government agency to use a billboard of a famous public service trademark, a national icon. The producers okayed going ahead with the day's shoot, feeling certain they would get the signed permission later. The government agency refused permission based on the script they were sent (which they hated). The producers had to reshoot the day's work without the billboard at a huge override of their budget.

Another time, one of our short film producers was offered a chance to release his film theatrically. It was to play in front of a feature. In order to take the deal the producer had to go back to all his actors and get signed permissions from them to upgrade his initial SAG contract. He also had to pay them all again (over $20,000). One of them wanted a $1000 signing bonus in addition to his salary or he wasn't going to give his permission. That one actor was in complete control of what would happen to the film. The producer paid. His short film got rave reviews. Unfortunately, the feature did not. No money was made. If the producer had foreseen such an opportunity he could have made sure he controlled all rights to his film's destiny and the risk of any theatrical exposure wouldn't have been so expensive.

One of our student filmmakers used a famous rock group's song in his end credits. When he tried to get a clearance for commercial use he was quoted, according to him, a $1 million licensing fee. It didn't matter that he was a student. It didn't matter if he ever actually sold it. That was the fee, take it or leave it. He changed the song. But it took months to learn what he should have done in the first place.

Think ahead and cover your bases wherever possible.

Most buyers of film content, whether short or long, who pay money for programming, are at a huge liability risk. They require us, the distributor, to provide "Chain of Title" paperwork, proving the film-maker actually has written contracts and releases from actors, extras, real people, composers, record labels, trademarks and logos, products, copyright, clips or excerpts from other copyrighted material, and locations in some cases.

Other requirements are tape formats, dialog lists, music cue sheets, production stills—all of which can be done easily in postproduction but are very hard to create after the fact. We also highly recommend investing in a high-definition tape format of your final product. It's not a required element yet, but that's coming.

All of this un-fun side of filmmaking is crucial to know about and experience while you're making your personal-film-school-project. Hopefully one day you'll have other people taking care of all this for you, but wouldn't it be good to know what they're doing or if they're doing it all? Because, I guarantee you, every future project in your entire career will involve this business side of getting your vision produced.

So, get out there. Start putting it together in a realistic way. I'm personally in awe of anyone who can get a film made. It's almost a shock and certainly a delight to see one that hits the mark and is clearly what the filmmaker had in mind. You'll find lots of people who will want to help you swim upstream at this beginning stage (aside from the Bank of Mom and Dad). Some of them might even help you if you start to drown. But to avoid being left to flounder all on your own they've got to believe that you believe.

It doesn't have to be a stupid idea.

Bon voyage.

JENN CHEN is General Manager of Ouat Media Distribution, a premiere distribution company specializing in the international promotion, distribution, and sales of short films. She was formerly the head of Flow Distribution, home to the films produced by the Canadian Film Centre.

Ms. Chen studied cinema at the Sorbonne in Paris for a year before returning to Canada, where she worked in feature film production and directed/produced her own short films. She has shared her knowledge of the short film industry with audiences at film festivals around the world, consulted on distribution strategies for award-winning shorts, and represented shorts in many international film festivals, including Los Angeles, Sundance, Clermont-Ferrand, Berlin, and Cannes.

Life Starts When?

By Jenn Chen

For most filmmakers, the joys and pains of making and finishing their film is what defines filmmaking. In reality, the life of the film has only just begun. No one cares what hardships went into making your chef d'oeuvre if no one ever sees it. The true life of a film begins after it's in the can and it's sent off into the world to see if it can walk on its own.

I manage Ouat Media Distribution (www.ouatmedia.com), an exclusive short film distribution company. We acquire the rights to international short films and sell them worldwide. The most traditional platform we sell-through to is broadcast television, but the world of new media is opening new channels of distribution for short content. It's a really exciting time for short films.

For emerging filmmakers, of whom I've met so many working in short film distribution, the key to real success always lies in what happens after the film is made. To make my job easier, and to give your baby the best shot at life in the world, I share with you some key words of wisdom for making your short film a success. As someone who has also struggled through producing short films, I truly speak from the heart and wallet!

When I first meet the director and producer, I always ask: "What do you want this film to do for you?" Filmmakers rarely think about this because they've been sweating over just getting the film done. But this essential question will help dictate the responses to so many questions that will arise from here on. . . .

Festivals

In my opinion, the international festival circuit is the most cost-effective way to market your short film. Nowhere else can you get international exposure for your film. A strong festival strategy means taking submission and marketing costs into consideration early on in the production process and budgeting for them appropriately.

To capture the "face" of your film, production stills are a must. Later, when you make your postcards or posters, you'll have the images you want in the proper resolution. For ideas on what the photos should look like, take a look at festival program guides (they are available online) to see what images work best in a program.

When you move into post, you want to start researching submission dates that are fast approaching. Most festivals will look at rough cuts if you're pressed to meet a festival deadline. A word of advice: make sure it's not too rough a cut. There is a fine line between "rough" and "not ready" with each programmer at different festivals. If you can wait until the project is done, try to. Often you can only submit to a festival once and you want to know that the film was the best that it could be before you sent it. Another quick tip, include a dialog list or a shooting script with your submission to film fests in countries where English is not their first language.

Costs

Money has to be budgeted for film festivals. Give your baby at least that chance. Thoughts around your festival strategy also begin here. Where would you like to premiere your film? What is your backup if you don't get that festival? Have you timed production around a particular festival or should your festival submission strategy be timed around your production? These are all important questions to consider when determining your strategy. When you have a general idea of which festivals you would like to submit to, you can accurately budget for them.

What will you need to submit your film? DVD screener copies of your film, bubble envelopes, postage, one-sheet printouts, and festival submission fees are just the start. Multiply by the number of festivals you would like to submit to and then double it! After you've spent some time researching all the festivals (and you must do this) you will always discover another interesting festival that would work for your film. And all this before you get in! Additional costs to consider if your film IS invited to a festival: shipping, marketing materials, and press kits. Some festivals will only cover the one-way cost of sending your exhibition print or tape to them. The exhibition format itself is generally a film print (35mm or 16mm) or is most commonly a digibeta, beta sp, or sometimes, a DVD. All this before you add the cost of travel if you decide to go.

Must do's if you attend a film festival: Always meet the programmer who invited your film. At the top of your list should also be meeting the festival publicist. Every festival has a publicist who will help you if they can. You need to try to stay top-of-mind with them and if they're not swamped, they will help.

Usually, you can email your contact person at the festival before you arrive to get a list of the delegates attending. Set up meetings with those people, remembering what you want the film to do for you.

Rules around festivals

Researching the rules and eligibility requirements of film festivals is crucial. I suggest that you submit to the feature film festivals that have short programs before hitting niche events like shorts-only festivals or genre festivals, where regulations on the age and premiere status of the film are generally more lenient.

Markets

Markets should also play a big role in your festival strategy. You should definitely include submissions to film festivals with industry markets. In the case of shorts, only short film markets apply. At these markets, buyers shop for content for their respective platforms. Television, DVD, Internet, and now mobile content buyers come to the markets looking to license short films. Distributors also attend these markets, looking for films to add to their catalog.

Distribution

As your film gains "legs" on the festival circuit, distributors looking for new films can contact you to see a screener or, if they've already seen your film, will start discussions around acquiring the rights to your film.

Short film distributors function in a similar way to feature film sales agents. They look to acquire the rights of a completed short film to sell internationally. Most short film distribution companies take a commission of every sale. These commission rates range from 30 to 50%. Deductibles, rechargeables, expenses, terms, territories, and rights are also factors in negotiating the contract. The best way to feel out a distributor is to talk to them or other filmmakers who have worked with them in the past. It's the best way to go—and don't be afraid to ask questions.

Most distribution organizations are set up with two primary functions: acquisitions and sales. Acquisitions deals with the films and filmmakers. Acquisitions people seek new films to represent, either through unsolicited submissions or actively pursuing a title that they've seen at a festival. The more popular films are usually comedies under

10 minutes. Once the acquisitions team has made their choice, someone then manages collecting all the required deliverables to sell-through to a buyer. In distribution, this can sometimes be the longest part of the whole process.

Common document deliverables:

- music cue sheet
- music clearances
- product and/or location clearances
- errors and omissions (E&O) insurance

There are music and footage clearance specialists that you can hire to advise if you have properly cleared your music.

Depending on the story of the film and any products or locations seen on screen, we usually need documentation illustrating permission from the respective company or location. Furthermore, the permission will have to include allowance for you to receive compensation from all the territories and platforms you would sell to. Oh yes, even for a short!

Lastly, everyone will ask for E&O insurance but very few filmmakers actually have it. It's an insurance policy that protects the filmmaker from any claims made against the film. It also protects anyone licensing the film from claims. If it's at all possible, it's a good exercise to get it. Assuming that a short filmmaker will one day want to make a feature film, it's good practice.

After the film has been licensed, we work on who and how we're going to sell it. Depending on the length and genre of a film, we begin to develop a sales strategy. At the same time, we also prepare all the marketing materials. It's best to get a film while it's new and still on the festival circuit. Some buyers like very new films, while others look for genre-specific films regardless of age. A distributor has access to a whole range of buyers looking for content. If your film doesn't work in one territory or on a particular platform, don't worry, there are always other options. The sales arm of a short film distributor looks for short film sales opportunities as a full-time job. Your job is to continue making films!

Similar to the strategy for film festivals, there is a pecking order that should be respected when developing the sales strategy for a film. We ensure that those who require exclusivity in a territory or platform get a chance to review the film first. Usually, they pay the most.

In the short film world, you have to know that you will NEVER make big money. None of us do. It's about the love and fun of it all.

Short films are a great way to tell an original story. A great short will lead to other projects. So, a couple of final words as your baby goes out into that big cold world: Tell a good story in your style, with your voice. Think about what you want to achieve with the film and plan your festival strategy accordingly. Get a distributor because they WILL do a better job than you could. Keep it clean, meaning you have paperwork for all music/location/actor clearances. But most of all, have fun!

LINDA "O." OLSZEWSKI joined Shorts International in January 2006 as Head of North & South American Acquisitions & Podcasts to spearhead acquisitions for Shorts International's iTunes "Academy Short Film Nominees" launch, as well as the simultaneous theatrical, DVD, and television releases with Magnolia Pictures.

She is currently focused on acquiring shorts for iTunes, BT-Vision, and the recently launched Shorts TV France channel, as well as for television clients. She can be found at festivals scouting for cinematic gems in all genres and/or producing podcasts for Shorts TV on iTunes.

Former credits include Co-Founder/Director of DreamWorks Film Fest, Hanna–Barbera's Development Team for Cartoon Network's *What A Cartoon!*, Eveo's Director of Worldwide Acquisitions, Head of Shorts for The Hatchery, Senior Programmer at the Palm Springs International Short Film Festival, Feature Film Screener at the Sundance Film Fest, and documentary cameraperson in Afghanistan and Mexico.

Taking the Brake Lights Off Your Film

By Linda "O." Olszewski

Years ago when I was in film school, I had the opportunity to go to Cannes with a 16 mm film camera and a few filmmaker and actor friends to make a film (*Cannes or Bust!*) about the future of cinema. We had gotten the necessary credentials to attend the Cannes Film Festival, had the look and wardrobe to crash the right parties, and enough charm and humility to get movie stars to participate in our movie. We even had a producer carrying our equipment for us—he said he had always wanted to see what it was like to be a production assistant. As we filmed, Harvey Weinstein of Miramax Films became curious about our project and followed us around for the better part of an hour.

It was all very exciting. We were convinced we were on our way to success. Perhaps we would return the following year to show our film at the festival. Yet, despite our enthusiasm and film school educations, we were not to experience what seemed like a certain future because we did not take some of the basic steps necessary to ensure our film would be distributable. In this chapter, I want to point you in the right direction so you don't misstep the way we did.

Releases

A release is a signed permission form stating, "This footage is distributable." Have everyone who is in front of the camera sign a release. When we filmed in Cannes, we didn't realize we needed releases until an industry insider we interviewed asked to sign ours. We didn't have one so he asked a lawyer friend to draft a boilerplate release for us. (You can find the forms on the Internet.) Had we not gotten signed releases from everyone we filmed, we would never have been able to screen or distribute any of the footage we shot.

Unions

You can save time and money by hiring nonunion actors and crew. However, if a star is willing to be in your film, don't say no too quickly—having recognizable talent will make your film more interesting to distributors. If you decide to hire a union actor, you must get "signatory," which means signing with the union and agreeing to their terms and rates. Be sure to allow three months turnaround as the process requires detailed paperwork. If you do not get signatory and the film gets distributed, not only will the union seek compensation (perhaps by trying to get a lien on your house or anything of value), but it may penalize the actor and possibly throw him or her out of the union for participating in a nonunion project. It also may harm your chances of working with the actor or anyone else of that caliber in the future. For more information on unions, go to:

Actors: www.sagindie.com or http://www.aftra.org
Directors: http://www.dga.org
Editors: http://www.editorsguild.com
Producers: http://www.producersguild.org

Story

Try to make a film that is original. Choose a story that inspires you, that comes from within you or from your own personal experience.

58

I say this for two reasons: First, and most important, if you are working from a gem of wisdom that inspires you to make and actually finish a film, chances are it will inspire others as well. And that's the point—to touch other people, to cause them to laugh, to encourage meaningful action, to make them think about a situation or a person outside of their own sphere of existence. Do not make a parody of someone else's short. Spoofs are so last century—don't do it, no matter how much you are tempted. Great films and the great stories are not remakes but are original works by people that had the courage to reveal themselves in order to connect with others. The kind of films I am talking about are generally the ones that eventually are labeled "classic" because they stand the test of time and appeal to broad audiences. Many people want to make a film from a short story that inspired them in order to share the story with the world. That's great, but it might cost a lot of money and a certain amount of control over the film's distribution. The author or the author's estate will retain the rights to the story and can stop or limit distribution for any number of reasons. You may start out making a film for the festival circuit, and it might just win a festival, thus qualifying it for Academy Award consideration, and you might even receive a nomination. You might even win. Fantastic! Everything is going perfectly—until you have to get the permission of the rights holder. If someone else wrote the story, they have input on where the film will get seen. It might get quite expensive and could prohibit you from distributing the film. If you are planning to use a short story, negotiate the parameters for festival participation and distribution and get a signed contract with a detailed distribution option before you shoot. I frequently come across films I would love to distribute but cannot because they are stuck in legal limbo.

Film vs digital video

If you were to ask this question 10 years ago, few filmmakers would pick digital. Video imagery was flat. The cameras did not have near the capability they do now. You could not use film lenses on video equipment. Today film budgets are higher. Production schedules are longer because of rehearsals, practice runs, and lengthy setups for lighting. In film postproduction you had to think telecine, film syncing, reconfiguration, negative cutting, interpositive, film print. Now with the great high-definition digital cameras available, as well as inexpensive editing software such as Final Cut Pro, you can shoot and cut your film quickly. An Avid setup used to cost more than $20,000, and even though you could get a camera package for free, film processing and telecine alone could amount to 25% of your budget.

Times have changed. The only reason to shoot on film today is for the look; there's no reason to edit on film. (Most of the great film editors have retired.) As for theatrical projection, 5 years ago theaters still only screened 35 mm prints. Today, with the influx of digital projection such as Landmark's QUBE, you only need to create a D5 master for premium quality. Many of the recently Oscar-nominated independent and animated films used QUBE for theatrical projection. It saves a lot of money for distributors and ultimately puts more money into the filmmaker's pocket.

iTunes USA

Apple's iTunes is a great way for indie short and feature filmmakers to reach a wide audience. Short films only cost the consumer $1.99 and indie features $9.99, but the filmmaker's share, depending on the number of downloads, can add up to significant money. How does one get onto iTunes? Indie filmmakers need to go through a distributor such as Shorts International or a film festival such as Sundance. Generally, whether live-action or animated, films must have commercial viability to be sold on iTunes. If your short is about your grandmother's bad dye job, this probably isn't the place (we'll talk about YouTube shortly). Films that work best on iTunes are shorts that have a coherent story and high production values. Computer animation is particularly hot on iTunes and films like *Gopher Broke, Emelia: The Five-Year-Old Goth Girl, The Mantis Parable, Smile, Maestro,* and *The Freak* are all great examples of indie CGI shorts that easily compete with Pixar. Animated shorts should be 4 to 30 minutes, while live-action shorts should be 10 to 30 minutes. Comedies always sell better than dramas. Is your film appealing to at least half of the people sitting in an AMC Theater? If the answer is no, iTunes might not be the right venue. Some very successful live-action shorts are *Denial, Cashback, The Shovel, Boy-Next-Door, Full Disclosure, Message from Fallujah, Victoria Para Chino,* and *The Runaway.* All the past Oscar nominees and winners are getting high downloads as well.

Podcasting

A great way to keep the buzz going about your film is via your web site, MySpace page, YouTube posting, or iTunes video podcast. The most successful fan building I have seen has been by Chris Mais for *Smile,* Menithings for *The Freak,* and Josh Staub for *The Mantis Parable.* All three filmmakers have built a wide audience through their festival circuit presence, have nurtured it through their web sites, and expanded it with podcasts and trailers on their MySpace pages.

Smile was twice voted MySpace's "best short of the month," and Chris capitalized on the interest by creating two video podcasts about the making of *Smile* for his MySpace and ShortsTV, Shorts International's podcast on iTunes. All the exposure not only created more buzz for these filmmakers, but generated more sales for their films on iTunes.

Building a fan base

Self-promotion is key, and film distributors and talent scouts always Google filmmakers and films to find their web sites. A dynamic web site is important. Make sure to keep all your contact details updated and that you have downloadable press kits, festival and screening announcements, trailers, podcasts, and information about the director. Blogging about your festival experiences and production "war stories" will help create interest and may convince a distributor to look at your film. When you attend festivals, always bring postcards and eye-catching flyers. Distributors pick them up for your contact information. Fans love them, too. Maintain a mailing list and regularly send announcements for upcoming events. Keep your fans excited about your film so they will want to download your film when it gets on iTunes.

YouTube

This is a handy place to put something up immediately for your friends and family to view. However, if you plan to enter your film in festivals or try for an Academy Award, don't put your film on YouTube because you will disqualify yourself from consideration.

The Academy rule is 30 seconds or 10% of the total running time, whichever is shorter. Also, many film festivals will automatically disqualify you if you have put your film online prior to their screening. Check the festival rules carefully, and consider instead putting up a trailer or clip only if you intend to go on the festival circuit.

Shorts television channels

Shorts TV France, a TV channel featuring only shorts from around the world, recently launched in partnership with Shorts International. Managed by Julien Hossein and Carter Pilcher, its creative board members include Roman Polanski, Sophie Marceau, and Maurice Jarre. Shorts TV is scheduled to launch additional shorts channels in the coming year across Europe. Movieola is a 24-hour Canadian shorts channel. Other TV channels that buy shorts include The Sundance Channel and France's Canal Plus.

New distribution platforms

The possibilities for distribution are multiplying, with new platforms emerging every month. As you consider the options, your goal should be to get your film seen by as wide an audience as possible while making an acceptable amount of money. Can you get there independently or do you need to go through an aggregator (distributor)? Never give your film away for free! It devalues your work and the short film industry. In the coming years, we shall see if the current hype surrounding cell phone distribution and other emerging platforms will stand the test of time. Mobile media opportunities recently launched are BT Vision and Verizon, and a few new online platforms including VOD are Amazon Unboxed, JOOST, Google Video, and Indieflix.

Film festivals

The top festivals I always try to attend are Clermont-Ferrand, Aspen ShortsFest Toronto Worldwide Festival of Short Films, Tribeca, Palm Springs Short Film Festival, Sundance, Cinemajove, Los Angeles, Newport Beach, AFI, Drama (Greece), Sao Paulo, Vila Do Conde, Cannes, Edinburgh, and Rio de Janeiro. When submitting your film, the first rule of thumb is: Always submit early, in the first week if possible. This increases the likelihood that the programmers will see your film while they are still fresh and when there is still plenty of room left in the shorts program. An excellent festival submission tool is Withoutabox, an incredibly streamlined online submission process system. As recently as 1999 filmmakers trudged through a myriad of submission forms for each festival, but now for a fixed price, a filmmaker only has to input their film details once, push a button, and almost miraculously their film is under consideration at festivals around the globe. Participating in film festivals can help get your film screened by industry insiders, distributors, attorneys, and agents. Plus, winning the short film prize at an "Academy Qualifying" festival will automatically qualify your film to be considered for an Academy Award nomination. But just as importantly, going on the festival circuit will create opportunities for you to be with your audience as they embrace your film (hopefully), as well as meet fellow filmmakers who you may one day collaborate with. You will participate in Q&As and travel to many places you might never have visited. Many festivals will host filmmakers for part or all of the festival. Some even offer airfare! I interview filmmakers for Shorts TV video podcasts, and when I inquire what their best festival experience was, every filmmaker always has as least one fest they definitely hope to return to.

Sales rep vs distributor

Word-of-mouth is the best way to find a sales representative or distributor that is trustworthy and will meet your needs. Does this sales rep have the contacts necessary to get multiple global sales done? Sign with a sales rep for a year and try them out. A sales rep will not have errors and omissions (E&O) insurance; a distributor will. Does this distributor have interesting deals and/or partnerships in place? Google them. How many times do they come up? What kind of percentages do they have in place (this is not necessarily a deal breaker because some distributors can get you higher pay rates than you could have gotten on your own and still get themselves paid with more money in your pocket). Are statements and payments generated biannually or annually? Is the person you are doing business with willing to include an inactivity clause? When Disney bought Miramax's library, many good films ended up stuck on the shelf. Had they requested an inactivity clause, the filmmakers could have bought the rights back or had the rights revert back to them. You can find active distributors or sales reps scouting at the above-mentioned film festivals. Fees will vary slightly, but sales reps generally charge 20 to 35% of all sales plus costs. Distributors generally charge more, but will cover your film under E&O insurance, which ensures that if you somehow missed something in your film and get sued, you will be covered. International television stations generally require E&O and will work with distributors who can guarantee the films are distributable. This generally helps distributors have more reach into the world markets. Some filmmakers get different distributors for different territories/continents because they might specialize in a region. For example, Premium Films specializes in France.

Don't be a jerk

No one wants to give a jerk a break. A jerk is someone with an inflated sense of entitlement. If someone is too difficult to work with, no one will want to work with that person for long. It's a relationship. If your girlfriend or boyfriend is uncompromisingly demanding, eventually you might decide this is just no fun. This is entertainment and ultimately the reason most of us work in short films is because we love films. It's a very niche market, meaning there is not a lot of money to be made. But there is some. So be patient when people are reviewing your work. Nudge only once a month. And when you get an offer, listen about the plans the distributor has for your film. Let the distributor know about the fan base you have built and what ambitions you have for your film. If you're lucky, it will be a match and you will be on your way to sharing something special with the world.

Oh, by the way, we took our own advice and fixed our distribution missteps. With a little luck our film, *Cannes or Bust*, will be on the festival circuit by the time you read this.

Good luck! I hope to see you on the festival circuit both as an acquisitions executive and as a fellow filmmaker.—Linda O.

Make Your Mark

By Joe Amodei

The first short I ever laid eyes on was a 1945 Mervyn Leroy-directed film titled *The House I Live In*. My father had purchased a used 16 mm projector and a box of films and I can still recall seeing it projected onto an old pull-up movie screen in the living room of our home in Philly. I was only eight years old but already on my way to a life of film geekdom and also a love of Frank Sinatra who starred in the film. The film opens with Frankie in the recording studio crooning a tune and then going outside into an alley to, as he phrases it, "catch a smoke." When was the last time that line was used in a movie!

So he goes outside and is greeted by an angry mob of teens chasing after one poor helpless boy. He breaks up the fight and finds out they are about to beat him because the boy is Jewish. The skinny as a rail Sinatra goes on to explain that the war we had just fought and won was engaged to stop this kind of thinking. He sets the kids straight and heads back to the studio but not before warbling another tune. This was the first time I had ever been exposed to a film with any type of social message. Viewing the film helped shape my own intolerance towards racism and hatred. It was that powerful. And it was not a feature film. It was a short.

Now here I am 40 years later spending a good part of my life looking at shorts from both a personal and business point of view. My personal love still exists in the format, as I get a kick out of watching well-put-together stories with a very short running time. The business aspect is quite different. I look for shorts to jazz up a series of DVDs I release to the public through a distribution company I own. Part of what we do is release smaller independent-driven product that is not in the mainstream. So we look for interesting shorts to add on as special features. Sometimes we get them directly from the filmmakers themselves. Sometimes we search for them. Where we search is just about everywhere and anywhere we can.

The best places to find shorts for our type of use is at film festivals. The most common and well known, Cannes, Sundance, Toronto, and Tribeca, devote part of their programming efforts to short films and some have their own competitions as well. As an acquisition executive it sometimes gets tough as you have to choose between seeing a feature film that is available for sale or a series of shorts. But that's all part of the job.

Another source for films is the college circuit. Any school that offers filmmaking produces literally dozens of shorts each year. They hold their own short film festivals and hand out awards. Most of these films are amazingly good so the choices are many. The students use professional equipment and produce films from all genres, including narrative, experimental, and documentary.

The Internet has also opened up a whole new world where the viewing of shorts takes place. As with everything else on the World Wide

Web, this is good and this is also bad. The good is the simple fact that sites have cropped up that feature films by aspiring filmmakers waiting to get discovered. The bad is, well, the very same thing. Anybody with a video camera can now make a short and get it on the Internet. And unfortunately, they do.

But finding a good short that can go onto a consumer-driven DVD is not as easy as it sounds. Even though there are more venues than ever to see a short, when you get around to putting it on a disc that will be purchased by the public, the problems are many. And it all revolves around one word. Rights. Music rights. Publishing rights. All kinds of rights. Because most shorts that come through the pipeline do not have those rights cleared.

There should be a list created of the do's and don'ts for every young filmmaker who wants to create a short and then use it as their resume/calling card to get work. Here's mine, in no particular order:

- Use original music. If you use copyrighted tunes to tell your story your chances of getting it seen on a wide basis diminish greatly. And you take the chance of really pissing off the person who recorded that tune. And they will have a lot more money than you will when they sue you.
- If you are making a short please remember the word "short." Short means no longer than 20 minutes max. Since you only have a short time to tell your story make sure that you grab the viewer in the first 3 minutes or chances are they won't get to the last 15.
- If you want to focus in on the poster of Mick Jagger on the wall of the bedroom you are shooting in remember that you must get that image cleared. So only use those types of images if you have to. The filmmaker is the one responsible for providing all clearances.
- Don't expect to make any money on your short. In most cases you will not. But as stated earlier it is a perfect resume for getting work in the industry you love.
- Submit your shorts to as many festivals as you can. Don't be afraid of rejection. That's what the film business is all about. If it bothers you please be prepared to take advantage of that "backup plan" that Mom and Dad always talked to you about. You'll need it.

But always remember one thing. And that is that the short you make could have the same effect on people that a feature film can. It can make people think. It can inspire. *The House I Live In* won honorary Oscars for Sinatra, LeRoy, and writer Albert Maltz. More importantly it taught a young soon-to-be film fanatic the importance of tolerance for all people. An 11-minute short can be as powerful when released in 1945 as it still is today.

Strive for the best and you will go far.

SHANE SMITH is Director of Programming for Channel Zero, Inc., an independent Canadian broadcaster and owner of the digital TV channels Movieola—The Short Film Channel and Silver Screen Classics. Prior to this, he was Director of the Canadian Film Centre's Worldwide Short Film Festival in Toronto.

Mr. Smith graduated with a B.A. in film studies and mass communications from Macquarie University in Sydney, Australia, before hitting the road and ending up in Canada. Shane is the former programmer for the Inside Out Festival and sits on the board of directors of the Centre for Aboriginal Media and the organizing committee of the International Short Film Conference. He directed the short film *Goodbye to Love* (screened at more than a dozen film festivals around the world) and has written about film for the Canadian publications *Xtra!* and *Cinema Scope*.

A passionate advocate for the art of the short film, Mr. Smith is a frequent guest speaker on the topic and has served on the jury of festivals in Iran, Brazil, Thailand, Germany (Teddy Jury at the Berlin International Film Festival 2005), the United States, Bermuda, Sydney, and Toronto and curated programs of short films for festivals and events in Canada, the United States, Brazil, Bangladesh, Argentina, Sydney, and Mexico.

He is Founder and Co-Director of OzFlix: Australian Film Weekend in Toronto, and in 2006 he joined the shorts programming team for the Sundance Film Festival.

So You Want to Sell That Short? Not So Fast...

By Shane Smith

Congratulations! You've made a short film. That's something to be proud of, and I bet it took longer, cost more money, and was more exhausting and time-consuming than you ever thought it would be.

Getting that puppy in the can and out of post may seem like the hard work, but you've still got a long road ahead. Now you get to become a publicist, a festival strategist, an entry form "wiz," a shipping and receiving operation, a salesperson, and, oh yeah, a business affairs expert. Short filmmaking sure does make you a well-rounded multitasker.

Consider this valuable on-the-job experience that's going to serve you well for the rest of your career. It's not called the film "hobby," it's called the film business, and the skills (not to mention contacts) you'll acquire while making short films are invaluable.

This section is intended to give you some insight into the broadcast acquisitions of short film and to offer tips on how you can navigate it effectively, efficiently, and maybe even painlessly.

Why would I want to buy your short?

I've got a shelving unit in my office that houses over 1000 short films sent to me in the last year. And those are just the ones from distributors. The shelf from filmmakers holds another couple hundred. I love short films and I'll watch them all—eventually—but I program another TV channel and handle the contracts and scheduling for that one, too. Okay, cry me a river, I'm busy, but the point is—given those circumstances, what's my motivation to watch YOUR short film?

+ **It has a kick-ass original story, awesome production values, and stars Brad Pitt.** That trifecta isn't going to happen often, if ever, but two of those three will help move your film closer to the top of the pile.

+ **It's played 60+ film festivals, so it must be good right?** As a festival programmer myself, I can't disagree with that, but there are a couple of caveats. First, a "festival darling" doesn't always equal a film that's suitable for TV. Setting aside the obvious broadcast hindrances of excessive swearing and lots of nudity (although depending on the channel these can be pluses), the film may be long and the pacing may be too slow for TV. Most broadcasters have difficulty placing a short that's longer than 10–15 minutes, as shorts are still often used for interstitials (filler) or limited to 30- or 60-minute slots where several shorts are competing for placement. Movieola is the rare exception—we only broadcast shorts so we're open to all genres and lengths up to 40 minutes, and indeed some of the films which have garnered the best viewer response are longer. A methodically paced (read "slow") film, especially a short, can be deadly in the short-attention-span-600-channel universe we live in. I've got to try to keep people tuned in to my channel. Secondly, WHICH festivals did it play in? There are a lot of festivals out there that will play almost anything that comes their way (want names—buy me a drink and we'll talk!), and although you may think it looks good to have a list of festival screenings as long as your arm, it doesn't always help. Buyers and programmers know which fests are big deals and which aren't, and seeing some of the less reputable festivals on a screening list can set alarm bells ringing.

+ **It's won awards at several of those festivals.** Now you're getting my attention (unless those awards came from the *less reputable* fests — see above), and I want to see what all the fuss is about. Niche festivals can also be helpful in this way; awards from doc, gay/les, African-American, Asian, Jewish, animation, children's' festivals, etc., can tell us a lot. A buyer may just have the perfect strand or theme slot for your film.

+ **It's won an Oscar.** Bingo! I don't know of a buyer out there who isn't interested in seeing or licensing an Oscar-winning, or nominated, short film. The Oscars are seen by more people than any other platform for short film in the world — yes, even YouTube. They give your short instant name-recognition and they give buyers a powerful marketing tool to promote the broadcast of the film.

And that's the bottom line. Buyers are not interested in your film just because it's a good film; there are thousands of great short films out there. We're interested in ensuring people watch your short film on TV/airline/web sites/DVD — whatever the platform may be. How do I do that? By having a marketing or promotional hook that can get some attention. Attention = eyeballs. Eyeballs = advertisers. Advertisers = revenue. Revenue = money to license and broadcast more short films. Crass isn't it? But that's the "business" part of the film business. . . .

To be honest, short films face an uphill battle being seen and we need to do whatever we can to get people to watch them. You and I may love short films, but the majority of the population doesn't have a clue about them, and thanks to the proliferation of user-generated content, probably doesn't have a very high opinion of what they think short film is anyway. That's why things like awards, prestige, and celebrities can help cut through the clutter and get your film seen. But don't despair, there's always going to be a place for beautifully made, low-key shorts. It's called my heart.

What else helps?

+ **A distributor is representing your film.** Why? Because I know that everything is in order and I can sleep at night. They've (hopefully!) done their due diligence and confirmed that you've got all the paperwork you should have. If they don't and there's a problem, the distributor runs the risk of pissing off the buyer. No distributor wants to do that — especially in the short film world.

Sidebar—other reasons you should try to work with a distributor:

- They know the orderly chain of distribution and who should be buying your film first (i.e., the guys that pay the big bucks!).
- They have the knowledge of, and relationships with, the guys that pay the big bucks and can get your film seen by them.
- As a buyer I can license ten films from a distributor in the same amount of time (or less) that it takes me to license one film from the filmmaker directly. And with a whole lot less explaining and hand-holding. Who do you think I'm going to approach first, especially with the proliferation of new platforms that I'm going to need films for?
- Having a distributor frees you up to do your job—making more films.

Sidebar to the sidebar—do your research and pick the right distributor. You're going to have a long-term relationship with this company and it should be the right fit. Check out the kind of films they already distribute and ask other filmmakers on their roster for their thoughts; ask festivals and buyers who they'd recommend. You'd be amazed at some of the horror stories filmmakers have about distributors that are still operating today, and you can avoid making the wrong choice just by doing a bit of legwork. One simple question to ask your distributor: Have any lawsuits been filed against you? If they hang up the phone, you have your answer. . . .

What's going to stop me from buying your film?
A few crucial things:

+ **That Elvis/Beatles/Dylan song on the soundtrack.** Even if you're willing to change the music, if I see the film at a festival I'm going to scratch it off my list immediately, as will pretty much every distributor. With the proliferation of bands and music on the Internet it's never been easier to work with cool, unsigned bands who are eager to get their music heard. Save yourself the hassle of falling in love with a piece of music you're never going to get the rights to, and help discover a new musical sensation.

+ **You can't show me all the clearances and paperwork I need to see.** If I have a shred of doubt that you've not got all of your paperwork in order—see ya! It's the biggest drag but one of the most crucial elements in filmmaking. Practice it here because it's only going to get harder as you move onto larger productions. I'm not going to risk my job for your film, no matter how much I love it. That's one of the main reasons I like to deal with distributors.

+ **You're an ass and I know you're going to be a nightmare to deal with.** That one pretty much explains itself.

But wait—should you even be selling it to me?
Jump back, and think about these things first:

+ **Should I get a distributor instead of trying to sell the film myself?** I say yes and thank you—you've just made my life easier.

+ **What other opportunities might I be jeopardizing by selling the film to you?** Oh, just things like potential exclusive deals in the same territory that pay way more money; festival screenings if your film plays on TV before it should; Academy Award consideration if your film plays on TV/Internet before it qualifies for the Oscars. Minor things...

+ **Is this the right place for my film?** Know your film, and the appropriate place for it. The Sci-Fi Channel doesn't want to see your musical comedy, and your experimental documentary is not going to work on Comedy Central. This may seem obvious but filmmakers still do it—wasting not only our time but theirs too.

Hunting the buyer—and what to do when you've found one
Now that you've decided your film is ready to be licensed, it's time to put on your camouflage gear and bag yourself a buyer. At the risk of precipitating my own demise under a deluge of DVDs, here are a few hints:

+ **The natural habitat of the buyer**
- Behind a desk in a small office, hidden behind a precipitous pile of DVDs (not VHS—they take up too much room and you can't watch them on a laptop—consider them extinct).
- At quality film festivals dedicated to shorts, usually in the screening room, not in the theaters—we're looking for films for TV or smaller screens and need to power through as many shorts as possible. You'll find a lot of shorts buyers and distributors at the Clermont-Ferrand Short Film Festival and Worldwide Short Film Festival to name just two.

+ Approaching the buyer—the Pitch

- In person at a festival: be succinct and able to explain the story of your film in one or two sentences. We're meeting lots of people just like you, so get in and out and leave a good impression. Offer a DVD and contact info, and remember that we're going to be offered a lot of DVDs so the smaller the package it comes in the more likely we are to take it. There's no need to offer press kits and other extras—we want to see the film.
- Contact info is crucial—make sure it's on everything you give us—the DVD, the DVD cover, the postcard—everything! A buyer may not view your film for a few months so make sure that when we do, we can get in contact with you easily.
- If you're sending the film by mail fill out all requested forms (check the buyer's company web site for submission forms/guidelines—and follow them!). Contact info on everything!
- Follow up around 6 weeks later—email is always better than a phone call—and don't be discouraged if you don't hear back for a while (or at all). Remember the 1500+ DVDs on my shelf? Your film is at the bottom of that pile.
- If you have a distributor and you've met a buyer, let your distributor know ASAP—they can follow up on your behalf and may already be talking to that buyer—don't muddy the waters.

Sealing the deal

You've tracked them, trapped them, and hey, that buyer likes your film and has sent you a contract. How to seal the deal:

+ **Get your distributor to do it.** Did I mention that you really should think about getting a distributor?

+ **Doing it yourself?** Read the contract thoroughly and be ready and able to supply everything it asks for—dialog lists, music cue sheets, broadcast master, stills and promotional information, actor contracts and agreements—all those pesky business bits again. There will be lots of lawyerly words like "indemnify," "warrant," "underlying rights," "nonperformance," "liability" that may scare the crap out of you, so seek advice if you need it and don't sign anything unless you're sure about what it means and what the implications are if you happen to be in breach of the contract.

+ **Want to make changes?** Make sure you're not being nit-picky and only focus on requesting changes to the things that may be negotiable, like exclusivity (do you want to give up your right to license your film in this territory/platform?), term (can the license term be shorter?), territories (are you willing to have your film seen in all of these countries?). Pick your battles wisely and know that many of these things may be nonnegotiable. It doesn't hurt to ask—the buyer can only say "no"—but don't ask unless you really want it.

+ **Respond to an offer or contract in a timely fashion.** Within days of getting the offer or contract, please and thank you. You don't have to sign the deal right away, but let the buyer know what the hold-ups are. It may have taken me three months to get in touch with you, but now that I have I want to close the deal NOW (yeah, it's not fair, but I'm paying you so hustle your ass).

+ **Remember, you don't have to sign the contract if you're not comfortable with it.**

It's not over yet—help your film be seen

The deal is sealed, the film is delivered, and the air date is set. You can relax now. Or can you? This is YOUR movie, so spread the word far and wide, promote the screening on your web site or MySpace page, have a screening party at home, email everyone you know (even if the broadcast is in another country—you never know who has friends in Luxembourg these days), contact the local media—do everything possible to let people know your little film is on TV!

Not only will that do wonders for your ego (and maybe even convince your parents you've got a "real" job), it can help your career immensely. Along with endearing you to the buyer who acquired your film . . . the same buyer who will be more than happy to put your next short on the top of their DVD pile.

And then?

Go to the beginning. And repeat.

Swimming Lesson #3

The Deep End:
Exploring All Options

The expanding world of short films has opened up a variety of opportunities that filmmakers could, and should, explore. This chapter will elaborate on some of them and give you some thoughts on how to figure out which of them might work for you.

With so many mergers and acquisitions resulting in large corporations that house many smaller entertainment entities, "branding" has become a very important goal, as evident with Disney and its association with Pixar as the "family friendly" source of entertainment. Disney = Family, plain and simple. That's the "brand."

Furthermore, corporations with products and services outside the realm of entertainment have been faced with a quandary of how to utilize the Internet to their advantage. In the past several years, there has been a preponderance of competitions in which filmmakers create a short film specifically for that product or company, such as the well-known BMW or Nokia shorts competitions. These competitions create visual pieces for the company to assist in its branding and identity and lure more traffic to their web sites. Perhaps more importantly, companies are looking to capitalize on the YouTube phenomenon and then take it one step further. Competitions allow companies to obtain original branded content and consequently reach out to a broader demographic for their products.

The addition of viewer control, in that for many contests the audience "votes" for the winner, further increases that reach, such as with Delta Air Lines' "Fly-In Movies" competition in which viewers "voted" for their favorite short from among the finalists selected both in the air and online. This has generally become the case with every reality program on television, in which viewers select the finalists or winner, most recently on Mark Burnett's short film reality show *On the Lot*, in which three celebrity judges provided feedback on the short films, but it was the audience who determined the filmmaker's fate, a la *American Idol*.

Why Should You Investigate Competitions?

In 2007 HBO held a competition for gay/lesbian themed shorts, and the finalists were given money to produce them. The shorts were then broadcast on HBO on Demand. Filmmakers therefore got not only funding to make the short, but also exposure by that short being broadcast on HBO, which certainly will help further their careers.

Each competition designates a maximum running time for the short film, ranging from 60 seconds to several minutes. The Nintendo "Short

Cuts Showcase" film competition had a maximum length of 5 minutes, with the winner receiving a $10,000 prize.

If you search "short film competitions," you will see creative contests to make shorts for everything from the Honda Prius to Pizza Hut. Sure, you're creating something "commercial" and sure, whatever you create has to incorporate the "product," but think of it as an end to a means. Think about what you could do with that money to further your filmmaking dreams or how you might use that opportunity to get paid work.

Competitions provide funding and/or cash prizes and visibility. Big visibility. I implore you to look deeper into what competition participation can do for you. In the case of the essay by the filmmaker who entered the Chrysler competition, winning the $1 million prize for his short film allows him to finally make his dream feature. Investigate competitions, troll through corporate web sites, and read publications such as *Crain's* and *Advertising Age*. You don't have to want to direct commercials to participate in competitions, but one might work for you to help you create the film you eventually want to make.

Why Should You Think Beyond Traditional Narrative Film?

OK, I have to be honest here and basically admit something about being part of this whole film universe. Everyone in it is an oddball, and I say that with the utmost affection and include myself in that illustrious group. To work in this industry, you have to walk/sing/dance/swim to your own beat, otherwise you could never survive it. Being part of this world means acknowledging that aspect of you and embracing it.

It's only natural, then, to consider that perhaps traditional narrative storytelling is not your cup of tea/vodka/vitamin water and look for some other format that rocks your boat. Many filmmakers don't take the time to explore other short film formats, such as animation and experimental, which are equally viable routes to creating what matters most to you. Each format offers its own challenges in terms of both creation and finding distribution, and the essays on experimental and animation illuminate each author's passion and personality with respect to that format.

The word "experimental" has been bandied about and is unfortunately used as a term to describe those films that don't conform to a traditional narrative storytelling structure. People fear the word "experimental" and often confuse it with "avant-garde." Films are often lumped into this category when they don't quite "fit" anywhere else, and that does this particular format a true disservice. This essay will dispel this myth and enlighten you on what the word "experimental" really means.

From the days of Disney's *Steamboat Willie* to the amazing technological achievements today, animation is a very popular form of entertainment. I use the word "entertainment" because animation is one of the most entertaining art forms around. When we talk about the "rules" of short film, I say, "The golden rule is that there are no rules," and nowhere is this more evident than with animation. Simply drawn or created using complicated CGI, this short film format permits the ultimate breakdown of barriers. Dialog that might be construed as offensive seems humorous when coming out of a frog's mouth, as evidenced by the many adult-oriented animated series on television. Suspension of disbelief comes easily with animation, and style is individual by nature. An Academy Award-nominated filmmaker shares his thoughts and positive attitude about animation in his essay.

An interesting new development in the short film world is the release of Academy Award-nominated short films via theatrical distribution, on DVD, and on iTunes. As this book is being written, this is proving to be a successful endeavor, and the conversation with the project's creators illuminates the genesis of the program and their thoughts about the multiplatform release and what it portends for the future of short film distribution.

Why Should You Care About The Academy Awards?

Have you heard the old expression "it's an honor just to be nominated"? Well, in the short film world it is one of the most prestigious accolades you can garner. Similar to those actors who use "Academy nominated . . ." in all their press, a short film nomination is the seal of approval from the industry.

Short films are eligible to be nominated for an Academy Award in two ways: first by theatrical exhibition in Los Angeles and second by winning a "best-in-category" award at an Academy-recognized film festival. At the time of this writing, there were 60 recognized film festivals listed. Detailed eligibility rules and a list of recognized festivals and approved award categories can be found on the web site www.oscars.org.

Honestly, the likelihood of your short film getting theatrical exhibition (other than four-walling the theater yourself) is pretty slim, since shorts generally don't play theatrically, but the chance of you getting into a festival, and winning a key festival award, is indeed possible. It's important that you understand what will make you ineligible for consideration, such as putting your short in full on the Internet or by broadcasting it prior to receiving a "best-in-category" award. That basically means you better be sure you have exhausted the festival circuit before you exhibit that short anywhere else. Note that the Student Academy Awards has its own eligibility requirements separate from the above, also available on the web site.

What Else Should You Think About?

Programs such as the Sloan Foundation grants, offered to the major film schools to encourage the creation of shorts with a scientific theme, allow filmmakers to create something that may further their career and, of course, provide funding to write the script or produce the project. Grants can be a very appropriate source of funding for documentary short films, particularly if they align with a foundation's mission. The Foundation Center offers a plethora of information, at www.foundationcenter.org.

Exploring all options means thinking about yourself and how you best fit into the filmmaking world. I started at the NYU film school with the same dreams that my students have today—to be a great director. But guess what? I made a couple of short films and they sucked. Really sucked. I credit my first professor, Nick Tanis, who has become a beloved colleague at NYU, with brutal honesty. He said, while giving me perhaps the worst grade of my college life, he didn't believe I would make a good director. While I was contemplating a swan dive from the Brooklyn Bridge, he continued that he thought I would make a great producer—that I had the ability to see the "big picture" and passionately put a film together with all the details in place. His comments made me think about my talent and strengths in a different way and allowed me to pursue the right path for me. As you forage through the film industry, you too may find an alternate path from the one that you initially envisioned, and the essay by Ryan Werner tells a similar personal story.

It's hard when starting out in this world not to get overwhelmed by the constant balancing act of the creative and business aspects of the film industry, so I thought it was important to remind you of the imaginative spark that set you on this road to begin with. Filmmaker and Professor Andrew Lund encourages you to "embrace your inner poet," and his essay will help you to keep thinking of yourself as an artist, and encourage you to keep your balance even when the road is filled with potholes.

This chapter should make you think. Think about yourself, your strengths, your passion, and the many options that are available to you.

BILL PLYMPTON has always been fascinated by animation. He was born in Portland, Oregon, and credits its rainy climate for nurturing his drawing skills and imagination. He went to Portland State University and first attempted animation there, making a yearbook promo that was accidentally shot upside-down, rendering it totally useless.

In 1983 he was approached to animate a film about the Jules Feiffer song "Boomtown." After *Boomtown* he began his own animated film, *Drawing Lesson #2*, which garnered the film a 1988 Oscar nomination for best animation. His string of successful short films includes *One of Those Days, How to Kiss, 25 Ways to Quit Smoking,* and *Plymptoons.* He self-financed his first animated feature, *The Tune.* Sections of the feature were released as short films to help generate funds for production, including *The Wiseman* and *Push Comes to Shove,* the latter of which won the 1991 Prix du Jury at the Cannes Film Festival. *The Tune* made the film festival rounds, winning the prestigious Houston WorldFest Gold Jury Special Award and a Spirit Award nomination for Best Film Score.

After personally drawing and coloring 30,000 cels for *The Tune,* Mr. Plympton then moved to the live-action features *J. Lyle* and *Guns on the Clackamas.* His animated features include *I Married a Strange Person* and *Mutant Aliens,* which won Grand Prix at Annecy 2001 and was theatrically released in 2002. His latest feature film is *Hair High.*

Mr. Plympton's short film *Guard Dog* has been a hit at film festivals and brought him his second Oscar nomination in January 2005.

Plympton's Dogma

By Bill Plympton

Call me crazy, call me Pollyanna, call me an optimist, but I believe it's possible to make a living off of short films. Yes, I believe that short films are a viable source of income.

I've been making good money from my shorts for over 20 years, and it seems that now I'm making more money than ever.

I have three iron rules that must be followed, though—call them Plympton's Dogma:

Rule #1—make the film short! The film must be under 5 minutes. I judge a lot of festivals, and when I read the list of films to be judged, and I see a film that runs 15 or 20 minutes, already I don't like it. Film festivals don't like screening long short films, DVD collections don't like long short films, and most importantly, audiences don't like long short films.

Rule #2—make the film cheap! Around $1000 a minute is the rule. And now, with video and Flash technology, the cost of making a film is greatly reduced. Obviously, if you make a film using big-name actors, or famous music, or tons of fancy CGI effects, your budget's going to go through the roof, and it will take that much more time to make the investment back. If you ever make your investment back...

Rule #3—make it funny! I don't know why it is, and I certainly don't make the rules, but when people watch short films, they want to laugh.

There is one film that I know that is the perfect synthesis of my Plympton's Dogma—it's called *Bambi Meets Godzilla*; it's an animated cartoon done in 1971 by Marv Newland. It's about one minute long and consists of 12 drawings—he made it over a weekend for about $500. It's hilariously funny and has gone on to make over $100,000—that's success. *Bambi Meets Godzilla* is the *Deep Throat* of short films.

Now, of course, a lot of films have not followed my rules and have been huge successes—take, for example, *Ryan*, a wonderful animated film from Canada by Chris Landreth that won an Oscar in 2005. It's serious, it's long (18 minutes), and has a huge amount of CGI that probably cost over a million dollars, and it will never show a profit. It will always be in debt, but that's OK because it was financed by the Canadian government (the National Film Board) and it's good publicity and prestige for the NFB and Canada.

But, I don't have government funding. I don't do grants, or sponsorship, or corporate tie-ins. I fund my films out of my own pocket, so that way, I have no interferences—no producers telling me a film is going to offend a certain audience demographic.

So, say you've made your film—short, cheap, and funny. How do you sell it? A lot of filmmakers send it to the various TV stations— that's all well and good if you have an uncle or sister who works at MTV or Comedy Central. But, when I was doing a lot of work for MTV, I would visit my producer in his office and see one wall, floor to ceiling, loaded with tapes and DVDs. I asked him what they were, and he said he got up to a hundred submissions of short films a week, and just didn't have the time to watch everything sent to him, and

81

besides, most of it was amateurish crap. Also, now that there are so many lawsuits by filmmakers who claim their ideas were ripped off for successful TV shows, most TV executives are afraid to look at any unsolicited material.

So, what do all the TV executives do to find new artists and great films? They go to the film festivals, because the film festivals screen out all that crap and show only great films. So, my recommendation is to send your film to the festivals—that's where I was discovered, and they're even more important today than 20 years ago.

Now, there are thousands of film festivals. Festivals for films about food, festivals for films about dogs. There's even a film festival for pain in Sweden—if you have a film about pain, there you go. But, not all festivals are great for making sales—here is a short list of festivals and events that I've found are excellent for doing business:

1. The Oscars. If you get nominated for an Oscar, you're set. You'll have to fight off the agents, buyers, and press—and if you win the Oscar, you can retire. But, who wants to retire?
2. Cannes Festival. Cannes shows a lot of shorts and there are tons of buyers there looking for product. Although most of the buyers are European, that's OK, because that's the biggest market right now for shorts. Plus, it's got the sun, the food, and the topless babes—how can you beat that?
3. Sundance Festival. Robert Redford's January festival is like Cannes in the snow. They don't showcase a lot of shorts, but the media, buyers, and agents are there in force. And sometimes, you don't even have to have a film in competition to make deals.
4. Clermont-Ferrand. In an ugly, sleepy little city in the center of France is one of the most amazing festivals I've ever been to. It has many cinemas and four of them seat over 1000 people. They're packed all day long—people wait in line in the cold to see SHORT films! And they're passionate about shorts! It's the largest market for short films in the world; consequently all the media buyers are there—TV stations, distributors, agents, DVD companies—looking for short, cheap, funny films!
5. And my favorite, the Annecy Festival. It's a little medieval French village, nestled between a crystalline lake and the French Alps, with white swans cruising the many canals that wind through the wonderful French bistros. It's strictly an animation festival, so you'll get to hang out with the likes of Nick Park, Jan Svankmeyer, the Quay Brothers, or maybe even Bill Plympton.

The second year I went to Annecy (1987), I brought *Your Face*, and after the first screening, I was surrounded by people wanting to talk to me about buying the film rights and offering me money. Now, I was quite naive at that point and didn't even consider making money off of my shorts—but as soon as the offers started coming in, I quickly realized, "Hey, there's money to be made here!"

When I returned to New York, I called the magazines and newspaper that I'd been doing illustrations for and told them I was going to become an independent animator. They laughed, and said I was crazy, that animation was dead (remember, this was in 1987). I said, "No, I think I can make a living doing animated shorts." Then, I banged out four very successful short films in a row—*How to Kiss, One of Those Days, 25 Ways to Quit Smoking*, and *Plymptoons*.

I'm now going to list the places I sell my work, in chronological order:

1. Theatrical. My first exposure is in movie theaters. I started out showing my films in the "Tournée of Animation," then the "Spike & Mike" show. Now, I deal mostly with "The Animation Show," which I love. But there's also Magnolia Films' collection of shorts that tours theaters and, also, Carol Crowe of Apollo Cinema distributes short films theatrically. Occasionally, a short of mine will play before a released feature, such as *Guide Dog* before *Fuck: A Documentary*, but that's rare.

2. Nontheatrical. These are screenings in schools, libraries, museums, corporations, airlines, etc. *25 Ways to Quit Smoking* was a huge hit on the nontheatrical circuit because it was perfect for cancer societies, lung associations, and health organizations— I did very well with that film.

3. Television. This is probably my biggest moneymaker. Especially in Europe, with channels like Arte, Canal+, BBC, etc. But I also sell a lot in the United States, to MTV, Comedy Central, Sundance Channel, Cartoon Network, and many others. I'm also doing well in other countries, like Israel, Australia, Korea, and Japan. The thing is, each country has two or three channels that are looking for short films, and sometimes they renew the rights, year after year.

4. DVD. This is a fast-growing sector—I've been making a lot of deals in the United States and foreign countries for DVD rights, on all sorts of compilations, and the DVD growth is just starting.

5. Internet. The Internet is back, and this time to stay. I've done a lot of deals with AtomFilms, and now with iTunes, iPods, and such, it looks like a whole new market.

6. Merchandise. I sell all my work, usually on my web site or in stores — my DVD collections, books, posters, T-shirts, music, even original art. I've got a special deal, where for $125, you can purchase the Bill Plympton Super Fan Package — everything I've ever done. It sells very well.

7. Commissioned work. Occasionally I'll do outside work, if it's fun and pays well. I've done a number of commercials, for Geico, United Airlines, Taco Bell, etc. I've done music videos for Madonna, Kanye West, and "Weird Al" Yankovic, and then sometimes I do trailers or bits for feature films like *Fuck: A Documentary*.

8. Appearances. I often do lectures about "Surviving as an Independent Filmmaker," for example, at schools, corporations, film festivals, and conventions.

So, you see, there are many ways to make money on short films. Just remember my Plympton's Dogma — short, cheap, and funny.

JON GARTENBERG is a film archivist, distributor, and programmer, who has been actively engaged in the experimental film world for several decades. Formerly a curator at The Museum of Modern Art, he acquired avant-garde movies for the permanent collection of the Department of Film and restored the films of Andy Warhol. Currently, his company, Gartenberg Media Enterprises, distributes experimental films on DVD and licenses clips from these films for documentaries on Andy Warhol, Bob Dylan, and other cultural figures. He advises independent filmmakers on placing their works into the commercial distribution and exhibition network. Jon is the programmer of experimental and underground films for the Tribeca Film Festival. He can be reached at jon@gartenbergmedia.com.

The Fragile Emotion

By Jon Gartenberg

Introduction: What is an experimental film?

One of the most vibrant, yet underexposed, currents of the short film format is experimental filmmaking, which has historically also been referred to as avant-garde film, underground movies, expanded cinema, and visionary film. Experimental filmmakers create their works as labors of love, in the pure spirit of self-expression, without regard for financial profit, or to use as a calling card to Hollywood. Making experimental films is most often a solitary experience by a single individual, without benefit of a cast or crew. The hand of the artist is privileged, so that the seamless illusion of reality in commercial cinema is rejected in favor of techniques that expose the filmmaking process itself. In fact, production "mistakes" are often incorporated into the fabric of individual avant-garde movies. Linear narrative is subverted in order to foreground other ways of perceiving the flow of cinematic time and space, resulting in the expression of motifs related more to poetry, music, and subjective, psychological thought patterns.

Experimental filmmakers begin with observations of the world around them, but process these experiences through their subjective mind's eye, often resulting in films of abstraction. Avant-garde movies are replete with flickering frames, individual shots deliberately under- and overexposed, accelerated and slowed-down motion, repeated and looped frames and images, and attention to the grain (of films shot on celluloid) and the individual pixels (of works created on digital video). When, in the early 1970s, Jonas Mekas tutored young John and Caroline Kennedy in filmmaking—an experience which was later compiled in Mekas' own film, *This Side of Paradise* (1999)—Jackie O. wrote him that she never knew that movie cameras could zoom in and out, and speed up and slow down action, which, in her children's hands, now could produce poetic effects. Numerous experimental films are also created via direct film processes (i.e., painting directly onto the emulsion, or exposing objects onto the raw film stock without running the film through the camera). For example, Stan Brakhage's *Chartres Series* (1994), an abstract, hand-painted film of vivid colors, is a meditation on his experience of visiting the famous cathedral, while *Black Ice* (1994) conveys the artist's mind's-eye sense of slipping on the frozen surface.

Many avant-garde filmmakers are still committed to working in the ever-shrinking universe of small-gauge celluloid film stocks (e.g., 8 mm, Super 8 mm, and 16 mm). Thematically and texturally, many of these artists deliberately link the extinction of these film stocks both with their own tenuous existence as avant-garde filmmakers and with the fragile state of human affairs. To further underscore this concept, a recent trend by numerous filmmakers has been to treat the image with chemical processes. Highlighting a sense of environmental decay, these filmmakers directly impress their delicate emotions onto the sensitive surface of the film emulsion.

A brief history of experimental filmmaking

The formal beginning of the avant-garde moviemaking tradition extends back to the 1920s in Europe, where it intersected with art movements in painting and photography. In the United States, a parallel experimental filmmaking effort arose, with the production of such key films as *Manhatta* (1921), *The Fall of the House of Usher* (1928), and *The Life and Death of 9413—A Hollywood Extra* (1928). In *The Life and Death of 9413—A Hollywood Extra*, the filmmakers employ minimal sets and avant-garde filmmaking techniques to parody the depersonalized, assembly-line nature of Hollywood moviemaking. *Meshes of the Afternoon* (1943), made by dancer Maya Deren (and photographed by Alexander Hammid), is considered by many to be the most emblematic avant-garde movie ever made, because it clearly pointed to a new direction in visual expression, moving away from a strict linear narrative and toward a visual style incorporating self-reflexive images refracted through mirrors and windowpanes, repetition of shots and disjunctive editing, and the foregrounding of subjective states of mind suffused with sexual desire and repression. A more active avant-garde filmmaking tradition developed in the United States during the immediately post-World War II era. In the ensuing decades, the practice of experimental filmmaking fully exploded, culminating in the 1960s in New York, when Andy Warhol's twin-screen epic film *The Chelsea Girls* (1966) burst above ground. Over time, the experimental filmmaking practice has evolved and matured into many different stylistic threads and directions by an extensive underground network of artists. The numerous established subgenres in which these filmmakers work include found footage and animation, films of the body, structural films and film diaries, landscape and portrait films, film and video installations, and performances incorporating projections of moving images with live music or dance.

Made outside the commercial mainstream, experimental filmmakers function apart from the built-in production constraints of the Hollywood system. Avant-garde artists are able to freely address provocative political themes, explore outlandish subjects, and frankly depict nudity and sex. However, the public projection of this kind of work has, on occasion, run the risk of encountering censorship problems. When Jack Smith's *Flaming Creatures* (1963), replete with shots of naked, writhing bodies, transvestites, and other theatrical characters, was shown in New York City, police raided the theater and impounded the film.

Even though experimental filmmaking functions completely outside the commercial film economy, the historical interweaving of the two traditions is in reality quite strong. Many avant-garde artists have studied commercial cinema in some detail, in order to employ techniques and formal strategies to subvert narrative in their own films. One of the most proficient avant-garde students of Hollywood film was Warren Sonbert, who wrote about such classic filmmakers as Alfred Hitchcock and Douglas Sirk. The Hollywood cinema has appropriated visual styles of avant-garde films, including the abstract films of Jordan Belson and Ed Emshwiller, that inspired moments from Stanley Kubrick's *2001: A Space Odyssey* (1968). The visual aesthetic of Mark Romanek, the director of *One Hour Photo* (2002), starring Robin Williams, was profoundly influenced by Stan Brakhage's *Mothlight* (1963), which he saw as a teenager. Moreover, the pioneering styles so ever-present in avant-garde films (including image and sound counterpoints, the use of superimpositions and multiple images shown in the same frame, accelerated and slow motion, and rapid montage) can all be seen as precursors to MTV and reality television.

Getting involved in production

Experimental filmmakers produce their works on shoestring budgets. Some artists obtain production grants from local and state arts councils, and others supplement their filmmaking activities with income from unrelated day jobs, as film production teachers at universities, or as professional film editors for sponsored films. Many seasoned experimental filmmakers welcome interns from film school to help in their day-to-day production activity. Certain universities also have production faculty proficient in teaching experimental filmmaking; a few such colleges of note are Bard College and the School of the Art Institute of Chicago.

Exhibition, distribution, and broadcast opportunities

As difficult as finding a market for short narrative films or documentaries is, the economy for experimental film exists even more outside the commercial mainstream.

Since their films are not about making money, the filmmakers' main focus is on exposure to get their work seen. Whereas commercial films are fixed in form and replicated many times for maximum exposure in

theater chains, on DVD, and for broadcast, experimental films historically have most often existed only as single copies, which were at various times altered in form by filmmakers from screening to screening.

Experimental filmmakers view themselves first and foremost as
artists, rather than as moviemakers. As such, they often also create
works in other media of visual expression, including photography,
painting, and drawing. They frequently generate still-life artworks as
by-products of their filmmaking process. A few moving image artists
have been fortunate to show in galleries where their works can command high prices. However, artists working in the true historic tradition
of experimental filmmaking fall outside the gallery and art world universe, which is focused more today on product and personality than
on process and creativity.

Numerous experimental filmmakers working in the short film format have gone on to produce feature-length avant-garde movies. The
economic opportunity for these films to get commercial distribution
is rare, indeed; some features garnering prizes at film festivals fail to
secure theatrical distribution. Filmmakers who produce their movies
in digital format are nowadays also confronted with the added cost of
a conversion to 35 mm film, even for short films that are eventually
shown in theaters.

There is a tight-knit network of venues where experimental films
are programmed. This tradition extends at least back to the 1940s in
the United States, when a mix of European avant-garde, international
classics, and experimental shorts were regularly screened through the
Art in Cinema programs at the San Francisco Museum of Modern Art
and the University of California, Berkeley (1946–1954), and through
Cinema 16 at various venues in New York City (1947–1963).

Today, many film festivals worldwide are committed to showing at
least some experimental works. In the United States, these include
The New York Film Festival, the Tribeca Film Festival, TIE (the
International Experimental Cinema Exposition), the San Francisco
Film Festival, the Chicago Underground Film Festival, the Ann Arbor
Film Festival, the New York Underground Film Festival, Mix, and
LA Freewaves Experimental Media Art Festival, and in Europe and
elsewhere, the Oberhausen Film Festival and the Berlin Film Fes-
tival (Germany), the Rotterdam Film Festival (the Netherlands), the
Toronto International Film Festival (Canada), and the Torino Film
Festival (Italy), among others.

There is also an extensive network of nonfestival exhibition venues,
which are committed to showing avant-garde works. In the United
States, these include museums, universities, libraries, galleries, and

alternative spaces, such as microcinemas, lofts, storefronts, film cooperatives, music clubs, independent theaters, and informal gatherings of filmmakers showing new works to each other. An international list of venues showing experimental films, together with a weekly schedule of exhibitions, can be found on the Flicker web site (www.hi-beam.net/cgi-bin/flicker.pl).

Historically, experimental films and videos have been primarily distributed via film and video cooperatives. In the United States, these include Canyon Cinema (San Francisco) and The New York Film-Maker's Cooperative, as well as Electronic Arts Intermix (New York) and Video Data Bank (Chicago). In Europe, there are parallel cooperatives in countries including England, France, Germany, the Netherlands, and Sweden and also in Canada. Boutique film distributors such as Zeitgeist Films and First Run/Icarus Films have occasionally released more high-profile experimental works, primarily feature length, by world-renowned avant-garde artists such as Guy Madden, as well as documentaries about well-known experimental filmmakers, including Stan Brakhage, Maya Deren, and Marie Menken.

Increasingly, artists' works are published and distributed on DVD by boutique presses or through self-distribution. Anthologies of avant-garde cinema have been published recently on DVD by Kino Video and Image Entertainment; Re:Voir has published works by numerous experimental artists; and other publishers have put out works by individual artists, including Kenneth Anger (Fantoma), Stan Brakhage (Criterion), Maya Deren (Mystic Fire Video), Su Friedrich (Peripheral Produce), John Canemaker (Milestone Film & Video), Oskar Fischinger (Center for Visual Music), Mike Kuchar (Other Cinema), and Bill Morrison (Plexifilm).

Experimental films are rarely shown on television, although on occasion, selected works have been broadcast on the Sundance Channel and on 13/WNET in the United States and on the Arte network in Europe. Experimental filmmakers often take broadcast matters into their own hands, showing their works on public access television or making them available as video-on-demand through the new Internet technology, via such outlets as iTunes, YouTube, and UbuWeb.

Conclusion: Working against the commercial grain

Experimental filmmakers work against the tide of commercial feature films and narrative shorts. These filmmakers are richly rewarded in the personal fulfillment their craft provides and in reaching out to a receptive audience who yearn for more challenging cinematic fare.

RYAN WERNER is Vice President of Marketing at IFC Entertainment. He oversees the marketing campaigns for films such as *Penelope*, starring Christina Ricci and Reese Witherspoon, the Academy Award-nominated *After the Wedding*, and *You Kill Me*, directed by John Dahl and starring Ben Kingsley and Tea Leoni. He also oversees the marketing and PR on the company's IFC First Take program, a landmark day-and-date distribution program that has released films by Hou Hsiao Hsien, Patrice Chereau, Daniel Berman, Ken Loach, Alain Resnais, and Lars Von Trier and the New Zealand film *Black Sheep*.

Prior to IFC, Werner was Head of Theatrical Distribution at Well-spring, where he oversaw all the company's releases, including Jonathan Caouette's *Tarnation*, Jacques Audiard's *The Beat That My Heart Skipped*, and Todd Solondz's *Palindromes*. He also was Head of Theatrical Distribution at Palm Pictures and VP of Acquisitions & Distribution at Magnolia Pictures and Shooting Gallery.

He has served as programmer for the Woodstock Film Festival for the past four years and also as chair of the Spirit Awards Someone to Watch committee for four years.

Life in Short

By Ryan Werner

Working in New York City in independent film for the last 10 years has given me an incredibly fun and rewarding career. I've had the good fortune to work with some of the great directors working today such as Godard and Ken Loach, on controversial work by Todd Solondz and Vincent Gallo, and to introduce such amazing new talents as Jonathan Caouette (*Tarnation*), Jacques Audiard (*The Beat That My Heart Skipped* and *Read My Lips*), and Julia Loktev (*Day Night, Day Night*). But one could argue, probably pretty successfully, that I wouldn't be where I am today had I not made a really, really, awful short film.

I was an undergraduate student at Boston University. I'd spent the last four years steeping myself in the works of the great masters, Fellini, Bergman, Godard, Kieslowski, Antonioni, Sturges, Cassavetes, Wilder, and Hawkes, not to mention discovering the works of exciting new film-makers like Gregg Araki, Quentin Tarantino, Whit Stillman, David Fincher, and Jane Campion. I was determined to jam everything I'd learned, every idea, every observation into one five-minute epic.

The results were horrifying. It was pretentious, badly assembled, and very poorly directed. Watching it projected in a classroom full of equally eager and ambitious film students was an excruciating, cold-sweat-inducing, nerve-racking nightmare. That their own efforts, while brimming with ambition, were, for the most part, equally preposterous and misguided creations, was of little comfort to me.

Every year thousands of film students around the world pour their heart and soul into that all important short film, the one that will transform them into bankable filmmakers. Maybe you've seen them in cafes and bookstores staring at their laptops, busily making revisions to their scripts, or on the streets, toting lights and C-stands from one location to the next. Some of them will decide like I did that a career change is order. But some of them, a few of them, will make something that changes how we see cinema.

Today there are more venues than ever before for short films. There are festivals, which can immediately legitimize the work of a previously unknown filmmaker. Sundance is perhaps the most coveted festival for a short filmmaker, but there are many other important festivals that showcase emerging talent, such as South by Southwest, Tribeca, Telluride, Los Angeles, New Directors/New Films, New York, San Francisco, and Seattle, just to name a few. Not only is there information about all these festivals online, but now you can apply to almost all of them online with only a few clicks of the mouse.

A screening at one of the major festivals gives you a captive audience of agents, producers, financiers, and development executives. Make sure you come prepared, armed with production notes pointing out what went into making your short, having a very strong batch of stills and several postcards to hand out to people with your screening times and locations. You never know who you will meet waiting in line for screenings, riding on buses from one location to another, or at a party.

I often get asked what happens after the festivals are done. I've worked at a lot of places that have been involved with short films in one way or another. The most important thing to remember is that you more than likely will never get rich from making a short film. They are investments in your career. You want as many people as possible to see it. If people don't see it at a festival, you should consider sending out DVDs or even setting up a web site where you can stream your shorts. It's always a good idea to inject some of your personality into your site. When producers or agents are looking for new talent, they are looking for not only a talented filmmaker but also one with some personality.

THE DEEP END: EXPLORING ALL OPTIONS

Having worked at Sundance Channel and now at IFC Entertainment, whose sister company is IFC TV, there is also a market for short films on television. Among these networks, there are Current TV, Logo, and a handful of others that air shorts. These networks generally pick up your short for a couple of years and will ask for downloading rights also. You should get a lawyer who specializes in film to help you. These networks often discover shorts at festivals. You should also make sure you create a DVD box that jumps out at people. When you are sitting at a desk with hundreds of DVDs, your eye undoubtedly goes to the most interesting packaging.

I would say it's incredibly important for filmmakers at the beginning of their career to really understand the landscape they are working in. Joining organizations like IFP or Film Independent can help you understand how things work through seminars and meetings. You can also really get a better understanding of deals by reading *Variety*, *The Hollywood Reporter*, or *indieWIRE*. Filmmaking is ultimately a business and some knowledge of this will allow you to get what you want made easier.

As technology changes, there is a whole new world for shorts. In the nineties during the Internet boom, companies were racing like crazy to pick up shorts for new web sites. These days, it's all about cell phones, iPods, and downloading sites. Short films are quick to download and often provide great entertainment on the go. It's important to stay on top of these developments as they will offer you opportunities to get your work seen and possibly to make a little bit of money.

While all of this must seem somewhat daunting, there are success stories. Two recent successes started as short films and bloomed into features. These are Ryan Fleck and Anna Boden's *Half Nelson* and Peter Sollet's *Raising Victor Vargas*. These were incredibly popular short films that attracted a lot of attention and, in the case of *Half Nelson*, allowed the directors to cast Ryan Gosling in the lead. Other great filmmakers whose shorts helped them move into features are Mike Mills (*Thumbsucker*), Sylvain Chomet (*The Triplets of Bellville*), and Andrea Arnold (*Red Road*).

As a young filmmaker you might feel compelled to make something huge and ambitious that incorporates every idea you've ever had into its brief running time, that dazzles with its high production value and pristine craftsmanship. This can seem very daunting, especially if you have limited resources. But the reality is you don't need a lot of bells and whistles, all you need is a good idea, a good story, and don't be afraid to keep it small. Observations about nuances of everyday life can be just as powerful as crane shots and period pieces about World War II.

The Duplass Brothers' (*The Puffy Chair*) first short, *I Am John*, was made in their kitchen for $6.00 over the course of one afternoon. It was accepted into Sundance and netted them agents at the William Morris.

The basic equipment to make a film is increasingly accessible and affordable, and thanks to the pervasiveness of the Internet there are more outlets to screen and promote your films. A film doesn't have to be an impossibly overwhelming task. Use what you have around you, your friends, your neighborhood, whatever you might have access to. You can do it, now more than ever, and if you can't, you can always do what I did.

TOM QUINN began his film career in Los Angeles doing domestic publicity at Dennis Davidson Associates, working for the Senior VP of West Coast publicity, Nancy Willen. He later moved on to work for Samuel Goldwyn, Jr., eventually becoming the VP of Acquisitions, and was responsible for acquiring *Raising Victor Vargas* and *Super Size Me*. He is currently Head of Acquisitions at Magnolia Pictures, where he reports to President Eamonn Bowles. His acquisitions for Magnolia include *Oscar Shorts, Ong Bak, Woman Thou Art Loosed, Pulse, The Host, World's Fastest Indian, Jesus Camp, District B13, Tears of the Black Tiger, Cocaine Cowboys*, and *Great World of Sound*.

CARTER PILCHER is the Chief Executive of Shorts International. In 2006, they created the simultaneous theatrical and iTunes release of the Academy Award-nominated short films, with DVDs following thereafter.

Conversation with Tom Quinn and Carter Pilcher

SB: Why don't we start with the genesis of the Academy Award Short Program.

TQ: I used to work at Samuel Goldwyn in Los Angeles, and a friend of mine pitched me the idea of doing the Oscar shorts ages ago. Coming to Magnolia Pictures years later, the same individual reached out to me and pitched the idea again, and I thought "You know what? It's just crazy enough that we could pull it off." Nobody was doing it, and for us at Magnolia, owning a theater chain and our own DVD label, we were trying to push the envelope with full-length features, so why not do it with shorts?

We started from scratch trying to predict what this could be worth and how we could accomplish it, and at that point, the only company I was aware of that was doing this was Apollo. The idea was (as opposed to doing it year-round) and what excited me most was the idea of doing it as a nominated collection before the awards. A lot of the success on the theatrical side is really about timing, and the right weekend, so the focal point would be the nominated films of the year, including the animated branch and the live-action branch, which were two awards guaranteed. There was a marketing hook and we felt that there would be enough critics that would jump on board in the major markets that we might get some additional traction.

We put together a plan and started making offers, and were honestly swimming around in the dark. Our head of business affairs and I structured a deal unlike anything we had ever done before. There were so many moving parts as far as rights issues were concerned, and the one piece that we had not taken into account the first year we did it was where new media was going to fit into this program. Initially we were only dealing with TV, which was going to be HDNet, our own TV window; DVD, which was Magnolia Home Entertainment; and the theatrical portion that Magnolia Pictures would release through our own theater chain Landmark Theatres, which is the largest chain of art theaters across the country in the top 20 markets. We had all the pieces in place except for the new media part. In the background, Carter (unbeknownst to me) had the same idea and was working on his own program.

CP: Our beginning point was slightly different. We had been distributing short films since 2000. We launched a web site that showed short films on the web, and it did not initially generate the kind of revenue that we had anticipated. We focused just on building a distribution business, and we launched a deal in the autumn of 2005 with the American Film Institute to represent their films and were putting some of these films onto PlayStation Portables.

I was in LA and had a meeting with Jon Bloom, who is the one of the governors of the Short Film and Animation Branch of the Academy (AMPAS—Academy of Motion Picture Arts and Sciences). He said that this is all great, but couldn't we do something with Oscar shorts. We were talking about different things we could do. The following day I had a meeting in San Francisco with Apple to talk to them about how we might launch Shorts International films onto iTunes. While talking, I thought about the Academy-nominated short films and since they are a "time" commodity we could get them up before the awards and see if that worked. They were very excited and we went off making offers to filmmakers just for the new media portion. We hadn't thought, and didn't really understand, the theatrical side so we were motoring along doing the new media side and collided into Tom.

TQ: It was a serious competition. We both had the same idea separate from each other, and here we are trying to buy these films at a breakneck pace.

CP: You have no time, and every year is the same. You have a couple of weeks to get the films and a couple of weeks to show them and then it's done.

TQ: From start to finish, from nomination to the awards, you have about four weeks. You have to negotiate the films, close the deals, deliver the films, and get them ready for theaters. That is its own delivery nightmare because every film is in a different format and we're digitally distributing these films, so that in itself is a whole book. To do all that and promote it and launch it within two weeks is insane. We knew each other was out there. I knew what Carter was doing. He knew what I was doing.

CP: We didn't really understand, from our side, that theatrical made a difference. Our experience had been with Apollo Cinema, and they had gotten three of the ten, or six of the ten nominated films, and I had been out of the States for a while so I wasn't really familiar with Landmark, and I envisioned another kind of Apollo situation.

TQ: Carter and I decided we were going to compete head-to-head, and I called Carter and told him "You're going to lose this battle." We spent a week trying to beat each other. We just kept ratcheting up the offers and finally a week later we realized we were cannibalizing the program so we finally came to our senses and said let's be friends and let's work together. Somehow we all had the perfect parts and it was the perfect partnership and a week later (the day of opening) we still were negotiating.

There were two films with multiple lawyers, multiple managers, multiple rights issues, and other distributors. It was an "Acquisitions 101" class, and a great way of learning all the pitfalls of this program. Everything was cleared and we got it out. The beauty of it was, we opened in five major Top Ten markets and these films performed at the top of their engagements except for one, which was second. We thought that was great—by hook or by crook we launched the program. It was out in the marketplace and people were going.

There were some reviews such as *The New York Times* and *The Los Angeles Times*. It was a small beginning but the films really grossed. People had a huge interest in this with very little awareness so it proved everything we believed about what the program could be, and the timing of it. At the end of the day it grossed $180,000 theatrically, but it was actually profitable because we had spent most of our allocated budget buying the films in conjunction with Shorts International and on delivery.

CP: I think you never know when you do something like this if it will work at all or not. It could be a total flop.

TQ: Carter then launched the shorts on iTunes the following week on Tuesday, which was the launch date for everything on iTunes. Our fear was initially that the minute that these became available elsewhere, since this is such a small niche program, that ultimately revenue was going to shift in the new media direction. What actually happened, which proved the day-and-date idea, was that the grosses, because of the awareness on iTunes (which is probably the sexiest online store available to consumers) drove people into the theaters. Grosses went up after they were launched on iTunes.

CP: Nobody knew that would happen but it showed the more you can break into people's consciousness, the more they realize about the films, that seeing them in a theater is a great way to see them, and they can still buy them online.

SB: Did the filmmakers have all their clearances and paperwork in order or was this also one of the hurdles with the clock ticking?

TQ: The best advice I can give anyone who has a nominated film is absolutely make sure that your music is cleared. If it's not cleared make sure you have some substitute music. Make sure there are no lingering SAG issues. Some of these filmmakers honestly had never been in the position of having a piece of content that a distributor wants to buy. This is the first time they're on the scene and they are slightly naive and green about the issues. I also found an inhibition to disclose some of this information, which was very interesting—it's not something to feel embarrassed about. These are real issues and we dealt with them.

CP: In fact, there were a few filmmakers where the problem was that they were young or new at distribution negotiating and were quite unsure of what to do.

TQ: We had multiple negotiations that went on and on. It was like peeling an onion and finally getting to the core, where you're like, "Oh, this is the issue."

SB: Were there also filmmakers who were hesitant about participating in this project?

TQ: Absolutely, that comes back to the idea that they had never been in a negotiation before. There's an education process that happens and you have to basically walk someone through the process. The flip side of that is everybody knows who you are and at some point wants to make sure that they negotiate the best deal for their client. There are a lot of lawyers involved even at this level, which was surprising to me.

Both Carter and I have developed a program from scratch that has real revenue attached. We really went out on a limb and paid advances that have never been paid before to show people that we were serious about making this program work. There was nothing behind it. Some people take advantage of that. We're willing to walk away if, in fact, we cannot make a deal. We're out to get all ten films but at the end of the day if you do not want to participate in this program you're ultimately doing yourself a disservice because it is a huge program. The first year we released these films in over 80 engagements, this year we will be in over 100 engagements.

CP: The number of downloads on iTunes tripled this year. From our perspective, there is, to an extent, a significant value in the films together that doesn't exist with one or two nominated short films, which is untrue with any other Academy category, where each film stands on its own. In terms of commercial interest, the audience doesn't just want to see one short film. For the good of the branch, one thing that has made Jon Bloom and the Academy excited about our program is the fact that it is not possible in the U.S. to theatrically release one short film. There are a few distributors, like Pixar, who can release a short film in front of a feature, as they did with *One Man Band* in front of *Cars*, and a huge audience got to see it. But that's an exception, so we're finding that this release gives all the short films the chance to be seen by a wider audience who wouldn't look at them nearly the same way individually.

TQ: This year, we worked with Pixar, Disney, and Fox, so the fact that these competing entities are working together to service the program with two competitive companies is pretty amazing and a unique situation. We sell the program as "the program" in two sections, the live-action section, which is one ticket purchase, and the animation section, which is its own ticket purchase. In addition to that, we have also acquired some of the short-listed animated films for the animation section. We had a whole range of animated shorts from all over the world, as well as *The Wraith of Cobble Hill*, which won Sundance, and we have included Bill Plympton shorts, and made some curatorial decisions based on what was challenging and goes beyond just the nominated program.

SB: Was the filmmaker arrangement exclusive or nonexclusive?

CP: Every filmmaker is slightly different. Generally we try to make them exclusive for a few months on the theatrical side to make sure that they don't pop up as random releases around the country. On iTunes we normally take a little bit of exclusivity, maybe a year, and then they become nonexclusive. We are providing advances to filmmakers that are frankly unheard of.

TQ: In many cases I'm paying more of an advance on these films than some of the full-length features that I'm releasing, so these are really competitive. Although we should be asking for 15 years of exclusivity we're building something that hasn't proven itself as a source of signif-icant revenue. From the first year out, we're into overages theatrically, which is a rarity for any film, so the fact is that we're doing it with these films in a really tough situation. I couldn't be more proud of anything we've done here.

SB: Do you think this program has opened the door for other possible shorts packaging?

TQ: Yes, Carter and I, based on our partnership the first year, have been kicking around a bunch of ideas as to how this can evolve into an omnibus program of shorts. There are all these preconceived notions of "what is a short?"—over or under 40 minutes—and these are definitions that I don't adhere to or understand. I'm more than happy to go see a film that's 60 minutes for ten bucks and get my full money's worth, and then have an extra half hour at dinner.

CP: Definitely there's a much greater understanding of shorts in Europe. We have launched a television channel, Shorts TV, that shows only shorts in France. The reception is unbelievable. Everyone knows what a short film is, and is excited to be able to watch them. They do show occasional shorts in Paris at a standard time, but in the U.S. it's not quite there.

TQ: The shortest film I've seen, treated as a feature with full ticket price, was an Israeli film, which I believe was just under 60 minutes and grossed $300,000, so at some point it's in the eye of the consumer if this is worth going out to the theater for. The animated program could have been 40 minutes this year and we would have gladly gone forward with that, but we took it as an opportunity to include other films that we like and we would do the same for the live action.

The interesting part is that we do not curate the program. This program is chosen for us. You're never sure what you're going to get.

The one thing I want to get across is, I love what Sundance has done with their shorts program and I love what we do with the Oscar shorts. I would encourage filmmakers to go to oscars.org and figure out how to get your film qualified. There is an opportunity for more films to be part of the selection process. If there's anything we can do to encourage that, actually participating on the front end helping to get these films qualified, screened in LA or NY, is something I'm very interested in. I encourage filmmakers to do their homework.

CP: I've had so many filmmakers say, "We had no idea we could be considered for an Academy Award nomination." Filmmakers should be careful how they use the Internet in order not to disqualify themselves, and investigate how they can get qualified. Believe it or not, they have a better shot than they think.

DEREK CIANFRANCE was drawn to filmmaking at an early age and attended the University of Colorado film school, where he studied under avant-garde film legends Stan Brakhage and Phil Solomon. His first three student films took the university's top prize for student film in three consecutive years. One received a Special Dean's Grant for Achievement in the Arts and the Independent Film Channel's top award for Excellence in Student Filmmaking. He shot and edited his first feature, *Brother Tied*, at the age of 23. The film made its American premiere at Sundance, traveled to over 30 festivals, and won international awards at six of them.

Mr. Cianfrance ventured into documentary work upon joining @radical.media. His work includes profiles of artists Sean "Diddy" Combs, Mos Def, Run-DMC, and Annie Lennox; a portrait of Vietnam veteran biker clubs for *Rolling Thunder—Ride for Freedom*, produced for Harley–Davidson; and *Shots in the Dark*, produced for Court TV and Britain's Channel 4. As the director of photography for *Streets of Legend*, he won Best Cinematographer at Sundance 2003.

He directed the second and third seasons of MTV's *Battlegrounds* series, produced for Nike and Wieden+Kennedy Entertainment.

He has directed numerous commercials and various high-profile branded content work, including 51 films for Lincoln–Mercury's *Meet the Lucky Ones* campaign. He codirected a long-term documentary about the American automotive industry with Joe Berlinger and Bruce Sinofsky. Mr. Cianfrance recently won the Chrysler Feature Film Competition and will begin production on his second narrative feature, *Blue Valentine*.

Rudiments of the Short Film

By Derek Cianfrance

I started playing the drums in first grade. Using only a snare, I learned the rudiments. First, a roll, then a simple march beat. The principal assigned me flag duty, and each morning and afternoon I marched with my single drum out to the flagpole and hoisted the red, white, and blue high above Irwin elementary. I was proud of my job.

By the time I was in second grade, my parents could see that I was serious about drumming. So they bought me a high hat for my ninth birthday. Soon after, I stopped hoisting the flag, stopped with the marching beats, and with the rudiments. I can't remember another time in my life when I practiced playing the single snare drum. I needed more to hit. By the time I was a senior in high school, I had 36 different pieces to my drum set and by the time I graduated high school my drumming skills reached a plateau. The brief period I spent with the single snare drum failed to provide a substantial foundation for my larger ambitions. My playing was walking with a limp.

While I was playing the drums, I was also making movies. Short movies shot on a home video camera that I borrowed from my high school's librarian. My family and friends starred in many little epics, like *Does Your Dad Have Any Big Knives?* and *Don't Let Your Life Expire*. Making these short movies was like playing the snare drum. They taught me a basic grammar of film language. I abandoned the drums and entered film school. In my first production class I could see that this practice put me ahead of the pack.

After five semesters I dropped out, started a production company, and in six months raised $40K to make my first feature, *Brother Tied*. At 20 years of age, doubt never entered my mind. Faith was my arrow. In my mind and in my heart, I needed to graduate to the 36-piece set.

I spent four years making *Brother Tied*. The film did okay, it went to festivals and won some awards, but a distributor never picked it up. Ultimately, not that many people saw it. The film is very soulful and stylish. But it certainly has its problems. Just like with my drumming, naïveté and ambition were its battling dualities. Perhaps I needed to go back and spend more time making shorts, practicing the rudiments of the craft, before I tackled something so large.

But ambition drove me forward and I immediately started work writing my second feature *Blue Valentine*. Joey Curtis and I hammered the keyboard late night for six months at a Denver production company that specialized in making children's cereal commercials. I remember this feeling, this premonition, standing over the printer as it printed out our first draft. I envisioned the script landing in the hands of a smart producer, and by the fall of that year I would be in production of my second feature. The year was 1998.

The year is now 2007. And the film is yet to be made.

Over the course of the past nine years I've had the film set up many times—with studios, with private equity sources, etc. And each time something goes wrong—the president of the company gets fired, the money turns out to be tied to some bogus Saudi Arabia oil mogul, etc. My patience and will have been tried and tested, but I have refused to give up the hustle. My stubborn nature is either a blessing or a curse.

I kept busy over those years, making documentaries and commercials, honing my craft, sharpening my skills. With every break in between paying projects, I would hit the computer to bang out another draft of *Blue Valentine*, this time with my cowriter Cami Delavigne. Together we must have logged 1000 hours writing over 36 rewrites. Each time, the script got tighter and truer. Still, financing eluded us.

Last spring, my new producer Jamie Patricof called to tell me he was submitting the script to the Chrysler Feature Film Award. He said that the winner of the award would receive a million dollars to produce their film, plus a million dollars P&A budget. I learned a long time ago that when you are searching for money, you must overturn every stone. "Sure," I said, "go for it."

A couple of months later, while I was in Las Vegas working on a documentary, I got a call from Jamie telling me that *Blue Valentine* was selected as a semifinalist out of 650 scripts. I caught a plane home to New York to interview with the Chrysler people.

They kept me waiting in the waiting room for at least a half an hour as they dealt with production issues—they had a small documentary crew there to record the interview. Dan Cogan and Scott Osman were the producers of the competition. They asked me to pitch

Blue Valentine. I looked over at the camera crew, knowing they would record my every stutter and ineloquence, but I wasn't nervous. Over the past nine years, I have sat in so many meetings and given the spiel so many times that it has become second nature. And the film is very close to my heart so it isn't hard talking about it. I could tell that everybody was engaged. They knew I was serious and they knew that my passion was real. They knew I was going to make a great film.

They told me that they wanted to consider *Blue Valentine* for the award. But, there was one more hurdle—a final stage of the competition. I had to make a short film. They would give me $15 K and one month to make it. It had to be less than five minutes and it had to feature a new Chrysler vehicle in the narrative.

I listened to the rules and kept my composure. I shook hands, smiled, and left the meeting. But inside, fear turned my heart to ice. I was being asked to play the snare drum again. I walked down the street in a daze. I didn't know exactly how to do it.

I focused and fought through the fear and doubt. Within five minutes, an idea struck me. I went home and immediately started writing a script called *Golden* about my grandfather, Hilmer Palisch. The story took place in Golden, Colorado, and followed a widower's mundane life alone, until he ultimately faces his wife's death by opening a letter from the insurance company. This leads to test-driving a new car and a drive to the cemetery. Eventually I changed the title of the script to *Days Have Gone By* after the John Fahey song.

Chrysler read the new script for *Days Have Gone By* and they hated it so much that they forbade me from making it. They were trying to get away from the perception of Chrysler as an "old man's car."

I was furious. I felt like walking away, but I didn't want to be responsible for sabotaging *Blue Valentine* so I sucked it up and went back to the drawing board. The clock was ticking. I had less than two weeks before I had to be in production. I was desperate for an idea.

I told my friend Kirt Gunn of my woes. He told me not to worry, that he would come up with "the prizewinner." The next morning he called with an idea about a family who isn't getting along. One morning, the father wakes up and looks out the window and sees a brand new car parked in his driveway with a big red bow on it. He assumes that it is a make-up gift from his wife. Meanwhile, his wife wakes up and looks out the window, sees the car, and assumes that it must be a gift for her from her husband. Meanwhile, the daughter wakes up and thinks that her parents bought her the car. The family convenes in the kitchen where they all make up and are nice to one another. Underneath their kindness is greed, and they all can't wait to go outside and see their gift. When they go outside, they see the car pulling away. It was delivered to the wrong house.

It was sure to be a real crowd pleaser, but it didn't really feel like me. It felt too much like a skit. Kirt reminded me that this project wasn't about getting what I want; it was about giving them what they want so that they will give me their money to make what I want. He's like Yoda that way. I thanked him kindly and started writing the first draft, but the only thing good that came out of the session was the title, *Lately There Have Been Many Misunderstandings in the Zimmerman Home.* I put it on the back burner and tried to come up with another idea that was a little closer to my heart.

Monday morning and I hadn't slept well in days. It was the 4th of July, one week from my scheduled start date. My good friend and my long-time collaborator Jim Helton came over to my house and we banged out a script called *The Voice of the Turtle* (another Fahey title), about a basketball trainer who finds a turtle in the road and tries to teach him to move faster. I wanted to use the great trainer Jerry Powell, who I worked with on the basketball documentary *Battlegrounds.* He agreed to be in the film, but warned me that it was "impossible" to make a turtle run.

That night I went to the rooftop of Radical Media, my employer for many years, and photographed the fireworks exploding over the city. It sparked off another idea. I raced home and wrote a script about a man escaping a burning city.

It was a horse race—the idea that made it the farthest would be the one I would make. Two days passed and I had still not committed to a single idea. My producer Alex Orlovsky insisted that we hold auditions for the *Misunderstandings* script. I met him at his office the next morning at 10:00 A.M. I was a wreck and totally unprepared to hold auditions. The first person I saw was a stand-up comedienne. I asked her to tell me a joke. It didn't make me laugh. It almost made me cry.

I fled the office and hid out in the coffee shop downstairs. I tried to pull myself together, to focus. I knew it was too late to drop out. I finished my coffee and made the decision to commit to the *Misunderstandings* script. It seemed to make Alex happy when I told him. He slapped me a "high five" and introduced me to Alan Greenberg—a short, balding actor with a self-depreciating sense of humor. The three of us went to the audition room, I turned on my mini DV camera, and I asked Alan to imagine that he had been an asshole to me for a long time. Then I gave him an imaginary gift—a new sports car.

THE DEEP END: EXPLORING ALL OPTIONS

I asked Alan for an apology. He gave a 10-minute improvisation that made Alex and I smile broadly. That quickly, we had found the father.

I repeated the tactics throughout the day, and by the end of the auditions I had a decent family cast. I took the DV tapes home and studied the improv apologies. From these I rewrote the dialog in the script. Things were shaping up. That night I slept well.

The actors arrived around 3:00 the next afternoon. I introduced everyone and gave a big speech about how I was ready to quit the film until they all showed up the day before at the audition. But there was a weird feeling in the room. I could tell that Alan (the husband) and Darlene (the wife) weren't really attracted to one another. At all. I could feel them both staring at me (the matchmaker) as if to say, "I would never marry someone like THAT." I tried to ignore the bad vibes and suggested we start a full rehearsal of the script. We did. It was so bad that I seriously considered recasting. Seriously.

Saturday morning. I had a strategy. Before Alan showed up I had a moment alone with Darlene. I told her part of the comedy in the film would be that such a beautiful woman like her would marry such a hairy sausage of a man. She blushed and said that I was sweet. Later, when she went to the bathroom, I told Alan pretty much the same thing. It worked like a charm. They flew through the rehearsal and I had time to visit the location with the crew.

I love getting into production. It is the most enjoyable part of film-making. All the planning of preproduction can drive you crazy. You get too much time to think. Too much time to create problems. Too much anticipation. I like the action, the life of production. There's no time for thought during production, only time for instinct and action. I love it. It is living.

We had one week to complete the edit. And it was a busy week. Earlier that winter, I had survived seven months without a job. Now, here I was juggling a half-dozen in a month. Such is the nature of freelance filmmaking—feast or famine. I soldiered through and, with the collaboration of great teammates working many late nights, finished everything on time. *Lately* . . . made a nice little film and I felt it would serve its purpose well—to reel in the money for *Blue Valentine*.

Chrysler set up a special jury of industry professionals to judge the five shorts. It took a couple of weeks to coordinate everybody's schedules and so the five finalists had to wait for the results. The anticipation racked my nerves, but I still had a lot to do. So I just kept busy. Finally, while in Indianapolis on a job, I got a call from Dan Cogan. He congratulated me on being chosen the unanimous winner of the prize. But, he said, I couldn't tell anybody for a month.

Chrysler planned to publicly announce the winner during a press conference at the IFFM in New York.

I told everyone I knew. How could I keep it in? I had finally raised the budget for my dream film. A million dollars meant I could stop talking about *Blue Valentine* and start making it. But I felt skeptical. The film had been started and stopped so many times that I was certain something would happen to make it all fall apart. Jamie Patricof told me there was the possibility that Chrysler could change their minds before the announcement. Watch out. Years in the Hollywood system can condition you to be a pessimist.

A month passed with no bad news. My wife and I went to the premiere of *A Guide to Recognizing Your Saints* where they announced the winner of the Chrysler Film Project. They showed *Lately . . .* on the big screen in front of the premiere audience and gave me one of those "big" checks. After my acceptance speech, the press took pictures of me. I made sure they could see the money, so I held the check up high. *Blue Valentine* had been green-lit many times in the past, but I had never had my picture taken with the money. This was evidence. Proof they couldn't take it away. *Blue Valentine* would be made at last. The dream would be real. I would make the film I was born to make.

I remember afterwards, a reporter asked me why I didn't seem excited to win the money. I told her, "this isn't the lottery and I didn't win by luck. I've been practicing and preparing for this opportunity for years now. I am more than excited. I am ready."

Ready, again, to tackle the 36-piece set.

ANDREW LUND, a New York City native and the son of artists, is an assistant professor in the Film & Media department at Hunter College, CUNY, and an adjunct professor in the film studies department at the University of North Carolina at Wilmington. He also serves as an adjunct assistant professor in the graduate film division of Columbia University, where he received J.D. and M.F.A. degrees.

Mr. Lund is the executive producer of a number of independent feature films, including *Vanaja*, *Confess*, and *Arranged*. He has also served as a producer on several award-winning documentaries. As a writer and director, Lund's short films have won numerous awards at film festivals around the world; have appeared on PBS, ABC, and major networks in Europe and Japan; are distributed both theatrically and nontheatrically; have garnered multiple grants; and have been included in DVD compilations and film textbooks.

Drawing on his extensive experience as an entertainment lawyer, Mr. Lund consults on legal and business aspects of film, theater, television, publishing, and fine arts. At Hunter, he has launched CinemaTalks (a guest filmmaker series), designed a digital film clip library (an interactive tool for film production courses), and created the Short Film Repository (a special features resource for makers of short films).

What's a Short Film, Really?

By Andrew Lund

With too little money and too few readers to go around, the aspiring poet faces a formidable task. What does one say when confronted by such an imposing calculus? Give up, don't bother, why try? No, because writing poetry isn't about playing the odds any more than it's about following prescribed formulas for success. Despite the obstacles, poetry flourishes—in coffee houses, in bookstores, in universities, and on street corners. So what advice would I give to the aspiring poet (putting aside the fact that no poet will ever ask for my advice)? Write from the heart, about things that matter to you, with precision and specificity. Write for the rewards of the creative process itself and not for some best-case-scenario result. Cultivate your voice, a distillation of your unique experiences, perspectives, attitudes, and beliefs. Judge yourself according to your own aspirations (and limitations) and not by external standards. Applaud your work for what it is rather than torture yourself over what it isn't. Make writing a habit and hone your craft. And above all, enjoy it.

Okay, so maybe poets don't need my easier-to-say-than-to-do platitudes. And you may be wondering what poetry has to do with making short films anyway. Writing a poem doesn't cost money, require special equipment, talented actors, or a dedicated crew. Plus, the poet can't hope for a three-picture deal or a big payday for that spec script. So why am I writing about poetry in an essay about short films? It's not an attempt to lend my words greater import, to take a highbrow approach to the topic, or to please the poetry lobby. Given the challenges that face the short filmmaker, adopting the disposition of a poet serves creative survival more faithfully than a speculative, result-oriented approach. By embracing the poet's temperament, we can recalibrate our conception of a successful short film to include more than just "lottery" winners.

Do I have further insight on the subject? Not much (but that won't stop me from continuing). My personal experience has taught me that there's no "secret formula" for a winning short. When my first film screened at a festival with another film that I loved, I asked the filmmaker for a copy; she told me I would have to speak with her distributor (this was when I learned that short films could have distributors). Her distributor agreed to send me the film, provided I sent him a copy of mine. Coincidentally, he grew up in the Brooklyn neighborhood where it was shot. He had a soft spot for his old stomping grounds, and I suddenly had myself a distributor. The smart move would have been to shoot my next film on those same Brooklyn streets. Instead, I shot it entirely in New Jersey (I have yet to meet a New Jersey film distributor). But, it managed to attract the attention of a Swedish distributor. Why? I think because my last name (Lund) is a common Swedish name, and the Swedes like to support their own. Well, I'm not Swedish (not even a little bit), but I didn't advertise that fact. And sure enough, my second film found itself a home. My next short featured a character named Bjorn at a smorgasbord, right? Wrong; it did attract a distributor for an entirely different, yet no less arbitrary, reason. Who knows what fate awaits my latest film. The vagaries of distribution remind me of how, after finishing each project, I optimistically take stock of my mistakes so that I won't repeat them. Yet, each film's novel circumstances render past mistakes moot while providing ample opportunity for new ones. Similarly, the elements that attract a distributor to one film may not draw them to another. Aspire to make a film that others will enjoy and hope one of its fans has a business card with the word "distributor" on it.

Now that I've urged you to make your film for its own sake without considering its potential return, I'm going to propose several practical approaches that might help give it "legs." My seemingly contradictory advice can coexist in the same way as the film production imperatives to be totally prepared for principal photography and yet be ready to abandon elements of your plan in order to take advantage of opportunities that arise in the moment. Striking the right balance between these two approaches can be like walking a tightrope (but if you perfect it you'll be able to run away and join the circus). These suggestions may be tried in tandem, in isolation, or ignored completely.

The term "short" film is a misnomer. A three-minute film and three-hour film share a cinematic heritage, just as a short story and a novel both tell a story. Yes, the feature-length film is the most common and commercially viable format, but it hasn't always been that way—remember, the first films were all "short" films (by technological necessity). But even if the feature-length film remains the benchmark, films that fall short of that running-time bar should not be lumped into one overly broad category. An aspiring poet may need to establish a framework for her work beyond the umbrella term "poem." Will she write an epic poem, a haiku, a sonnet, or a limerick?

Since we've covered poetry, now let's do a little math. Assume the average feature film lasts between 90 and 150 minutes, a spread of 60%. A short film is defined as anything less than 40 minutes (at least according to Academy Award-qualifying rules), so let's say shorts run anywhere from 5 to 40 minutes (even though many great films are shorter), a spread of 400% — that's quite a lot of territory for the "short" to cover. The short designation should really be divided into more precise categories (some festivals have begun to do this). By recognizing that the short film moniker has developed as a catchall for any film that's not a feature, you have the opportunity to define your film according to what it is instead of what it's not.

A film's running time should be determined by the shortest time needed to tell your chosen story. But, determining the minimum can be tricky (consider the adage that every short film can be improved by cutting it in half). Why not approach duration from the opposite perspective? Start with the goal to make a five-minute film, and then tailor your story to fit within the confines of your chosen running time. Why place this artificial boundary on your creativity? In my experience as a film professor, students are liberated creatively when forced to work within strict limitations. Conversely, the do-whatever-you-want-as-long-as-you-can-pay-for-it approach often results in bloated, self-indulgent work. In James Schamus' legendary no-budget producing class at Columbia, he urged us to make the aesthetic fit the budget. So now I implore you to supplement that sage advice by "making the story fit the desired running time."

Just as runners expert at different distances rely on different muscles and training techniques, the tools used in shorts of different running times vary widely. In short shorts, the characters, setting, and premise don't come under too much scrutiny (just as a short joke that isn't that funny is judged differently than a long joke that's a dud). It's often enough for a short short to present a compelling situation, an engaging incident, a clever hook. While the audience may grant a short short greater leeway (on the time invested watching to expected payoff ratio), it takes formidable talent to effectively communicate with an audience so quickly. Short shorts have very little time for setup, elaboration, or character development; the filmmaker must immediately thrust the audience into the story, providing the necessary information and context to follow the rapidly unfolding action. When festivals can program six 5-minute films, three 10-minute films, two 15-minute films, or one 30-minute film in the same time slot, it's understandable that they favor the shorter end of the spectrum. Shorter shorts also make more sense if your distribution plan targets Internet streaming, digital downloads, or playback on a handheld device like an iPod.

However, as a training ground for feature film work, longer shorts boast some real benefits. They provide the opportunity for character development, narrative arc, three-act structure, subplots, visual motifs, genre conventions, and many other cinematic and narrative tools commonly employed by the feature filmmaker. The longer running time tests a filmmaker's ability to engage an audience over an extended period (if you have me riveted for 30 minutes, I bet you can do it for 90). Longer shorts also provide the chance to collaborate with actors in meatier roles. The fundamental cinematic skills consistently called into play on these longer shorts make them great training experiences. And while it may be harder to get a longer short programmed at festivals, and while it can be tough to have an "objective" screening of a longer short when it is surrounded by shorter shorts (as well as more difficult to stream, download, and watch on a handheld screen), festivals are not the only place that a short screens. In fact, if you have contacts interested in seeing your film, they will probably watch it in the comfort of their own home. Consider approaching your film like an artist whose paintings are meant to create a personal relationship with the viewer, not to hang with other paintings that compete for attention.

Knowing how you want your film to be seen—the big screen, video projection, television, the web, etc.—may influence how you decide to shoot it. Depending on the size of screen, the same shot reads differently in terms of duration, movement, and composition. And the audience's ability to gather visual information also varies with screen size—the smaller the screen the harder it is for audience to pick up on certain visual clues, forcing you to consider other options (to prolong the shot, to foreground the visual information, or deliver it in a more direct way).

Each shorts category has its respective benefits. Maybe you want to start out with a shorter film that will have a better shot at festivals, where you'll get to watch many other shorts and meet other filmmakers (an integral part of a film education). Maybe you want to showcase your work with actors, and you don't care how many festivals your film gets into as long as the right people have the right reaction to your work. Maybe you want to start developing a group of collaborators who you can work with on successive projects, so you take their preferences into account when choosing the appropriate project/length. Maybe your concerns are strictly practical (which is okay): you only want to spend so much money and devote so much time, or you're constrained by the availability of equipment, locations, actors, and crew. Deciding what category of short you want to make helps you choose, mold, and shepherd the appropriate project (which will improve your chances of achieving your goals for it). Make limitations work for you by incorporating strict guidelines into your creative process.

Now that I've told you to embrace your inner poet and to time your films as if they were soufflés, I'm going to further confound you by recommending that you borrow some feature film attitude. Think about some of the things that we're usually happy to avoid as short filmmakers. Like marketing. Imagine the poster for your movie (even if you don't plan on having a poster); what is the iconic image that everyone will identify with your film? Does it encapsulate your story? Now pair that image with a good title. We've all laughed at the horrible titles of coming attractions—generic names that told us nothing about the films except that we'd be better off avoiding them. It's not so hard to choose a title that provokes audience's curiosity, that has a connection to your film, and that people will remember (okay, maybe it is hard, but that's all the more reason to devote some creative energy to the task).

And speaking of coming attractions, imagine your film's trailer. If you actually script a trailer during preproduction, it may help you to focus your story; imagine it first as one of those trailers that whets your appetite for a film and then as one of those tell-all trailers that makes seeing the actual film seem redundant. Once you reach post, why not cut an actual trailer? Write up a catchy blurb and a clever tag line so that readers will feel like inconsiderate idiots if they miss your film.

Before you grow tired of my rant (if you haven't already), I have a few more things to say about elements that contribute to a short film's viability. If your short is an excerpt from a feature, make sure that it stands on its own as a work that feels complete. Don't just talk about the look of a film—bleach bypass blah blah blah. If you don't have a story that engages the audience, the look won't rescue you. Don't pawn your next film just to shoot this one on 35 mm or to rent that perfect lens. But, don't just say you'll shoot the hell out of it on video and then figure things out in the editing room. Video may be effectively free in comparison to film stock and processing, but all that time spent shooting endless footage will wear down your actors and your crew (not to mention that the limitations of film force you to make the creative choices that are the bedrock of directing). Make sure you have a polished sound design. If your film doesn't look great, the audience can focus on the story and assume the degraded image was a conscious artistic choice. But when we can't hear what's being said, or when there are uneven audio levels, or background sounds pop in and out, it's impossible not to be distracted. Keep your credits short, but if you hope to work with these generous and talented people again, you better make sure they, their friends, and their families can read their name in the credits without a magnifier. Remember, the most important thing you take away from a film is your relationship with your collaborators. Nurturing those relationships will help sustain you as a filmmaker.

Make specific choices, not generic ones. But keep in mind that an inside joke that's too inside will potentially alienate those of us on the outside. I have seen numerous films wow a local audience at the schools or in the communities where they were made. But outside that specific (and too narrow in distribution terms) audience, those same films fall flat. Hopefully, you're not making your film exclusively for your crew or the students in your school (there's nothing more tyrannical than the too-cool-for-school film student audience). Imagine the reaction of someone who doesn't know you, hasn't read your script, and doesn't recognize your actors or locations.

My first film was picked up for distribution in the educational market; more than 10 years later, I still get periodic checks from the distributor—it won't finance a mortgage, but it allows me to remain current with the latest iPod. Teachers like using films as teaching tools. It's an angle that most filmmakers don't think about. That doesn't mean you have to make the equivalent of a public service announcement or an after-school special. You just have to pass this simple test: if your film were shown to a class, would it trigger a valuable, instructive discussion among the students?

Don't only apply to the best-known festivals. While my films have screened in some very prestigious festivals, my breaks have always come from "second-tier" festivals. I've also enjoyed myself more at some of the lower key festivals where the vibe is more about appreciating film and meeting other filmmakers than about cutthroat competition. As you submit your film, remember that rejection is a natural and necessary part of the process. While writing this, I learned that I had been passed over for a prestigious fellowship; I wanted to punch the computer, but instead I just kept punching the keys, spitting out one word after another (it helps to think of it in terms of not being accepted rather than being rejected, but semantics doesn't always dull the pain).

And don't try to make a film that everyone will love, because you'll fail. When the Woody Allens and Martin Scorseses have their critics, we should welcome ours with equanimity.

In the aftermath of graduate school, when everyone was struggling to get their features made despite their extremely successful, award-winning shorts, one talented director shocked everyone by making another short. It was an act of preservation not strategy. He wanted to be a filmmaker, and filmmakers make films any way possible. Ultimately, the most important thing I can tell you is to keep making movies (and writing poems). Why? Not because it's practical. Not because it's easy. Not because it will pay off. Not because it will advance your career. Not because it will make you rich and famous. But just because that is what filmmakers do. And if by chance, while you forge ahead with your films, one of those other things occurs, then hooray for you! So keep making films. And remember, a film never made will never be distributed.

Swimming Lesson #4

How I Learned to Swim: Filmmaker Survival Stories

Repeat after me:

"Other filmmakers are not my enemy."

Say it again, louder, and mean it this time.

Many filmmakers look around and see every other filmmaker as their competition, with a "me or them" mentality. I want you to think about it differently because in reality, other filmmakers can be your allies, potential collaborators, or BFFs if you let them.

For example, when your film is in a festival, you really have only one task—to promote your film. Along those lines, you really only have one responsibility—your screening. So what are you going to do the other three, five, or seven days? Why, go to other people's screenings of course! When you are standing in the middle of that first fabulous festival party with sweaty hands clutched around a chilled drink, frozen smile on your face and fear in your eyes, instead of stalking the film buyers, turn to the filmmaker next to you and say hello.

Invite them to your screening and offer to go to theirs. You definitely want a full house, particularly if you have a comedy, and there's no better way to fill the seats than with other filmmakers. If you're a first-timer at the festival, other filmmakers can offer you some helpful hints to get through what can be a daunting environment. Find out what parties are the "must-go-to" events. Ask them about their experience.

Every filmmaker is in a different place in their career, and you can learn a lot from what they have gone through. Whenever you meet a fellow filmmaker, ask questions! What festivals were they in? What DP did they use? Did they get distribution—where/how/when? What buyers might they be able to introduce you to? Filmmaking is such a collaborative art form that your success is always dependent on other people. You don't work or live in a vacuum, and you can make great contacts if you take the time to interact with other filmmakers.

There is no one right path in this industry. Everyone creates their own journey based on who they are, what their project is, and where they want to go with it. Whether it's in a class or in a screening room, each filmmaker has a story to tell about their experience making and distributing (or not) their short film.

Thus the chapter title *How I Learned to Swim: Filmmaker Survival Stories*, because these firsthand experiences give you a good sense of what other filmmakers have learned from the process. I hope they help you with yours.

JENS ASSUR is one of Scandinavia's premiere photographers/directors and a regular contributor to leading Scandinavian and international magazines. From 1990 to 1997 he was a staff photographer for *Expressen*, then the leading daily newspaper in Scandinavia.

During his seven years at *Expressen* he produced extensive, thorough photo essays depicting aspects of life in nearly a hundred different countries. At the age of 23 he left *Expressen* to form Studio Jens Assur and began his photographic project *Under the Shifting Skies*, which comprises two books of 256 pages and a traveling exhibition.

In 1999 Jens was contacted by the prestigious *Life* magazine to complete a special-edition issue in connection with the Olympic Games in Sydney. Jen's photo essays were published in the last-ever issue of *Life* in the summer of 2000.

In 2006 Jens completed his first short film *The Last Dog in Rwanda*, which portrays the Rwandan genocide of 1994 and was shot in South Africa and Sweden. The short film won the Best Live Action award at the Palm Springs International Short Film Festival, the Best Film award at Australia's Flickerfest, the Grand Pix award at the Clermont-Ferrand Short Film Festival, the Award for Best Narrative Short Film at the 2007 Tribeca Film Festival, and recently the awards for Best Short at the Nashville and Rome festivals.

Jens is currently working on his first feature film as both writer and director.

Full Circle

By Jens Assur

This is a short story about doing your first short film.

During the nineties I worked as a photojournalist, first for a leading Scandinavian daily newspaper and then for *Life* magazine. During that period I had the opportunity to see the world.

I visited more than a hundred countries.

I shook hands with Nelson Mandela the night he declared himself South Africa's first democratic president. I hid in a basement in Sarajevo in former Yugoslavia when grenades were falling outside. I saw thousands and thousands of skyscrapers being built in Shanghai. I visited Somalia during the civil war—not just once, but four times.

And I went to Rwanda.

No journey and no experience moved and shocked me as Rwanda did. Nearly one million people were slaughtered over a period of only three months, and they were murdered by ordinary civilians.

I could write a book about Rwanda, but since this is an essay about film, I will instead tell you what I think about motion pictures.

I love motion pictures.

I grew up spending Friday and Saturday nights watching block-busters like *Raiders of the Lost Ark* and *Beverly Hills Cop*. When I was in high school I joined the film club and had the opportunity to see films made by Scorsese, Kubrick, Kieslowski, and Coppola.

That film club became my first film school.

What was so fantastic being a photojournalist was that I, through my pictures, could spread awareness and knowledge about the world and the day-to-day life we ourselves create. That is also what I think is so fantastic about films. I don't know any medium that is as strong, powerful, and important as the film medium.

What I also love about movies is that they contain so many different arts—photography, of course, but also writing, acting, art direction, music, and many others. When all these parts come together, I don't think that there are any limits as to what you can achieve with a film.

You can entertain.

You can create opinion.

You can create debate.

You can, from my point of view, actually change the world.

And you can do all this at the same time.

My only experience with motion pictures before I wrote and directed my first short film, *The Last Dog in Rwanda* (besides seeing a lot of movies), was that I read a book called *Easy Riders, Raging Bulls*, written by Peter Biskind, a well-known journalist and author.

Easy Riders, Raging Bulls is a great book about a great era in the American motion picture—the seventies. It was an era when writers and directors ruled Hollywood, an era that created some of the best films ever made.

That book became my second film school.

This is what I learned by reading Biskind's book:

1. It's okay to be nervous when you direct your first film. (Even Coppola thought *The Godfather* should be a failure.)
2. A well-written script and a well-planned shoot will reduce the nervousness. (Two words: *Apocalypse Now*.)
3. To make that well-written script and that well-planned shoot into a great film—work with the best people in the industry.

(What would *The Godfather* have been without its cinematography? What would *Dr. Strangelove* have been without its set design? What would *Jaws* have been without that tune? Probably good movies, but would they have been great?)

I am not sure that even if I had directed hundreds of commercials and music videos or attended film schools all over the world, I would have been prepared for all the questions and decisions I had to make when I went to Africa to shoot *The Last Dog in Rwanda*.

Three examples:

1. Mr. Director, I have finally found that missing container with props. It has been confiscated by Customs since they found six skeletons in it. When I talked to Customs they had to hang up because they were being subjected to an armed robbery. Can you go there and sort everything out?
2. Mr. Director, I discovered two six-meter crocodiles at the next location. Should we shoot them or find a new location?
3. Mr. Director, I made a mistake when calculating the costs. I just found out that you should multiply the South African Rand by the Swedish Krona instead of dividing it—what should I do? Should I fire the extras or reduce the principal photography by one day?

The answers to all these questions:

1. No.
2. Find brave actors.
3. You are fired.

Moviemaking is about decisions. All the time. Sometimes it is more important to actually make a decision than the decision you make.

The Last Dog in Rwanda had its first screening at Gothenburg's Film Festival. It was in a competition with six other short films that had been made in Sweden that year.

They gave away four awards.

We got none.

For six months the film lay on a shelf in a storage room.

Then the Swedish Film Institute—who had so generously supported the film financially together with Swedish National TV, SF, and Film i Västernorrland—sent the film to its first international film festival.

The film won First Prize in Palm Springs, California.

Then it won First Prize in Sydney, Australia.

And in Rome, Italy.

And in Clermont-Ferrand, France, this time in competition with 5600 films from 99 countries.

When the film was selected for Tribeca I bought a ticket to New York to attend my first festival. I had a great time. I was thrilled being part of a global community that works with global questions and that reaches a global audience. I felt that the film industry was generous and inspiring.

After a fantastic week in New York, and before the festival was over, I packed my bags, checked out from the hotel and took a taxi to the airport. When I reached New Jersey I asked the driver to make a U-turn and go back to Manhattan.

That weekend I had one of the most rewarding evenings in my entire life.

First I went to a small reception.

At that reception I met a man that I had met in the jungle in Rwanda during the genocide in 1994. We met north of Kigali, the capital, when he was a soldier and commander and was liberating Rwanda. Thirteen years later we met in New York.

He was now the President of Rwanda.

Two hours later *The Last Dog in Rwanda* won the award for Best Narrative Short Film at the Tribeca Film Festival.

I do not think I have to explain how moved, touched, and happy I was that evening. My work had become a full circle. From Rwanda to New York and back again.

This is a short story about doing your first short film.

JESSICA SHARZER made her directorial feature debut with *Speak*, based on the acclaimed best-selling novel by Laurie Halse Anderson. *Speak* premiered at Sundance in 2004 and was later simulcast on Lifetime and Showtime in an unprecedented network event. *Speak* was nominated for both a Writers Guild Award and a Directors Guild Award in 2005.

Ms. Sharzer has written screenplays for Universal, Showtime, HBO Films, and Endgame Entertainment. In television, she recently directed an episode of Showtime's acclaimed drama *The L Word*. She has written a one-hour drama pilot for the Fox network with Ashton Kutcher's company Katalyst and a Nashville-set drama pilot for CBS. She has just been hired to be the showrunner for a new series on MTV slated to premiere in August 2007. Ms. Sharzer is attached to direct the Dusty Springfield story for Universal Studios based on her screenplay, as well as *Cruddy*, based on Lynda Barry's cult novel.

Ms. Sharzer holds an M.A. in Russian literature from Berkeley and an M.F.A. in film and television from NYU Tisch School of the Arts. Her thesis film *The Wormhole* won various grants and awards including the Student Academy Award in 2002.

Trial and Error in Hollywood

By Jessica Sharzer

I am always a little perplexed what to say when people ask me how to get ahead in the film business. Because the truth is — I feel I got rather lucky. When I moved to Los Angeles in 2002, I didn't know what the hell I was doing — and I was lucky enough to fall in with a great agency and to start working with some of the most highly regarded producers in the business. I put my foot in my mouth on a weekly basis and I'm still not over the taste of shoe leather. So there's the first two pieces of advice: get lucky and be careful what you say. Hollywood is a painfully small town — like a suburban high school, except this time around, the nerds call the shots and the jocks fetch their coffee. So before you trash the latest box-office disaster in a meeting, it's always good to be sure no one in the room made said disaster.

Now, in addition to luck, I have also worked hard. Very hard. I'm still your garden-variety film school geek. I still attend weekend writing workshops. I watch about three movies a week and often outline them scene by scene. In other words, though I happily make my living writing and directing in Hollywood — I don't feel "done" with my education. I am still in awe of the craft and daunted by it. And I'm never satisfied with my own work. There is always a better draft to be found — so I'm fair game for feedback and another attempt to get it right. An essential skill in Hollywood is learning how to control the scowl muscles in your face when you hear outrageous notes that will tear apart the very fabric of your script. You learn to nod with an expression of thoughtful consideration. The key is to uncover the note underneath the note: what is the real problem they are having with the material? These notes meetings can occasionally devolve into mass brainstorming sessions in which everyone suddenly "spitballs." Occasionally, I will gently ask, "What problem are we trying to solve?" Dead silence. Nips it in the bud.

I loved NYU Film School, but I didn't learn how to pitch there — and that turned out to be the one skill I needed to get a job in

Hollywood. I learned it on the fly. I wouldn't say I have a natural aptitude for pitching, but I'm happy to report this is a skill that can be honed and refined along the way. Having just pitched and won a job this week, I can really see how far I've come in these five years. Early on, I asked my agent what I needed to accomplish in a meeting to get a job. He said that I had to make the executive or producer confident that they could entrust millions of dollars to me for whatever film and that I could handle it, both professionally and creatively. I couldn't help but think if I had millions of dollars at my disposal, I would probably put it into real estate rather than hand it over to me to make some movie. To my agent's sage advice, I would add that you need to command the room. You need to make eye contact with every person at the table and tell a great story. An A-list screenwriter friend of mine calls it "campfiring." First, I love that he uses "campfire" as a verb. What he means is that he tells the story like it's a ghost story being told around a campfire to a bunch of kids. It needs to be that tight, that suspenseful, that simple, and that *good*. You can't afford to be academic or have your nose down in a bunch of 3 × 5 cards. And God protect you if you go over fifteen minutes. You'll see eyes glaze over or glance at their Blackberries. One of my favorite executives sat with me and timed my pitch with a stopwatch over and over until I got it down. I talked so fast I thought I was going to bite my tongue—but I got the gig. And she is now running a major company.

My ego expected me to crank out great scripts from the first time I tried. Ha! Possibly the most comforting thing I ever heard in Hollywood is that it takes ten years to master a craft like screenwriting, so you have to buckle in and do the work with a whole lot of faith. I truly believe that. Sure, some people are thoroughbreds right out of the gate. I'm not one of them. I'm an up-early, at-the-coffee-shop-by-nine-with-my-laptop kind of writer and I get better in fits and starts. It's like anything else in life; the victories are hard won. It takes a Herculean effort to get a movie made, any movie, and there's never a guarantee that it will be good. In fact, Murphy's Law is always poised against you. Which brings me to my last point . . .

You better have an iron stomach if you want to make movies. You better be able to weather disappointments, ridicule, failure, rejection, and financial dry spells. You better have other things in your life that console and fulfill you when the business kicks you to the curb, and they will, no matter how big you are. You better have a big enough ego to stand your ground when it counts and enough humility to know when to fold. You better be willing to go the extra mile to outshine your competition. And, more than anything, you better be having fun. Because otherwise, in spite of the phenomenal Southern California weather (and, yes, it does help), you will eventually succumb to the inevitable cynicism that the business engenders in all of us. And your only real defense against it is a love of the work itself.

Based on all the mistakes I've made, here are my top ten tips in shorthand for the Hollywood newcomer, in no particular order:

1. Do not wear a Tahari suit to a "meet and greet." Everyone else in the room will be in jeans and sneakers and you will stick out like the neophyte that you are.

2. Only ever ask for water when they ask. Things that stain, spill, make you burp are out of the question.
3. Be extremely nice to every assistant you ever meet and try to remember their names. I guarantee you will be seeking a job from that person one day soon.
4. Always be prepared to abandon what you prepared to pitch once you "take the temperature" of the person to whom you're pitching. If you're pitching an update of *Grease* and they tell you flat out they hate *Grease*, abandon your mission. You will never win.
5. When they say, "I'd really like to work with you," *you did not just get a job*. This is a figure of speech in Hollywood and it carries as much cash value as "Nice to meet you." It does not come with a job or money. It simply means that if you turn into something one day, that person can call you up and remind that they said it and check in about what you're working on.
6. Don't go pitch movies that you would never dare pay ten bucks to go see. Should you be so lucky to get the job, you will wind up hating every minute of it and you won't respect yourself in the morning.
7. Do not bug your agent. Use email whenever possible and trust that they will call you if they have a job or job prospect for you.
8. Be prepared to run into everyone you work with at the gym. So if it matters to you, shave your legs ahead of time.
9. Bad idea to sleep with people you're working with. (I actually never did this, Scout's honor, but I know it's a colossally bad idea.)
10. Show up early and always leave 'em wanting more.

DAVID BRIND has directed three short films, including the current *Twenty Dollar Drinks* starring Sandra Bernhard and Tony-Award winner Cady Huffman, which premiered at the 2006 Tribeca Film Festival. Additionally, Mr. Brind wrote and produced the award-winning short film *dare*, which, after a successful festival run, was picked up by Strand Releasing as part of *Boys' Life 5*, a successful series of gay-themed short films.

In spring 2006, he directed the Off-Broadway production of *Sandra Bernhard: Everything Bad and Beautiful*. Mr. Brind is currently in preproduction on his feature-length screenplay of *dare* with director Adam Salky and producer Mary Jane Skalski. He is also hard at work on his next film project, a screenplay adaptation of William Wright's nonfiction book *Harvard's Secret Court: The Savage 1920 Purge of Campus Homosexuals* (St. Martin's Press). Mr. Brind received his B.A. in theater studies and American studies from Yale University and his M.F.A. from Columbia University's graduate film program.

dare to Create

By David Brind

September 2003. I started at the Graduate Film Program at Columbia University. In our first year, the faculty enacts a tradition called the "8–12." In it, every new film student is required to write, produce, and direct a short film that should be from 8 to 12 minutes long. The catch being that you can't direct your own script, but rather must apply to direct a classmate's script in a process known as "the swap." I entered my short script, then titled *Truth or Dare*, a dark high school story about two boys, an outsider and the cool kid, hanging out one night after play practice and having an encounter that breaks the lines of traditional high school social boundaries. I chose my classmate Adam Salky, now my creative and business partner, to direct the film, later retitled *dare*. Adam and I collaborated exceedingly well and (mostly) had a blast doing it. We set out to make the best short film we possibly could, but never thought too specifically about what would happen after. The film's production budget was just over $5000.

dare ended up playing over 50 film festivals worldwide, including most of the prestigious gay/lesbian film fests in the United States, like LA's Outfest, the Miami and Philadelphia Gay and Lesbian Fests, and San Francisco's Frameline. The gay festival circuit is a bit insular and so we quickly got requests from dozens of festivals to screen *dare*. We also screened at a slew of mainstream fests such as Palm Springs, Nashville, Alabama's Sidewalk, Rhode Island International, and Cinequest. At the end of the day, we sold *dare* to Marcus Hu and Jon Gerrans of Strand Releasing, where it ended up as the cover image and lead-off short on Strand's *Boys' Life 5*, currently available on DVD via Netflix and in stores nationwide. I subsequently turned the short into a feature-length script that Adam and I are now in the process of getting made with incredible indie producer Mary Jane Skalski (*The Station Agent, Mysterious Skin*).

October 2005. I started production on my next short, *Twenty Dollar Drinks*, an adaptation of a short play by playwright Joe Pintauro, starring the brilliant duo of actress/comedienne/singer Sandra Bernhard and Tony-winning star Cady Huffman (*The Producers*). This time I was both screenwriter and director, but once again set out to make the short as part of a class assignment at Columbia.

This was an altogether different process than *dare*. I was already thinking actively about the short's afterlife. It seemed clear that with Sandra and Cady on board, the film would be an easy sell, if we executed it well. My producer Jennifer Westin and I had the big dream of premiering the film at the 2006 Tribeca Film Festival, going on to many other fests after that.

Premiere at Tribeca we did, and triumphantly. Filmcritic.com singled out our film as the best in its program. But afterwards? We played four other great festivals, including Provincetown and San Diego, but ended up getting lost in the mix after that. The film, a talky affair about two actresses who came of age together, but now find themselves at odds, screened very well for audiences. But apparently was not for everyone. Was it hard to program thematically? Was there too much talking? Was it not cinematic enough? Or do films without a specific niche (gay, African-American, current events) or a huge, surprise plot twist at the end simply not get programmed as much? *dare* set the bar (and my expectations) high. *Twenty Dollar Drinks*, a film of which I am quite proud, performed solidly, but wasn't the home run in terms of festival play or opening doors that *dare* had been.

With few exceptions, the gay festival circuit hones in on its most successful films—they tend to play every major fest. Whereas the mainstream film fests are patchier—if you premiere at Tribeca, playing Sundance or any other of the major competitors is unlikely.

So what did I learn that could help the filmmaker about to shoot his or her big short?

Well, the perils of short-filmmaking are many. During my time at film school, many of my classmates (and myself) put a lot of time,

123

effort, talent, and money into making shorts whose subjects we were passionate about. There was plenty of critique and input along the way of course, but often, passion causes us artists to turn a blind eye (and ear). And more often than not, these expensive, overlong, shorts failed to inspire passion in anyone other than the filmmaker him- or herself. And so the filmmaker goes back to the drawing board and begins again (more often then not), creating the next short, which, chances are, will follow a similar path.

So what's the secret? I wish it were that easy. I can, however, share some guidelines that I learned through my experience.

1. Believe the cliché—write what you know.

Some of the best shorts I've seen are deeply rooted in the point of view of the filmmaker(s). They start with a subject close to their heart, delving deep into characters they know well, and the end result ends up really resonating for an audience. This does not mean to tell your life story in 10–20 minutes. Nor does it mean to replicate something from your life exactly in a screenplay. What do you find yourself thinking about when you're daydreaming? What excites you? What do you secretly wish someone had shown in a film that is rarely seen or depicted? Start from there and then . . .

2. Be specific—it's all in the details.

Use who you are in telling your story. The festival market is inundated with short films—make yours stand out. Niches are key. In my case, it was the gay angle. There are dozens upon dozens of quality gay and lesbian film festivals both in the States and around the world. They are all looking for quality material that will excite their audiences. Similarly, there are festivals that focus on films by or about women, African-Americans, South Asians, Latinos, religious groups, etc. You'd be a fool not to consider using your affiliations in your point of view. It is a part of who you are, and something you know from the inside out, however . . .

3. Avoid the stereotypes, be bold and daring in your storytelling.

There have been hundreds of short films about coming out, death of a parent, divorce, lost love, racism, mistaken identity, coming of age, etc. Most films fall under one of these or another more genre-specific category. But why should a programmer watch yours?

In the case of *dare*, I wrote a story that could certainly qualify as a "coming-of-age coming-out" story. But that wasn't what I set out to create. I was interested in a very specific emotion—what happens when you decide, for the first time, to go after what you want, to break out, and, fueled by frustration, ambition, and desire, take the ultimate risk. I wanted the journey of Ben, the protagonist, to feel familiar and slick—like any other high school film. And though the audience may have some idea of where the story is going, I wanted the journey there to take an unexpected path, creating suspense and titillation along the way.

At an early screening of *dare* in one of the festivals we played, my partner Adam was dismayed when an audience began to laugh during one of the climactic moments set in a swimming pool. I paused, listening as the nervous laughter quickly subsided to dead silence at the climax and turned to Adam and said, "They're laughing because they're nervous and excited, not because they think it's funny." That was a great moment for us as filmmakers—feeling we had accomplished what we set out to do.

A few other quick bullet points of advice:

- **Keep it short**—a smart, interesting short that is under 10 minutes significantly increases its chances of getting programmed.
- **Take great publicity stills**—the still photo from *dare* helped us out enormously, and ended up being the cover image of Strand's *Boys' Life* collection box set. You can see it at http://www.darethemovie.com.
- **Casting, casting, casting.** Don't use people you know just because it's convenient. Your cast of actors can make or break your short. Aim high, you never know who might be interested in appearing in your film. Sandra Bernhard was a friend who agreed to star in my short because she liked my previous work—having Sandra allowed us to get Cady Huffman on board.

So I'm taking my own advice in my words to you, my fellow filmmakers. I am writing what I know, in hopes that some of it will prove helpful as you begin to undertake your own work. Good luck and Godspeed. It is a crazy, fucked-up business, with no clear chartable path from short film to multipicture deal. But it can be well worth it. I leave you with some bonus moments from my trip through the world of short film.

A few of my favorite short film moments, good and bad:

Adam and I attended Frameline, the San Francisco Gay & Lesbian Film Festival, in the summer of 2005. *dare* was screened as part of a program of shorts at the famous Castro Theater, an old-fashioned movie palace, in front of an audience of over 1000. The crowd was literally screaming at the screen during the film, collectively gasped during the climax, cheered wildly at some lines of dialog, and madly applauded at the end. A filmmaker's wet dream. After the screening,

I was walking down Castro Street with a friend when a young woman came running down the street, screaming my name and holding out her cell phone. "Excuse me David? My boss is on the phone and he'd like to talk to you about buying *dare* for a DVD collection." Even more brilliant was getting to tell her boss via cell phone that we'd already sold it to one of their competitors. Had no idea this was even possible with a short—only at the gay fests, kids.

My short *Twenty Dollar Drinks* premiered at the 2006 Tribeca Film Festival, thanks to the taste and faith of the incomparable Sharon Badal. We screened in the NY, NY shorts program, a series of films about various aspects of life in the city. Also in our program was a short directed by Henry Winkler's son. Mr. Winkler attended several of the screenings. At the final screening of our program, a late-night affair in Battery Park, I was hanging out in the theater chatting with friends after it ended. Someone tapped my shoulder and I turned around to find Henry Winkler standing in front of me. He asked me if my background was in theater. I affirmed his suspicions. He complimented me on my direction of Sandra and Cady, specifically on their very specific performance arcs, and told me he looked forward to seeing more from me. So cool.

At the request of a short film programmer, of whom I am quite fond, I submitted *Twenty Dollar Drinks* to one of the top gay/lesbian film fests where *dare* had previously played. A short while later I received a note in the mail that read, "Thanks David! Really enjoyed it, but unfortunately we can't program it. Next time be sure to lez it up and we'll put it in!" Damn; I so don't wanna be pigeonholed, one of the shortfalls of doing well in a particular genre or niche. I still say it's the best way to go to get your short noticed, though.

The Provincetown Film Festival. It's like summer camp for film-makers. They are so generous, kind, and warm-spirited. A great festival that straddles the line of gay/mainstream exceedingly well and consistently draws talented filmmakers, new and established, to attend. The 2006 Fest was my favorite overall festival experience thus far.

One of the sets for *dare* was in the home of a close family friend of mine. We were filming in their indoor swimming pool. The house is gorgeous, and filled with breakable and expensive objects. As producer, I made two rules: (1) that I would be in charge of overseeing the movement of any of the residence's possessions; (2) I would never leave the set during production. We shot *dare* over the course of five nights. On the fourth night, we ran into a prop emergency. It was 3:00 A.M. and the soccer ball, a key prop, had gone missing. There was one at the home of the art director, about 30 minutes away. None of our

126

dispensable PAs could drive, so against my better judgment, I drove off in hot pursuit of a soccer ball before sunrise would forcibly end our shoot. Driving madly on I-76 in Philadelphia, I managed to make it back to the set in just under an hour. During that time, Adam, the director, had taken it upon himself to move a very large and very old African statue. And he had snapped its base in two. I arrived on set to a very red-faced director and a tense crew. Later that night, while room tone was being taken, the DP focused his camera on me. Sitting about 50 yards away, my legs crossed and one anxiously bouncing, I chain-smoked furiously and looked as though I was either plotting a murderous revenge or about to have a full-fledged nervous breakdown. Needless to say, it all ended okay, and Adam and I are still talking. But think twice about filming in the expensive homes of friends (or strangers) without a careful policy in place to avoid mass destruction.

SIÂN HEDER grew up in Cambridge, Massachusetts, in a family of celebrated artists and received her B.F.A. in theater from Carnegie Mellon University. She has worked extensively as an actress Off-Broadway as well as in television and film. In 2005, Ms. Heder was among eight women, chosen out of hundreds, to receive the prestigious Directing Workshop for Women Grant and Fellowship at the American Film Institute. Her directorial debut, *Mother*, won the Grand Jury Prize at the Florida Film Festival, the Cinéfondation at the Cannes Film Festival, and Best Narrative Short at the Seattle International Film Festival and at the Oxford Film Festival. In the past year, it has played in over 20 major film festivals worldwide.

Ms. Heder is now heading into preproduction on her first feature film, called *Tallulah*. She is represented by International Creative Management.

Mother's Journey

By Siân Heder

I made my short film *Mother* with no expectations. I was focused on what was directly in front of me, with no thought as to what would come after. I didn't see it as a calling card; in fact, having never made a film before, I wasn't even sure that I wanted to be a director. I just knew that there was a specific story I wanted to tell. I had written a script and had been accepted by the Directing Workshop for Women at AFI. My film was based on a personal experience that, although seemingly mundane, was particularly powerful to me, and I wanted to see if I could tell the story with the same kind of impact as the encounter that spawned it. I wanted to make a film for me.

My main concern when I finished the film was "Do I like this?" And I did. It moved me. Despite having sat in the editing room for countless hours, nitpicking over the two-second shot where I was convinced that my lead actress was walking like Superman (I could have sworn she looked like she had a cape on), I still reached the end of the film and felt goose bumps. It was as though three-quarters of the way through watching it, I forgot I had made it and was sucked right into the story, only to be continually surprised by the last moment. I loved my little movie. Then, as could be expected, I was overcome by a burning desire to have everyone else love it too.

Cut to: the arrival of my first rejection letter, from Sundance. Not overly surprised, I easily dismissed it with "Well, it's *Sundance*, for God's sake." A couple of days later, a second rejection letter arrived, from a much smaller festival. Then a "No" from Tribeca. Slowly, the "No's" piled up . . . there were five . . . eight . . . ten . . . you're kidding me . . . twelve?!

I crumbled with self-doubt. "It's *bad*. I made a *bad* film!" David, my producer, would roll his eyes and reassure me with "They probably didn't watch it." Or, "Did the DVD even play?" and finally, "Who knows *what* kind of meds the 17-year-old prescreener was on?" There are a million ways to justify why your film didn't make it into a festival. Believe me, I've used them all. Making a film is a vulnerable affair, and it's hard not to take the rejections personally. I grew convinced that Withoutabox was being single-handedly supported by my trigger-happy (and clearly futile) application attempts.

One day, four months after finishing the film, as I was sitting on my stoop, seriously questioning my newfound love of filmmaking and feeling quite broken-hearted, my phone rang. The guy spoke in broken English, with a thick French accent that sounded totally unconvincing.

"Allo? Is dis Siân Heder? Allo? I am calling from zee Cannes Film Festival . . . ."

"Shut up!" I said, convinced it was David, feigning a terrible accent and messing with me. I hadn't even applied to the Cannes Film Festival. It had to be a joke.

"Allo?" the voice said again.

"Who is this?" I asked tentatively. He told me his name was Laurent Jacob, the head of the Cinefondation at the Cannes Film Festival. He wanted to have *Mother* for the competition.

128

The "Woohoo!" that followed was so loud; Laurent is still suffering inner ear damage. It turns out that someone at AFI, a woman I barely knew at the time, who had seen my film and loved it, had submitted through the school on my behalf. Apparently, there were people out there who believed in my film even more than me.

So we went to Cannes. Overwhelmed by the yacht-choked marina, the impossible-to-get-into parties, the tux/gown wearing (which reminded us hourly that we were completely out of our league), we reassured ourselves that it was amazing just to be there, and that nothing else really mattered. The Cinefondation is the student com-petition at Cannes, for emerging filmmakers. I was the only American filmmaker among 18 selections from around the globe.

The best part of the festival was the inspiration I gained from the other filmmakers I met. The "American short" usually falls into a very specific aesthetic, one that my film did not necessarily fit into. There was no button at the end of *Mother*, no quick joke, or big reversal that made it easily, commercially, digestible. My film was character-driven and subversively comedic in a way that seemed much more at home in this global arena. I figured it would play beautifully.

It played to stony silence. A few weeks earlier, at a screening in Los Angeles, people had been rolling in the aisles. Here in France, not a peep. I stared, horrified, at the French subtitles as they rolled across the bottom of the screen, convinced that whoever had done the translating must be misquoting me. Clearly, my film had not gone over well with the French.

We were late to the awards ceremony, wandering lost down cob-blestone streets, and when I snuck into the back of the theater, full of hundreds of people and the international press, I was met with another uncomfortable silence. The festival Director Gilles Jacob was standing onstage, looking confused and the jury and crowd were beginning to murmur. I grabbed a glass of champagne and stood in the back, waiting for something to happen and thinking, "Wow. This is sort of an awkward moment for such a high profile event. You'd think that these people would pull it together." Finally someone turned around and saw me.

"Get up there!" She said.

"Why?"

"Because YOU WON!"

We did win. Third prize. I ran up to the stage and like a monkey in a ball gown, climbed up the front of it. There was a huge laugh from the crowd (may I never see the footage of that), and as I accepted my award from Tim Burton, he took my hand and said that he loved my film, he really loved it. He told me to get out of Los Angeles.

There are many lessons to be gained from this experience:

1. Most stages have stairs on the side, to make ascending the stage easier.
2. Tim Burton has the means to live wherever he wants.
3. Someone, somewhere, will believe in your film, and if you love it, it is important to be persistent and, above all, patient.

Sometimes it takes a while for a film to find its place. You have to make what you viscerally believe in as an artist and keep the faith that if it's good, it will be recognized eventually. *Mother* has gone on to play at many more festivals, and has received many awards, but what has sustained me, and kept me believing in myself as a filmmaker, is the feeling that I still have when I watch it. It moves me. I think it is good storytelling. I wish I hadn't let go of that along the way. Or allowed the initial frustration of festival rejections to sway my confidence so entirely. If you are solid in your belief in your own work, it makes traveling the festival road (and the long road after that) a lot easier. The success of the short has now facilitated the making of my first feature and has opened doors for me that I could never have imagined. It started with the simple act of making something personal and meaningful to me and putting it out there into the world.

BEN ODELL has produced a half-dozen features, including *Padre Nuestro*, which won the grand jury prize at Sundance in 2007. Prior to that, Mr. Odell lived in South America where he wrote Spanish-language soap operas and TV series. In 1999, he cowrote the feature *Golpe de Estadio*, which was nominated for the Goya in Spain in 1999 and was Colombia's nomination to the Oscar in 2000. He currently runs development and production for Panamax Films, based in Miami, Florida.

The Long and the Short of It

By Ben Odell

Film is Drama and Drama is CONFLICT.

Well here's a conflict for you: you got a chunk of change to make a film, do you make a superb little short on 35 mm that'll win Cannes, get you an agent, meetings with the majors, and a deal for your first feature within six months?

Or do you buy a mini DV camera, call up your friends and family to crew and act, and make a feature film that will play at Sundance next year, sell to Harvey and Bob, get you an agent, meetings with the majors, and a deal to direct your second feature within six months?

Now there's a dilemma.

If this is yours, you are not only crushed by the weight of your own angst, but you are also delusional, which means: you actually might make it. Because along with talent and luck, self-deception is a *key ingredient* to succeeding as a filmmaker.

I went to film school to learn how to produce. I produced a short and a feature in film school, each for first-time directors. Shorty raised most of the money and we won a small production grant from the film school to gap the rest. Feature raised the first third on his film and I raised the last two-thirds with a producing partner. Where did we get the money? Friends and family who were willing to depart with $2K, $5K, $10K, whatever.

Where are they now? Shorty did the festival circuit, won a few honorable mentions at a few respectable festivals, and sold his short to IFC, where it played on rotation for a few months back in 2005. He teaches at the New York Film Academy and tries to write on the side.

Feature's movie sold overseas and did a small DVD deal in the United States. The film lost money. But he just completed his second feature and is taking it to a major film festival.

Is there a lesson in this? They were both talented, they both made strong first films; one made a short, the other, a feature. The difference? Shorty didn't really have the drive to write a feature that he could sell to follow on the heels of his short success. He would throw around ideas and write a couple drafts of something here or there but it never really went anywhere. He was unfocused.

If he had written a magnificent script, they might have looked at his short and seen enough vision and talent in it to give him a chance. That is, if the script was *so good* that they wanted it enough to let him direct it. Who is "they"? Hell if I know—a studio, a producer, a financier. Depends on what kind of script he would have written. But he didn't write anything so it's irrelevant.

Did he think he would be That Guy? C'mon, you know who That Guy is, the one who made that five-minute short that some studio exec saw on web site, and who called That Guy to make a $70 million musical starring Bruce Willis? You know, That Guy. Your hero. The one who exists only in your dreams. And in the trades.

How I Learned to Swim: Filmmaker Survival Stories

Variety should start publishing articles on That Other Guy—the one who made a great short, didn't follow it up with anything, and is sitting on his ass doing nothing. But that's not news. Maybe if Shorty knew about That Other Guy, he would have been more motivated.

Feature, on the other hand, moved on. He wrote another script, found a lady that wanted to put $100K into a movie, and he was off to the races. And as I said, he's now at a major festival with it. He'll sell it, probably lose money on this one too, but he'll make a DVD deal and he will tell people who ask what happened that they can "rent it on Netflix." And he has three more scripts in a drawer somewhere. And he will make those too, one fine day. Kid's got drive. And talent. And, yes, he's been lucky.

So is there a correlation between making a short or a feature and success?

Yes.

No.

Maybe.

Depends on the short. Depends on the feature. Depends on the filmmaker's drive and his ability to take advantage of a little heat.

Here's another anecdote for you.

There was this friend of mine from film school who was kind of the star of our class way back when. We would be asked to do these little class exercises and his were always amongst the best. But these things are shot on video for a couple hundred bucks and if you didn't know the director lit them, pushed the dolly, *and* held the boom all at once, you wouldn't really be able to see past the flaws and feel the raw talent.

I knew he had it. So did anyone who went to film school with us. But the outside world wouldn't look at his little class exercises and think he was a genius. Hell, they weren't even worth showing.

Cut to:

A couple years later. I run into him on the street. He says he has a script and its been getting a lot of attention and would I like to read it? Sure, I say, fork it over.

And it was *amazing*. So good, in fact, that he got a top agent and a manager out of it. (His girlfriend's father was a dentist to the stars and slipped it to a top Hollywood screenwriter who actually read it, loved it, and called his agency—they signed him a week later: talent *and* luck). And all the studios were calling him to write stuff for them. But he just wanted to make his movie. It was a Spanish-language thriller about illegal immigrants in New York and he didn't want Benicio del

132

Toro to star, so no one would fund it in Lala Land. And I really wanted to make it. And he agreed.

So we started looking for money. Here he had this script that was so good that some financiers would forget that he wanted to cast unknowns in the lead, or that it was in Spanish, or that it was dark as hell.

—So what about his directing work? Has he shot any features?

—No.

—How about commercials?

—No.

—Any shorts?

—Nope. Just these little video exercises that we're not even going to tell you about.

With a magnificent short to show, it would have made some of the potential investors more at ease, especially the big studio types. There were real film financiers out there who loved the script but passed.

We found the money anyway.

Where? Friends. Family. Small film funds. A retired commodities trader. A crazy group of attorneys from New Orleans.

So we made the movie . . .

And it won the grand jury prize at Sundance. And now he's reading scripts from all the studio heads who want to consider him for multimillion dollar films.

He's The Shit. And he never made a real short.

So what's the moral of these stories? Do you make the short? Does it help? Is it better to make a feature?

Yes.

No.

Maybe.

One thing's for sure. They were *all* delusional. The rest is up to you to figure out.

PETER SOLLETT was born in Brooklyn, New York. He graduated from New York University's Tisch School of the Arts in 1998. His short film *Five Feet High and Rising* was awarded the Best Short Film prize at the 2000 Sundance Film Festival and the Cannes Film Festival, Cinefoundation Section.

His first feature film, *Raising Victor Vargas*, was developed with the support of the Sundance Institute in 2001. The film premiered at the 2002 Cannes Film Festival where it was acquired by Samuel Goldwyn/Fireworks Films.

Continuing on the international circuit the film was recognized at festivals in Toronto, London, San Sebastian, and Deauville, where it was awarded the Grand Prix. Mr. Sollett returned to Sundance for the film's North American premiere in 2003. Released theatrically in March of that year, *Raising Victor Vargas* ran for six months in major markets, earning critical praise and five Independent Spirit Award nominations.

Currently, Mr. Sollett is teaching film directing at Columbia University's Graduate School of the Arts and developing new projects.

Conversation with Peter Sollett

SB: Can you talk a little bit first about your festival strategy for your short film *Five Feet High and Rising*, and what you thought about the whole submission and acceptance aspect?

PS: Well, about a year before we were accepted to Sundance, Eva Vives and I (she was my creative partner on the film) submitted a work-in-progress cut of the movie to Sundance and it was too long. It may have been over their time limit and it got rejected, which was no surprise since we weren't adhering to their criteria. But it was still a little bit disappointing because we thought these folks look at works-in-progress all day long so we thought they'd be able to envision where it could go. We were a little bit discouraged to think that they didn't think it could go into the festival. But that was probably a premature submission and we continued editing on our own schedule and eventually finished the film in time to submit the following year.

As it turned out, the first festival that we were accepted to was South by Southwest, which I think announced the films they were accepting before Sundance and it was incredibly exciting and shocking, too, because it had already been rejected by Sundance once, and I thought, "My God, somebody's going to see this film other than our friends." Soon thereafter, the day before Thanksgiving, we got a message from Trevor Groth on our answering machine and he said we were going to be in Sundance, which was even sweeter considering that we'd already been turned away one time, and even more surprising because of that. Sundance was the premiere of the film, and we went to South by Southwest afterwards. I wouldn't say we had a carefully mapped out festival strategy, we just knew of the festivals that either people had told us about or we had heard about in our classes at NYU, and one of those festivals that we were told not to miss at NYU was Clermont-Ferrand, which we submitted to and got into. It turned out to be a very important experience for us because it was where we met the person who represented the company that would eventually finance *Raising Victor Vargas*. When the film got into Cannes after having won a few prizes at Sundance and South by Southwest, our acceptance and ultimate prize-taking at Cannes further motivated the financier we met at Clermont-Ferrand to get involved with us and it really solidified his interest in financing *Vargas*.

SB: So your short film really helped you make that next step.

PS: Yes, in a very direct way.

SB: In terms of Clermont and Cannes, did it expose you to international potential for the short film to be distributed?

PS: It sure did. One of the things that we knew just simply by living where and how we live is knowing there was very little market for shorts in the United States, or an extremely limited one. *Five Feet High and Rising* was in Sundance in 2000. Sundance 2000 was the year of AtomFilms and their influx of capital from Chase Bank, so they had a lot of money and flooded the festival with marketing and self-promotion. Thrust into a big pool of short filmmakers at that time was interesting for a lot of reasons. One of them was that Atom was just going crazy to collect the rights to short films; this was actually the first time I started hearing people use the word "content." They needed content for their web site and everybody was making deals with Atom as quickly as they could. We decided not to do that because there wasn't such an enormous financial upside; they were offering a couple of hundred dollars and we were already $20,000 in debt (or I was, from having made the film; that was all outstanding on my credit cards). So making a deal with AtomFilms wasn't going to solve my financial challenges and I wasn't really very excited about people seeing the film on a jittery postage stamp size, since that was the best you could do at the time with dial-up Internet connections.

So we decided to forego a deal with Atom and went to Clermont and that's where we were first approached by some foreign television stations that were interested in licensing the film. Now, we thought the length of the film (29 minutes) was going to be a real disability for us in terms of licensing the movie to TV.

SB: That's a pretty long short.

PS: It's very long. As it turned out, the length of the film turned out to save us, or save me, more specifically, financially, because we quickly discovered that for shorts they are licensed on a per-minute fee.

The film was long enough to, after licensing it a couple of times, to get me out of debt, and the film eventually turned a small profit.

SB: Did you have to provide any foreign language versions of the short?

PS: No, there were a few territories that asked us for translation and I was very up front with them and said we didn't really have the means to do that. I proposed to give them a transcript of the film instead and they agreed to that, so I had the film transcripted, which is an inexpensive thing to do and sent that along with the deliverables.

SB: So the festival arena really worked for you. Tell me a little about the "15 minutes of fame" thing that happened after you won the prizes at a place like Sundance or Cannes. As a young filmmaker, how did you deal with the attention? Did you have people advising you? I can imagine a lot of people came out of the woodwork after that.

PS: A lot of people came out of the woodwork, and we had an opportunity to meet a lot of people that we really admired, but had only observed from a distance. That was incredibly exciting. We had one really important ally that we made at Sundance who is our lawyer. We didn't really understand why we needed a lawyer. He explained that to us at Sundance. As it turned out, he was an invaluable asset with *Five Feet...*, for many, many reasons. One was because of his efforts we were able to license the film to so many places and make good deals for the film in those places—limit the terms of the licenses, get a good enough fee that we could get out of debt, etc. The thing that he also did was that he provided a great deal of mentorship for us in terms of how to handle the attention we were getting. Very basic things like, what the different expectations are of us or aren't of us in a certain type of meeting. He explained what kind of expectations we should have of different types of people.

SB: Especially dealing with the press and doing interviews for the first time, that has got to be a little intimidating.

PS: Interviews were very intimidating for me. One of the things you'd hear all the time from people who give interviews is how their words are always twisted in different directions and their meaning was distorted, and I had to learn how to manage that a little bit. Not that what I was saying was so important, but I did want what I was saying to be represented accurately. In lots of situations I just realized it's the situation where somebody's going to go for a juicy pull quote rather than what I was really trying to say. That was tough at times. I also learned how different doing press in one country is from doing press in a different country. American film journalists are very different from French film journalists and they have very different agendas. I definitely learned that the hard way.

SB: What happened with the short domestically?

PS: Domestically a few things happened. In terms of distribution, the first thing that didn't happen was AtomFilms, and that was by our choice. After that, there were two DVD companies that came along that were interested in putting *Five Feet . . .* on a compilation of shorts and we made nonexclusive deals so we could participate in both of those releases. After that, the Sundance Channel asked us if we were interested in licensing the film to them, which seemed like a natural and perfect fit considering the life of the film and how grateful we were to the institute and how desperate we were for people to have an opportunity to see our movie, which is really what it's all about. We have since relicensed it to Sundance a couple of times.

SB: If you were doing this today, how do you feel about online, the same way? Would you still use it as the last platform?

PS: No, if I was doing this today I would feel a whole lot better about licensing to an online distributor. There are lots of great ways to do content on the Internet now, content of all sorts, and it can be done elegantly and with high quality. The iTunes music store and what they're doing with short films is really encouraging, especially with the Apple TV announcement this week. I'm hoping to find a way to participate in that kind of distribution. I can imagine it's only a matter of time until there's a way for a filmmaker like me or others to distribute their films through iTunes.

SB: In the end how did that whole short film experience prepare you for the feature?

PS: There are too many ways to mention. Eva and I were making our student films and making *Five Feet . . .* in so many ways in a commercial bubble. We had no exposure to anyone or anything of that world. Everything came at us at the same time with *Five Feet . . . .*

SB: Here's what I'm getting at, and what I see happening, is that people think they can just make a feature, and they're going and making a feature from the get-go, as opposed to making a short, and testing the waters with a short, and then trying to do a feature. That's the root of the questions. Do you think making a short as a first step, regardless of whether that particular short segues to a feature or not, is a good first step for people who want to make features?

PS: Oh my God, yeah! I couldn't ever imagine making a feature film without having made a number of shorts. This is something I talk a lot about with people. I think it's very, very important to get to know yourself as a filmmaker before you make a feature. To gather the resources to make a feature and ultimately to get people's attention to look at your feature is extremely difficult and I don't see why one would invest those resources and take advantage of those opportunities without having made short films. People would really be doing themselves a disservice by skipping the opportunity to make shorts, I really do think so.

SB: I'm seeing a lot of that—filmmakers picking up a camera and making a feature and they fail because they haven't had any experience at all and they take on this large animal that they don't know how to make behave.

PS: There are just millions of things to learn before you start dealing with that. I don't think that's a winning idea.

SB: You got into Sundance Lab to develop the script of *Raising Victor Vargas*, so can you address very briefly how the short inspired you to go forward with a feature?

PS: Well, it was really the actors in the short that inspired Eva and I to write *Raising Victor Vargas*. We made the short with them, we didn't know them well when we made it, but we were totally astounded by how wonderful they were in the film and we said, "My God, they have so much more to offer, it would be great to pick up where this short film left off." Furthermore, the short film is really something I wrote about myself and Eva and I translated it in the script stage to their world and their neighborhood. We got to know them so well in making the short—their lives, their families, their experiences, and how they felt about things—that we knew we would be able to write something for them, and we thought that that would make it even better. It was really about us pursuing an opportunity to work with our actors again.

SB: Let's talk about the feature and its whole acquisition/distribution experience because I'm sure whatever you learned with the short now you learned 100 times more with the feature.

PS: Yes. The film was financed by Studio Canal via one of its sales agents.

SB: And those were contacts you had made at Clermont with the short.

PS: We met a representative of a company called Wild Bunch, which is a sales agent, which at the time was owned by Studio Canal. She liked *Five Feet . . .* and sent it to her boss, a guy named Alain de la Mata, and we eventually met him in Cannes. At the time, Wild Bunch had not financed any movie. They were looking for a first film to finance. We didn't know who Wild Bunch was but we obviously knew who Studio Canal was, because they were financing the films of all the filmmakers that I idolized—people like David Lynch (*Straight Story* had just come out) or Jim Jarmusch—so to have any association with the person who was financing his films, this was a dream come true. We were very interested in going with them. We got the script complete and they were prepared to finance it. Then we needed some actual producers in New York and we started with Scott Macaulay and Robin O'Hara, who are amazing producers. We made the film and it got back into Cannes. We went there for the premiere.

SB: Do you think because you had the short at Cannes, that they gave the feature a little extra eyeballing?

PS: I certainly do. I think it's in the best interest of, first and foremost, the audiences of the festivals, as well as the organizations and the filmmakers, to do that sort of thing. I know as a festivalgoer it's always a treat for me to see a film that I like and then a year or two later, to come back and see another film from that same filmmaker. It's really exciting, it's like getting that new album from that musician that you love that you've been waiting for. There are so many of these films and filmmakers that the only way they get to be seen is at festivals, so I think that's a really wonderful treat and I'm really glad they had me back. Obviously you get a lot more attention when you're there with a feature. It was a pretty exciting experience, and when we were there, Wild Bunch sold our film to Samuel Goldwyn Films, and Goldwyn partnered with a company called Fireworks Pictures, which is a division of CanWest, which is a Canadian company, and they bought the film for the United States and they also sold it to Momentum in the UK and Hopscotch in Australia and a few other territories.

SB: It has done really well.

PS: Thank God, we've been really, really lucky. With those sales they recouped their investment in the film. So we were very happy about that. They were very happy about that. Goldwyn then wanted to hold the film until Sundance the following year because they thought that's how they would get the maximum domestic push for the film, and that's what they did.

SB: It's filmmakers like you that inspire other filmmakers to keep going and I want to encourage them with this book. You're on the frontlines, and it goes back to, what advice would you give the 18-year-old somewhere in Small Town, USA, who wants to make a short film?

PS: I would say that there's really nothing stopping them, not anymore there's not. They have everything they need to make their short film in their home already or on their desk already. That's an enormous asset and something we didn't have at the time. It's something that I'm incredibly inspired by now, and it's something they should take advantage of.

SB: Considering you shot on 16mm, it's so different today with all these formats.

PS: Teaching at Columbia has been really amazing for me because every week my students bring in new scenes or new shorts that they've shot on HiDef with very inexpensive cameras, that they cut on their laptops, that we screen on big beautiful wide-screen plasma televisions, and the quality of this stuff is absolutely fantastic. The democratization of the medium is wonderful and in a way, repositions the emphasis on what is most important, which is the storytelling. What I mean by that is, I think, I hope that all of this technology is really saying to people, it's not that difficult to create a high-quality visual product. Here are the tools. They're very available to you. But what you need to distinguish yourself is a story well told.

SETH GROSSMAN was born and raised in Durham, North Carolina, and studied English and creative writing at Princeton University before attending NYU's Graduate Film School. At NYU, Mr. Grossman codirected the festival favorite *American Pork,* a short documentary about artificial insemination in the swine industry. His thesis film, *Shock Act,* won Best Narrative Short at the 2004 Tribeca Film Festival and Best Student Film at the Chicago International Film Festival. Mr. Grossman's debut feature, *The Elephant King,* premiered at the 2006 Tribeca Film Festival and has played at the Hamptons and Cairo Film Festivals. He has recently directed a new reality show for MTV and is developing an international coming-of-age thriller entitled *Unamerican Activities.* He lives in New York, close to Zabar's.

Losing Your Virginity

By Seth Grossman

At the NYU film school they teach a dubious catechism that goes something like this:

- First hone your craft on short films,
- Then make a well-crafted thesis film,
- Get that film into a high-profile festival,
- Attend that festival with a feature script under your arm,
- And with luck you'll meet the producer or agent or manager who will find money/talent/etc. for your feature.

I thought that was a ridiculous and unlikely path to directing a feature film, but it's exactly what happened for me. I went to Rotterdam in 2002 with a short documentary about artificial insemination in the swine industry (*American Pork*, codirected with Judd Frankel), and met a young producer there with whom I shared a sensibility, a few dinners at the best Chinese restaurant in Holland, and some wild nights of distinctly Dutch debauchery. When we came back to New York, he helped me raise money for my NYU thesis film, *Shock Act*, which won Best Narrative Short at Tribeca 2004.

That festival success gave me confidence, and confidence gave me momentum in the world. I would recommend that if you have success with a short film, you capitalize on it as soon as possible, while you are still shiny to the world. (I could go on and on about the benefits of being shiny, but it would just be confusing and probably lead to unnecessary polishing.) Some people in the film industry overstate the importance of hitting while the iron is hot—what's important is to maintain a level of confidence in your work, and recent validation from the outside world helps. The success of *Shock Act* came at the right time because I was graduating from NYU and at a transitional moment in my life, unfettered by responsibilities and able to focus on the next step. In the course of a few months, I signed with a major agency, I got offers, small magazines interviewed me as a rising star. Four months after winning at Tribeca, I began casting *The Elephant King*.

I got some advice from my friend Elliot Greenebaum, who directed the low-budget indie hit *Assisted Living*, when I started the casting process. He told me not to make the movie unless I could get a "name" actor to play one of the lead roles. He said he'd struggled with distribution for his film because he didn't have a name actor and didn't want me to face the same challenge. At the time, I was in LA with my short at a festival, and my new agents were pushing me to cast two mediocre name actors in the lead roles, guys who'd been on cheesy teenage television shows and bad romantic comedies and were looking to do darker, more original indie material. I was worried that not only did these fellows not fit the parts, but if I cast them, they would take over the movie, make it into something I'd never intended. There were only two actors I really wanted, Peter Saarsgard and Mark Ruffalo, but neither of them was available at the time. So instead, I cast two excellent New York theater actors in the main roles, Jonno Roberts, whom I'd seen in the play *Bug*, and Tate Ellington, who'd been in *The Shape of Things* and who blew me away in his audition. I ended up getting Ellen Burstyn, at the last minute, to play their mother, and I figured her indie-film credibility would be enough "name" for my movie.

I made the movie I wanted to make, and it's a good movie, with excellent performances by Tate and Jonno, but at the moment I'm not sure that anyone will ever get a chance to see it on the big screen. Distributors are wary of indie dramas without recognizable names on the marquee. I had assumed, from my experience with *Shock Act*, that audiences would respond to a good story well told, regardless of who's in the lead. But film distribution is a fickle business and only one or two small nameless dramas a year get out to theaters through regular channels. Last year it was *Junebug*, this year there was *Old Joy* and *Mutual Appreciation*, though that was apparently self-distributed.

The fact is that like me, many of you will make decisions based not only on notions of artistic integrity, but on economic imperatives. When I was preparing *The Elephant King*, I had no real source of income and over a hundred grand in film school debt. I'm not from a wealthy family and had no savings to fall back on. I agreed to a pittance salary for my work because I wanted all the money from our small budget to end up on the screen. But this economic reality meant that I couldn't bide my time, and maybe I rushed the production. I expected it to be a huge hit and then I'd get dozens of lucrative offers and endorsement deals, a golden door would open, and behind that door there would be underwear models floating in pools of caviar and cash, and all the gods of Olympus would invite me to fancy sleepovers. But that door doesn't exist, it's a fake carrot that I hung in front of myself so that I'd keep working hard, and there were other kinds of carrots, fantasies of acceptance speeches, European speaking engagements, and splashy magazine profiles, etc. Maybe it's good to be hungry, to be broke and desperate, and to gamble on a crazy idea, but don't rush it. Listen to the advice of peers in the indie film world. Cast a name actor: Ryan Gosling, for example.

How to do this, though—that's the question. What's the best way to be poor and nurse a project until it's ready? I've found that it helps to have rich friends, because they'll lend you money, but the best ones are the ones who earned it themselves. Also get used to sleeping on couches. If you stay with a friend and clean up his apartment while he's gone, you'll be welcome longer. If you consistently introduce him to attractive women as your "producer," you can probably get by rent-free for a couple of months.

On the other hand, you might not have the opportunities I've had, the agent and manager, the fancy film school, the festival success, the ability to move objects with your mind. You might just have a really good idea and a video camera. Then I suggest you practice. Hone your craft. See what works. The problem with filmmaking as an art form, the reason why it's so hard to get good at it, is that there's no opportunity for revision. You can revise the script (and I suggest you go through at least 25 real drafts before you shoot anything), but once you've shot the film, you're severely limited in the revision you can do in the editing room. (Unless you're Wong Kar Wai, in which case you can shoot for a year, keep looking for your story, return to locations, revise scenes, and eventually hone your film into something beautiful and well-executed.) Directors get out of practice between projects. Unless you're on a film set, the only way to practice directing is to "direct" your friends in evil social mind games, which can backfire and leave you friendless and alone, spending weekends unbathed on your couch, amongst the toenails, watching poker on ESPN2, and mumbling to yourself about fascism. But I digress.

What I've tried to do, since *The Elephant King*, is keep working on my own small digital video projects as I revise my next feature script. I've also discovered the glories of reality TV, which is like the Roger-Corman-B-movie incubation chamber for today's aspiring directors. Directing reality TV is like building the railroad while you're traveling on the railroad, with the "script" changing in the middle of a scene, and it forces you to think on your feet. The preponderance of reality programming on television is changing the way feature films are shot, and I think an education in documentary or reality TV can be a huge asset for a fiction filmmaker.

Which is to say I've become much more realistic about directing as a job that can sustain me, rather than a long-shot bid for pagan immortality. There's something kind of sad about this loss of innocence. It's a little bit like losing your virginity to a blow-up doll. (In this metaphor, directing is making love, and reality TV is the blow-up doll. Also, you're getting paid pretty well to fuck the doll, and afterwards

143

you brag to your friends about how this is the best way to practice, and ultimately you convince yourself that it's not pathetic. But still, sometimes, at night, you weep into its cold plastic shoulder and wish for more.)

But on the other hand, there's pleasure in doing something you're good at, and that's been the key for me. After experiencing success and disappointment as a filmmaker, I've learned to enjoy the process more than the anticipated results. Working for recognition or money keeps you on the treadmill of samsara, with each fulfilled desire leading to even more desire and dissatisfaction, whereas disciplining yourself to enjoy simply writing, as I'm enjoying writing this weird, rambling letter to you, or to enjoy directing, as I enjoyed working with actors like Jonno and Tate and the brilliant Ellen Burstyn (or even manipulating reality-TV stars like monkey-puppets on strings), means that you have settled into an identity as a filmmaker. And after rock star and bounty hunter, that's one of the coolest things you can be in our society.

TIFFANY SHLAIN has been honored as one of *Newsweek's* "Women Shaping the 21st Century" and is an acclaimed filmmaker and speaker, Director of The Moxie Institute, and founder of The Webby Awards.

Ms. Shlain has directed eight short films that have won many awards and have played at festivals including Tribeca, Sundance, and Rotterdam, including *The Tribe* and *Life, Liberty & the Pursuit of Happiness.* As Director of The Moxie Institute, a think tank and media company, she creates, develops, and distributes films and discussion programs about social issues using new approaches and emerging technologies.

Ten years ago she founded The Webby Awards, the leading international honors for web sites, and in 1998 cofounded The International Academy of Digital Arts & Sciences, which today has over 600 members and serves as The Webbys' judging body.

She lectures on her filmmaking and the Internet's role in reshaping popular culture, business, and society, having appeared on *60 Minutes*, ABC, CNN, and NPR. Her work has been profiled in publications including *The New York Times*, *The Los Angeles Times*, and *The International Herald Tribune.*

Ms. Shlain is a graduate of the University of California at Berkeley, where she studied film theory, and studied film production at NYU. She lives in Mill Valley, California, with her husband Ken Goldberg, an artist and professor of robotics at UC Berkeley, and their daughter, Odessa Simone. Her web site is www.tiffanyshlain.com.

Interdependent

By Tiffany Shlain

We used to use the term "independent filmmaker" as a badge of hard-earned, maverick honor that you wore on your tattered coat proudly. However, today, with all the new channels of distribution growing like a strong network of support around your film, I think the new term that we should all claim is "interdependent filmmakers." Each web site, URL, blog, and trailer strewn out into the vast Internet sea with images from your film are like hooks attached to lines that bring the viewer right back to you. It no longer needs to be some third-party distributor who held all the strings, while you relinquished all rights and control. With all the tools available to filmmakers today, it is *you* who is throwing those lines out with your film, and *you* who gets to be there to receive their interest, support, and money to fuel outreach or your next film. All the new technologies, reviewers, filmmakers, and audiences around the world create a supportive ecosystem for you to succeed.

It also used to be that getting a short indie film seen was like fly-fishing in a puddle. Today it's completely different.

2006, the windows blew open for us independent short filmmakers. Thanks to greater bandwidths and shorter attention spans, short films were really the only way to play in this new online frontier.

And if you are making a short documentary today, your work has the capability to make significant waves for social outreach and change. The 21st century will not only be known as the Information Age but The Age of Complexity. People need to understand the nuances of social issues as well as the big picture.

Culture is the true current to illuminate problems that need to be felt and understood. Film, music, and the Internet are powerful media to communicate ideas.

Just speaking about traditional culture channels for a moment, let's first look at film festivals as a way to get your film into the world. There used to be a handful of film festivals to enter. Now with specific communities, cities, and niche interests, each understanding the significance of gathering the best films to move social values, there are hundreds of film festivals in the United States alone and thousands in the world. Some of these focus solely on short films.

The next channel that is hungry for new ways to present ideas is the education system. The traditional classroom experience can be made more dynamic and effective with the introduction of fun, informative, educational shorts into curriculum. The model of students listening to someone speaking and watching simple white chalk on the blackboard can be catapulted to a whole new level by also presenting a two-dimensional screen surface that gives you the third dimension (and if it's a really good film, even the fourth dimension). Universities, high schools, and continuing education are all looking for short film experiences to present an idea or social issue. Now, the yummy fun stuff where there is no establishment, no roads, and hardly any rules: the Internet. Your social issue in a film can reach thousands if not millions in an instant. You have web sites that will play your film for money or for free, or for ad dollars, technologies like Apple iTunes, ITV, cell phones, web sites, and email to get the word out, just to name a few. I am excited to think about what new technologies and web sites will be available once this book gets published.

We're trying all of these things with my new film, *The Tribe: an unorthodox, unauthorized history of the Jewish People and the Barbie Doll . . . in 15 minutes.* We are interested in igniting a national conversation about American Jewish identity. We made a discussion kit that goes with the film which includes conversation cards and a film guide. Our only agenda is to get people talking. Talking always leads to some higher level of understanding. *The Tribe* premiered in 2006 and played at over 50 film festivals in its first year from Sundance in the winter, Tribeca in the spring, and then Rotterdam. We self-distributed the film and put proceeds back into funding our outreach. The Internet allowed us to experiment and test out all the new technologies to distribute the film. We're trying everything—we played online for free and online for money, we played in festivals, galleries, living rooms, on Second Life, the iTunes store, beautiful venues in NYC, SF, and LA that we packed through getting the word out online. We also did it the old-fashioned way with film festivals and DVDs. We found that the old and the new together make a fantastic marriage.

I founded The Webby Awards in 1996 and it was exciting to honor the pioneers in the intersection of the Internet and film early on. Self-distributing a film in 2006 and 2007, at a time when these sites have matured and new models have appeared, I feel like a DJ remixing songs that I get to throw into the changing rhythm and motion of the filmmaking landscape.

I look forward to continuing to engage in this experiment along with all filmmakers, web site creators, and audiences as we move forward interdependently.

www.tribethefilm.com
www.tiffanyshlain.com

JOE TURNER LIN is a native New Yorker and graduated with honors from Columbia University as an undergraduate screenwriting concentrate and proceeded to work on over 60 feature-length and short film, television, commercial, and music-video productions, including MTV's *Joe's Apartment, Jeffrey, HBO: Real Sex, The Rosie O'Donnell Show*, and *National Geographic Explorer*.

After producing a number of independent features, he returned to school at Columbia University's M.F.A. Film Program, where he received the Arthur Krim Award, HBO's Young Producer's Development Award, and Columbia University's Best Producer for the Student Academy Award-winning short, *Jesus Henry Christ*. He has written several feature-length screenplays, including a Nicholl Fellowship semifinalist. In addition, he has also directed short films, spec commercials, and industrials.

His short thesis film, *Seibutsu (Still: Life)*, was a national finalist for the Student Academy Awards in 2004 and recently won the Grand Prize at both the San Diego Asian International Film Festival and the Chinese-American Festival of Film and Culture. Currently, Joe is a partner in Kulture Machine LLC and continues to pursue projects that intrigue and fulfill him creatively.

Group Therapy

By Joe Turner Lin

Film school is a funny place. You never know who you're going to meet.

By the time I had returned to Columbia University for graduate school, I'd burned out on production—music videos, commercials, TV shows, and features were not giving me the time or opportunity to actually practice storytelling. I'd been writing screenplays, but besides that most of my life was spent moving from gig to gig, alternately working on a terrible commercial production for money and then trying to save my soul by slaving away on what would usually be an equally terrible independent film. There were a few good moments in there, but I'd gotten trapped in the "how" and forgotten the "why." So, four years after my undergraduate film degree, I limped back to school, hoping to rediscover why I had gotten into the movie business in the first place.

Columbia Film School has, in addition to regular directing exercises in each class, a larger, department-wide short film exercise that every student shoots at the end of their first year. It's known as the "8-to-12," and looking back, it was one of the most important catalysts for my graduate school education—in fact, and I've never thought about it this way before, but I think it is one of the things that really differentiates Columbia from other programs.

Essentially, at the end of the first year, everyone writes a script for an 8- to 12-minute short film. Everyone, no matter your intended concentration (writing, directing, producing, or cinematography). Then, the scripts are "swapped." You get someone else's script to direct. You become the producer for whoever has your script. This is the kind of large-scale social experiment that can only occur at an academic level. It's perhaps the biggest strength and argument for film school: the ability to fail with impunity.

148

What you get are not necessarily great films—what you get is the opportunity to interact with *everyone* in your year. You read everyone else's script, you work on their shoots, you help them edit their footage; whatever roles you can perform, you do. At the time, it was a challenging and deeply emotional process. There were more than a few friendships shattered by the 8-to-12. And the lessons learned were hard-earned: you have to pick people, not just scripts. But the biggest reward was something that happened so organically, I haven't realized until now what the 8-to-12 process truly was: institutionalized networking.

I had met Dennis Lee and Francisco Ordonez early on, and a group of us all became very close friends. But the three of us in particular gravitated towards each other when it came to story sessions and script notes, which is high praise at Columbia. What I discovered was that even though we didn't tell the same kinds of stories—the tone and plots of our material diverge wildly—we had the same narrative sense. The way that emotional arcs and action lines interplay, the way structure ebbs and flows across the spine of a script, the way plants and payoffs work: I recognized it in their storytelling. And it thrilled me to discuss story with people who were really working hard to figure out how to tell a good one.

It was our third year of film school. At Columbia you have two intensive years of classes and then three years of matriculation—basically time to write, rewrite, rewrite again, not to mention raise the money, to shoot your thesis film. The third year was, for many of us, a doldrum of creativity. Certainly for me it was. The lack of structure after such a rigorous course-load made self-discipline a requirement, and the procrastinator in me was having none of it. I needed help. Having had a background in producing and writing before grad school, I had often found myself as producer on many of my close friends' short film exercises while we were in class. Because of this, I had already been thinking about collaboration, support, and branding for a while, and so I pitched an idea that we'd all been kicking around, half-seriously, since we arrived: let's form a company. Dennis and Francisco were on board.

The goal of Kulture Machine (which had its origins as Shadow Machine—the literal translation of "camera" in Mandarin Chinese) was simple: the company was designed to help Francisco, Dennis, and me get our thesis films made. By labeling ourselves, we would get access to support from each other, constructive criticism we trusted, a consistent and dedicated above-the-line crew, co-branding of each others' films, and, if any one of our films did well, contacts in the industry.

Cut to: Three years later. Our company had expanded to include two more members, Julie Anne Meerschwam and Milton Liu, and in the process had become much more of a real entity. We had not only produced each of our short films (Dennis' *Jesus Henry Christ*, my *Seibutsu (Still: Life)*, and Francisco's *St. Paul*), but we'd produced two films for Julie (*Audrey & Einstein* and *Celamy*) and coproduced Caryn Waechter's *God Is Good*.

All the films played at film festivals worldwide. They did very well in competition, winning several major awards. Five out of the six films were nominated for Student Academy Awards. Three were national finalists. One won the silver medal in the Narrative category. I could go on, but the details are unimportant.

What was important: the Kulture Machine logo was working. The films had been branded together, and people in the industry began to recognize our little company in small ways. As we took meetings for the shorts (because they didn't all come out at once), we referenced each other. We got a write-up in *Filmmaker* magazine. Dennis was getting bigger meetings from studios. We had representation. Everything we'd wanted to accomplish with Kulture Machine had come to fruition. All in all, it wasn't a bad start.

Today, we're still moving along trying to make our way in this crazy business. It hasn't always been easy, and running a company in the real world has been more challenging than any of us could have imagined. We've gotten close with a few projects and been cut loose at the last minute. We've each been writing, struggling to generate our own property, which rules in Hollywood. The company itself has had to restructure a few times—typical growing pains—but the fact is that it was always designed from the beginning to remain flexible and to help us grow as filmmakers. To that end, certainly, the company continues to succeed.

Dennis, first out of the gate with his short, is first out with his upcoming feature. He begins principal photography, as of this writing, in about a week and a half. He has a whole group of "A-list" stars attached; and in an impossible, almost dreamlike turn, he has "the" A-list star attached. I won't mention the name, but you can look her up on imdb.com yourself. Milton is in LA, having won a writing fellowship with Disney. Francisco is in preproduction on his feature, which is scheduled for shooting later this year. And Julie and I got married; we're preparing a script we wrote together for the Tribeca Film Festival, and I'm finishing up a draft of a New York-based romantic comedy I hope to shoot next year.

What I know is that as each of us reaches the next stage in our career, we will continue to help each other. Through contacts, with script notes, as a company production, or just through moral support, we continue to uphold Kulture Machine's mandate.

My advice is this, and it's more difficult than it sounds: find people you love to work with, think big about how you're going to market yourselves, root for your friends—especially when they're doing better than you—and stay focused on telling stories you believe in.

Shake yourself loose from the "how," and remember the "why."

Because you love it.

RYAN FLECK began his artistic collaboration with Anna Boden in 2002 on the documentary short *Have You Seen This Man?* Their first feature-length documentary, *Young Rebels*, looked at the hip-hop community in Havana.

As a team, they have written, produced, and directed several short films, including *Gowanus, Brooklyn*, which premiered at the 2004 Sundance Film Festival and was awarded the Grand Jury prize in short filmmaking. *Gowanus, Brooklyn* was based on the feature-length script for *Half Nelson*, which Anna and Ryan cowrote and developed at the Sundance Screenwriters' Lab.

After *Half Nelson* premiered at the 2006 Sundance Film Festival, it went on to win numerous prizes, including three Gotham Awards for Breakthrough Director, Actor, and Best Feature Film.

In 2006 Mr. Fleck received the Best First Film award from the New York and Boston Society of Film Critics. In addition, he was nominated for Best Director at the Spirit Awards in the same year, where he and Boden were also nominated for Best First Screenplay.

Gowanus Brooklyn Festival Awards
Sundance Jury Prize for Best Short; Aspen Shortsfest Special Jury
Prize; Independent Film Festival of Boston Special Jury Prize

Half Nelson Awards and Nominations
Academy Award nomination for Best Actor; five Independent Spirit
Award nominations, winning for Best Actor and Actress; Gotham
Awards for Best Feature, Breakthrough Director, and Breakthrough
Actress; New York Society of Film Critics Best First Film; Boston
Society of Film Critics Best New Filmmaker and Best Supporting
Actress; National Board of Review Award for Breakthrough Actor

From Nelson to Gowanus and Back

By Ryan Fleck

Sometime back in 2002, I wrote a first draft of a feature script called
Half Nelson with my girlfriend, Anna Boden. We thought it was a
pretty good story that would make a terrific movie, but we had no
idea how to get it financed. Around this time I received the good
news that my old student short film, *Struggle*, was accepted into the
2003 Sundance Film Festival.[1] Going to Park City that year was an
amazing experience for Anna and myself. Not only did we meet other
filmmakers who we continue to maintain close friendships with—
The Duplass Brothers (*The Puffy Chair*), Ethan Vogt (*Funny Ha Ha*,
Mutual Appreciation), Steven Bognar (*Lion in the House*), but we saw
a movie that inspired us to move forward with *Half Nelson* in a way
we hadn't yet imagined—as a short.

The first time I saw *Raising Victor Vargas*, I was completely blown
away. I remembered Peter Sollett from NYU (we actually took the
same distribution class taught by Sharon Badal), but it was my first
semester as a shy transfer student and I don't think we spoke two words
to each other. A year later (1999) I saw Pete's thesis film, *Five Feet
High and Rising*, and I thought it was the best short film I'd ever seen;
so when I heard he and his partner, Eva Vives, expanded their short

---

[1] The same film was rejected by Sundance the previous year. Large festivals have
multiple programmers that can't see every submitted film, so if you think your
film may have been overlooked (or not seen by the right person), you should
definitely resubmit, even if the festival claims it doesn't accept resubmissions.

into a feature that would be at Sundance in 2003, I made sure to score tickets for the first screening, which did not disappoint.

After the fest, Anna and I returned home to Brooklyn determined to write a short version of *Half Nelson* that we would produce on video and submit to Sundance (and other festivals) the following year. When brainstorming ideas for the short, we discovered fairly quickly that the character of Dan Dunne was too complex to flesh out in 19 minutes, so we decided to make this Drey's story. In the script for *Gowanus, Brooklyn*, we explored how a girl's discovery of her teacher's dark secret informs her relationships with her family and friends.

Anna and I planned to shoot *Gowanus* in and around our Brooklyn neighborhood in May of 2003 on our Panasonic DVX 100 video camera. We had a few close friends who would lend us crew support (DP, art direction, PA), but finding Drey was the most important task before shooting. We contacted local junior high schools in our neighborhood and spoke with drama teachers about our project. Anna and I visited several classrooms and encouraged students to attend our "auditions" the following weekend, which were actually just casual interviews to get a sense of their personalities and comfort with the camera. We met a lot of great kids who we cast as Drey's friends or basketball teammates, but nobody stood out for Drey like Shareeka Epps, who won us over with a combination of sweet, adolescent innocence and Brooklyn-tough street smarts. The role of Dan went to our DP's roommate, Matt Kerr, who was a real schoolteacher with the wildest hair we'd ever seen, but the main reason he got the part was because he was so comfortable improvising with the kids during his audition.[2]

With our cast and crew working for peanuts (literally working for food), our biggest expense on *Gowanus* was the location fee for the interior of the school, which amounted to a little more than $400. We spent one full eight-hour day in the various locations in the school (more than that would have meant overtime for the school's custodian, which we couldn't afford). The other primary expenses on the movie were a 15-passenger van to transport the kids from Brooklyn to the school in Harlem ($100) and a nice pizza, pasta, and salad lunch for everybody ($100).

The rest of the shoot consisted of short pick-up days, grabbing a scene here or there in stolen locations or in our own apartment with minimal cast and crew. Anna edited the movie in our bedroom on Final Cut Pro and by the time we locked picture, about a month after shooting, we had spent around $800 total. Now it was time to

---

[2] We used Matt Kerr again in *Half Nelson* as Mr. Light, the substitute teacher.

submit to Sundance, but before doing so, we contacted one of the programmers we had met at the fest the year before just to let them know it was coming and to look out for it.[3] We crossed our fingers and a few months later, on Thanksgiving weekend, we got the call that we were in!

At this point, our little $800 movie turned into a $4000 movie. Our excellent DP, Chris Scarafile, had a friend working for a well-known post facility in New York, who offered to blow up our mini-DV movie to 35 mm film (this is not required by Sundance, but we thought it would be cool). And he would do it for no charge, as long as we paid for the cost of the materials, which was amazing, but still super expensive (the 35 mm film stock and printing costs totaled about $3000). Anna and I didn't have the money, so we contacted all our friends and family, told them our film got into Sundance and asked for small tax-deductible donations through our nonprofit fiscal sponsor, Film/Video Arts. We managed to raise most of the money this way, and our parents bailed us out on the rest. Thanks Moms!

Another $500 was spent on our sound mix (wonderfully rendered by Mike Damon in his home studio), and we were all set for Sundance (which has its own set of insane expenses I won't get into here, but remember that you can always stay in Park City for $30 a night in the Chateau Apres dorms—I did).

Sundance '04 was amazing! Shareeka got on an airplane for the first time in her life and we came home with the jury prize for Best Short Film. The experience also landed us a William Morris agent and an entertainment attorney, who both proved to be essential in getting *Half Nelson* financed. Of course, it wasn't easy. We had to deal with a lot of rejections and bad notes before finding the right financier, but when Jamie Patricof and Alex Orlovsky of Hunting Lane Films came on board, followed closely by Ryan Gosling, *Half Nelson* became a reality. And we owe it all to the little short we made in our backyard and the generous team of people who helped us do it for next to nothing.

---

[3] If you know somebody that knows a programmer, show them the movie and ask them to give a heads up for your film. It can never hurt.

Swimming Lesson #5

Little Fish, Big Pond: Thinking Globally

I was on the jury of the Worldwide Short Film Festival in Toronto, and I attended a panel discussion called "Who Buys What." The panel comprised 17 buyers from around the world, including some contributors to this book. Each buyer spoke specifically about his or her criteria for selecting shorts, and a couple of things that are important when we discuss international potential emerged.

The primary consideration is that a filmmaker must think globally now. Technology has permitted worldwide access to your film, and distributors, sales agents, and buyers have responded accordingly.

When one buyer was asked what type of deal was offered to film-makers, he responded, "Worldwide rights, all platforms, in perpetuity." What does this mean? It means that if you license your film to them, you're giving away the farm. Forever.

Forever is a long time, but what this statement conveys is a basic truth of the global marketplace — just as the independent feature world of acquisitions seeks to obtain the most revenue potential from a film, so now does the short film world, especially with the increased new technology avenues. Each buyer wants to have maximum potential for his/her acquisitions, and that means the inherent desire to license the film for as long a period as possible with as big a net as possible.

How does this affect the filmmaker in negotiations?

First of all, the filmmaker should know that he or she can, and should, negotiate. Some filmmakers are so grateful simply that some-one, anyone, wants their short (being in debt, eating cat food, and working part-time at Starbuck's) that they jump at whatever deal is being offered to them. Others are so intimidated by the distribution process and afraid that the distributor will walk away if they don't acquiesce to everything in the offer, that they blindly move forward without considering the consequences of the license terms, territory, and fees.

So here are a few basics:

How long will the distributor hold the license?

That's the "term."

The term is the calendar period of time that your film will be in the hands of the distributor. This is usually in years — as in 5, 10, 15 — or, as previously noted, "perpetuity." No matter how far away 15 years feels, perpetuity is a hell of a lot longer and gives you no recourse should the distributor fail to perform and you want to "take your marbles and go home."

Who else can distribute my film?

That's called "exclusivity."

Exclusive vs nonexclusive—Just as you will hear in the festival chapter in this book, everyone in this industry understands the fairly brief life span and time-sensitive nature of a short film and, which may be surprising to you, is generally amenable to that short playing in a number of different ways/places simultaneously. That being said, many will agree to a nonexclusive license, but some may want exclusivity. Exclusivity means that they are the sole license holder for that short in whatever territories you grant to them. The reasoning behind exclusivity is that the distributor is taking a risk on you, and their "discovery" of you entitles them to be the "sole holder" of the rights to your film since they are going to spend time and money promoting it. If a distributor wants exclusivity, it should be for a determined period of time (6 months/1 year) and then the license should turn nonexclusive, which opens you up to other distribution deals.

Where does the distributor want to license my film?

That's the "territory."

The territory is usually expressed as a geographical location, such as "North American rights." The word "worldwide" is exactly that—the distributor has global licensing ability. Especially for sales agents (the "middleman" between the filmmaker and the distributor), it's desirable that they have worldwide rights, since that gives them the most flexibility in selling your film.

One more note on "sales" and "selling"—these words are somewhat misnomers. A filmmaker is not really selling his or her film, in that someone else is purchasing it. We use those words to mean "license," which is giving permission for someone to do something with your film for a certain period of time in certain places. If you keep that thought in mind, you will keep the control of your short film in mind as well.

How much will the distributor get/pay me/take from the revenue?

That's the "fee."

For short films, distributors usually pay a filmmaker a dollar figure for every minute of the running time or offer a flat fee. The per-minute figure ranges drastically, from $25.00 to $500.00 per minute depending on the distributor, so it's important to find out "who is paying what" so you can approach distributors pre-armed with that knowledge. This information is not secret—distributors are quite willing to tell you how many films they acquire each year and what they usually pay for them. Distributors and sales agents will also take a percentage of the film's subsequent revenue, or there may be a revenue-sharing model, in which advertising revenue is "pooled" and a portion of that is distributed among the filmmakers, which is the case with some Internet sites.

What type of distribution will my film have?

That's the "platform."

A platform refers to the outlet by which the viewer will have access to the film. Multiple distribution platforms include Internet, mobile, broadcast, home video, etc., and distributors desire multiple platforms because, again, the more outlets they have, the more potential revenue for the film. It's common sense, really, if you put your mindset where they are and what their goal is—to make the most money from your film.

Remember the old expression, "It never hurts to ask"? That's the key to short film negotiation. Ask. Ask for what you want but be certain you know and understand what you are asking for.

To reiterate, it is important for any filmmaker today to think about his or her short films with a global perspective, because distributors are thinking that way. Not only is a 16-year-old aspiring filmmaker watching your short on the other side of the world, there are more chances for distribution internationally than there are domestically because the digital technology is evolving faster. To give an example, at Toronto someone said, "Do you know how to impress an American? Show them your cell phone." That's indicative of the progression of technology abroad, and filmmakers must consider their film appropriate to these new platforms and technology.

There are festivals in Europe, Asia, South America, and Australia, and in practically every major city around the world. Film buyers attend these festivals. They have web sites. If you understand your film well (and you should), you need to consider the global potential of your film and get it out there to those buyers and sales agents to consider. This chapter is written by international industry professionals to give you further information on their particular region as it relates to short film, both culturally and in terms of distribution.

KATHERINE SHORTLAND studied theatre and film at The University of New South Wales, from which she received a research scholarship to the University of Exeter, UK, to complete her bachelor of arts. She spent a European winter indulging in Spanish history and 18th century English painting and cowrote a play on Amelia Earhardt before heading back down under. She was then selected as one of only three students into the Masters in Film Producing program at the Australian Film Television and Radio School (AFTRS).

Ms. Shortland has produced short films, TVCs, and video clips. Her short films have appeared in dozens of international film festivals and picked up numerous prizes along the way. Her films traverse all genres, from documentary to drama, and all types, from digital to experimental.

She has worked across all aspects of the arts, including arts funding, digital broadcasting, publicity and marketing, public broadcasting, and film production. She is the inaugural research fellow for the Centre of Screen Business, a division of AFTRS, and is involved in a number of key academic research projects in the state of the film and television industry both locally and abroad. Ms. Shortland is also Business Affairs Executive at Flying Bark Productions, the largest production studio in Australia, overseeing a slate of animated and live action television series, feature films, and interactive content.

Part academic, part business exec, and all creative, she is obsessed with collecting children's books, fascinated by short content, and convinced that an animation series about a little turtle living in a snow globe is a good idea. . . .

Shorts Down Under

By Katherine Shortland

Ah short films. You bust a gut to raise the money and somehow hope it's enough. You pull favors with mates to drive across five suburbs to pick up a free redhead and a couple of scrims. You jump through hoops to get the "perfect" location, often promising to mow the owner's lawn for a month. The sets are dressed with art director/next-door neighbor/grandmother's furniture and the leading lady is wearing the costume designer's wardrobe. The editor pulls all-nighters surviving on coffee, words of encouragement, and the goal of shaving off seven frames. The sound designer is out in a paddock with a cow in labor and a mike at midnight. You beg your muso mates with a case of beer to record a set and your sister takes a bunch of stills on set for your "EPK." There is always a wrap party with beers and chips, where you slap each other on the back and wonder how you made it. You sweat and cry, laugh and joke—all for the sake of one thing—the story. So it's done and dusted. What happens now and was it worth all the blood sweat and tears? So how is it done down under? And is there any chance for your short films in the market? Read on and find out.

Telling stories is the expression to another human of our individual experience, our unique history, and our cultural voice. Art has always been a visual medium that moves beyond words, across language, religion, sex, gender, and culture. Art unites us as a people through media such as painting, music, dance, and photography. Film can be seen as an ultimate unification between stories and art. Individual and collective stories expressed visually, transcending time, place, and culture.

My unique perspective of filmmaking is inherently linked to my "Australian-ness." This quite simply is one perspective, or cultural context, that exists on the planet and is a vehicle for expressing universal stories. You may not identify with a crocodile man arriving in New York but you may identify with being an outsider in a new city. Your world may not be a sci-fi landscape where ferals and oil thieves emerge from the brown wide land, but you may know the pain of losing a loved one. Australian stories are not all about men on horseback, croc hunters, or drag queens, but they are the storytelling elements that deliver you the tale of lost love, the hero's journey, sadness, and survival. You are not limited by your culture and context. In fact, it's the stuff that makes your stories unique.

Short form content is the perfect vehicle for testing yourself as a storyteller. I ventured into the format with a passion for storytelling and for the opportunity to see those stories on film. Short stuff teaches the craft, exercises story skills, and forces drama and imagination into a contained space. It allows you to delve into those personal stories and if you truly succeed, those personal stories will ring true across cultures.

There is a history of Australians and New Zealanders using the short medium for telling unique stories of universal appeal. Some of the greatest antipodean filmmakers of recent time, and those that have made a mark on the international stage, cut their teeth on short films. Whether as a part of a film school, a filmmakers collective, or as individuals running around with a video camera, some of the biggest names in the international scene started short and proud.

It was at The Australian Film Television and Radio School in the 1980s that Jane Campion made a number of short films, including *Peel*, which picked up the Palme D'or in Cannes in '86. She then went on to write and direct many successful international films including *In the Cut*, *The Piano*, *Portrait of a Lady*, and *Holy Smoke*. In 2006, Campion returned to the short format with *The Water Diary*.

And it ain't just Jane. Gillian Armstrong, director of films like *Death Defying Acts*, *Charlotte Gray*, *Oscar & Lucinda*, and *Little Women*, wrote and directed a number of short films in and out of film school in the seventies and eighties. Phillip Noyce (*To Catch a Fire*, *The Quiet*

American, Clear and Present Danger) and Peter Weir (*Master and Commander, The Truman Show, Dead Poets Society*) also started out as short filmmakers banding together with other inspired youngsters.

And these are just a handful of Aussie + NZ filmmakers who started short. In fact the first Aussie short selected for Cannes was back in 1949 and since then 26 shorts have competed for the Prix de Jury for Short Film. A number of these directors, including Gregor Jordan, Shirley Barrett, and Alex Proyas, among others, have gone on to international feature careers. Of course there is always another generation of filmmakers waiting in the wings ready to tackle the world.

Okay, we get it. So those antipodeans can make short films and some go on to make a career out of features. That's all well and good, but what does it mean to other filmmakers all over the world? Well, a number of things. A successful short film needs good financing, marketing, and distribution plans. And there is a wealth of information available to filmmakers all over the world; you ain't limited to your own region.

There are a number of very impressive film schools and colleges in Australia and New Zealand that offer full-time study, part-time study, internships, and international exchanges. If you are fortunate enough to attend a film school or a university there are resources and facilities available to pursue the passion. YOU GET TO MAKE FILMS! Beyond being a student, those schools have incredible "back room" resources: libraries, distribution departments, marketing divisions, research facilities, and a plethora of info on what's happening in the local scene. And the best thing? It's all online.

Now as a filmmaker if you are not fortunate enough to attend a film school or college there are a number of key state and federal funding bodies that offer grants and equity investment into films. Virtually all of them have short and emerging divisions. And although they are restricted to Australian and New Zealand residents it indicates that there is plenty going on in terms of supporting filmmakers. The bodies will also feed you a lot of information, online, about festivals, budgeting, distributing, new media, marketing, and research. It's this kinda support that is often just as valuable as cold hard cash.

And let's not forget getting your film, wherever it has been made, in front of like-minded souls. The short film festival scene in the Southern Hemisphere is growing at a rapid rate. And in particular, Aussies know how to pull together a film festival. At last count Australia is hosting a film festival on virtually every week of the year. And that's for a population of about 20 million people. Festivals range from A-grade international festivals to niche or genre festivals for docos, experimental, gay/lesbian/transgendered subject, digital, children's, comedy, and extreme, to name but a few.

A number of our A-list international film festivals have significant short competition programs, such as The Sydney Film Festival, Melbourne International Film Festival, Adelaide International Film Festival, and Brisbane International Film Festival. Then there is a chunk of festivals that are purely for shorts, St Kilda Short Film Festival, Bondi Short Film Festival, Flickerfest, Fitzroy Short Film Festival, and the list goes on. There is also a series of traveling film festivals that get short films out to the regional locations.

And of course the Aussies love an outdoor film festival like Realm of the Sense, Fremantle Outdoor Short Film, In the Bin Outdoor Short Film Festival, and Flickerfest. Let's not forget Tropfest, the biggest outdoor film festival in the world. So how can you find out all about the festivals? The state and federal funding bodies are great resources for worldwide film festival listings.

Beyond the festival circuit what other opportunities are there for short films down under? Our public broadcasters will occasionally purchase short films, either from film schools or from festival programs. They may be station fillers up to 10 minutes or a slate of short films with a particular theme. Short form documentaries (up to 24 minutes) tend to get more of a run as they create a commercial half hour. To get noticed you either need to come from a film school or your film has had some level of success on the festival circuit. Not to say that a great short film with a neat marketing package can't crack it, but it's a pretty small market for TV sales. My advice? Go global, get your short shown in your own town, at international festivals, and try to nab a short film distributor to take on your baby. A good short film distributor will know the best festivals, who's looking for content for free to air television, cable, and on-demand.

And be sure that you are pulling together your marketing material from the point of inception. Go nuts if you can, 'cause a lot of these elements can be cost effective and can add value to your press kits, making-of additions, and viral marketing. Don't chuck out storyboards, costume sketches, early marked scripts, makeup test photos, and audition footage. They are a great example of the journey of your film. Be sure to take good stills on set, and remember that the photo will only ever be about two inches in a festival program, so keep it clear, simple, and striking. And always be sure to clear the material with the talent/creative first.

Read trade press from other English-speaking regions. The Australian funding bodies, trade magazines, and film festivals have email newsletters to subscribe to and will notify you of festivals, marketing tips, and inform you of who the upcoming talent is down under. And remember, if you like someone's work, contact him or her. It sounds simple, but these are the most effective ways to circulate your work.

So you've got your personal tale of universal appeal, you've managed to pull the film together, and it's almost exactly as you imagined. It's cracked into the festival circuit locally and internationally, maybe picked up a couple of gongs along the way. A couple of well-respected filmmakers /colleagues/mentors think it's pretty good and it gets you a couple of interviews or a knock on the door of someone you respect. And if none of this happens? You've had a blast, and YOUR story is immortalized.

RALPH ACKERMAN is the founder and Director of the International Short Film Association and the Film Program Cannes. He is a champion of alternative independent filmmaking. He made his first short film in 1963, and it was picked as a highlight of the Ann Arbor Film Festival and sent on a national tour.

His first feature, *Rock-It Box*, was the first Super8 feature film to be transferred to "broadcast video" using the then-new digital transfer method, in 1980. His multiformat experimental feature film, *Zoo Liquid Prototype*, shot in 16 mm black and white, was premiered in New York in 1997. His most recent feature, *Hold True*, was shot, edited, and distributed using digital video.

Mr. Ackerman is a past president of the board of directors of the independent film distributor Film-Makers' Cooperative of New York. He has been a consultant to the Digital Hollywood Conference for the past 14 years.

The International Marketplace for Short Films: Now with a Digital Assist

By Ralph Ackerman

I have witnessed many changes in film production and distribution since I made my first short film in 1964. Then independent filmmakers dreamed of a time when we could distribute our films directly to the consumer. We had to wait about 35 years for what is now called the "Digital Revolution" to bring this dream to a reality. This digital reach—the digital production and distribution of video referred to now as "content"—is enabled through Internet sites devoted to making the short film available to view online or download to portable video players or devices like the iPod, which connects to the computer and to the Internet to gather video content, or "third-generation" cell phones, referred to as "smart phones," that receive, download, and play a wide assortment of video content sent directly to the user's phone.

The international–no borders aspect of the Internet coupled with search engines allows viewers to access dozens of web sites that allow the immediate downloading and viewing of all kinds of video clips and films. Filmmakers are now able to reach out with the Internet using their own web sites or on community web sites like MySpace.com or YouTube.com to find a niche audience for their films.

One early indication that the Internet would help to find viewers for short films was when the short film *George Lucas in Love* debuted online at MediaTrip.com on October 12, 1999, and has proven very popular with both regular audiences and *Star Wars* fans ever since. When the film was released on VHS in 2000, *The New York Times* reported that the film made it to #1 on the Internet's Amazon.com's Top 10 sales chart, even beating out sales of *Star Wars Episode I: The Phantom Menace* for a day. The film's Internet success of selling copies through Amazon brought about a brick-and-mortar deal from the Blockbuster video store chain and from there it was a short jump to a broadcast deal with the Sci Fi Channel in the United States and on to deals with international foreign film market distributors.

The rapid growth of short films and their web sites on the Internet put short films in the media spotlight. Film professionals around the world were quick to take notice.

The professional international film community is well organized with film festivals and their related film "markets" held year round. Close to 10,000 film professionals converge at each of the three major markets of Cannes on the French Riviera in May; Berlin, Germany, in February; and the America Film Market in Los Angeles in the fall. In 2004 the world's largest international feature film market, Cannes, with its annual two-week gathering of thousands of film producers and distributors, responded to the growing explosion of the short film's popularity around the globe with the use of digital technology. A decision was made to introduce an official short film market as part of their official gathering. Labeled the "Short Film Corner," it was an immediate success and has grown each year.

This recognition of the potential for professional distribution of the short film at the Cannes Film Market is just one of many historic markers for this rising new star of the entertainment market.

That same year the International Short Film Association was founded in the United States. The Association is a web-based community for professional filmmakers. The Association's mission is to increase the professional opportunities for short films, to enhance the growth of the short film genre by providing services, information, and networking with industry distribution professionals and filmmakers.

A major hallmark of independent filmmaking in the United States is the Sundance Film Festival and Institute and in 2006 its founder Robert Redford announced the Global Short Film Project for mobile phones as part of the Sundance Film Festival. It was done in collaboration with GSA Association, whose members serve more than 2 billion mobile phone customers across the globe. This was another marker in the history to showcase the short film genre internationally. Redford during his announcement of the project referred to mobile phones as "fast becoming the 'fourth screen' medium, after television, cinema, and computers." John Cooper, of the Sundance Festival and Institute, who oversees the Global Short Film project, referred to the mobile phone as holding tremendous promise for "maximizing the impact and international reach of the short film genre."

With the proliferation of camera phones and their users shooting video with their "mobiles" and the availability of cheap video editing and publishing tools, it is allowing video shot on mobile phones to be distributed both on the web by email and between phones by Bluetooth. These nonprofessionally shot videos with home video cameras and mobile phones are typically intended for viewing by friends and families and are known as "user-generated video." Once they are posted on the web, they can be viewed by anyone. This casual nonprofessional posting and viewing of video on the Internet coupled with its recognition and promotion by mainstream media soon began to attract thousands and in many cases millions of viewers.

Google, Inc., learned that it could monetize this growing phenomenon by selling and posting small linked text advertisements on these sites.

In 2006, Google, Inc., bought the number one Internet video-sharing web site YouTube.com for $1.65 billion. This recognition of user-generated video was also good for smaller, more community-oriented online video services like Revver and Blip.tv, allowing them more room to grow and evolve. With the growing use of user-generated video on sites like Revver and YouTube, it begs the question, when does user-generated video become accepted as the latest genre in independent filmmaking?

With the success of the short film's digital reach and digital production that makes it possible for the viewer to become a filmmaker, is this part of the process in the world of "entertainment" that is related to reality TV shows that are growing in popularity internationally, where the viewers became the "actors"? The audience had joined the filmmaking process as actors in front of the camera—it was only a matter of time before the viewer/audience felt it could become the filmmaker behind the camera and then a short jump to joining the distribution/exhibition process with their own web sites with the posting and downloading of videos. This process of user-generated content has had the impact of allowing nonprofessional video makers to enter the professional content marketplace. Now anyone who wants to shoot with a home digital video camera can post their work on any number of user video sites. Now, in addition to everybody getting their "fifteen minutes of fame", they can also get their fifteen minutes of film credit by just turning on the camera, pointing it, and posting it on the Internet and in some cases having more viewers than traditional media distribution formats. It also is providing a new repository of video content with an archival nature similar to documentary filmmaking.

At the end of 2006, user-generated videos had already made up 47% of the U.S. online video market of 12.5 billion total video streams.

With user-generated video the cream rises to the top automatically with the viewer's choices. This is often accomplished with what is known as "viral" marketing of video, referring to video clip content which gains popularity through the process of Internet sharing, typically through email or IM messages, blogs, and other media-sharing web sites. User-generated content is releasing creativity in people who would never have had a chance to produce content using the traditional expensive film and video production systems of the past. Anyone in the business of content gatekeeping at this time of a digital revolution should be scared of this new growing trend of user-generated media with a digital reach around the globe.

Apple TV, introduced in 2007, syncs the user's iTunes library to their TV set so that anything that has been downloaded or pulled into the user's iTunes library, including their own videos or videos downloaded from the Internet, can be watched on their very own big screen TV next to their very own couch.

As the new international short film market becomes a "direct to download" on an iPod or iPhone and seen on the HD home movie theater with a device such as an AppleTV (this device has Apple, Inc., positioning itself as a digital content aggregator) will add to the trend of gatekeeping film "professional" web sites like iThentic.com, which act as a "middleman," selecting "quality" content worthy of professional ad money sales, as professional distributors do when they make decisions as to which films are the better ones to exhibit to the TV viewer on paid TV, thus taking the choice out of the hands of the viewer once again. Perhaps the digital reach will allow the filmmakers to remain one step ahead of the gatekeepers.

There is one thing for sure, even with the many questions that the Internet and user-generated content have brought the professional filmmaker, there are growing opportunities in a digitally connected international marketplace. The short film has taken its place as a major viewing experience with niche audiences large enough to support filmmakers. When we make a short film now we don't dream as we did in 1964 of how we will "distribute our films directly to the consumer," instead we dream how many will view our film.

SEIGO TONO has been Chief Director of the Short Shorts Film Festival (SSFF) in Tokyo, Japan, since 2000. The SSFF has grown to be one of the largest showcases for short films in Asia and was accredited by the Academy of Motion Picture Arts and Sciences in 2004.

Mr. Tono was born in Takarazuka, Japan, and studied journalism at Pepperdine University in California from 1987 to 1991. After living three years as a student in Clermont-Ferrand France, he directed a 35 mm black-and-white short film, *Ichigo-Ichie*, in Los Angeles. That short film was an official selection in the Tokyo International Short Film Festival in 1998. After working on two Hollywood film productions, he returned to Japan to write scripts for his own radio show at FM CO.CO.LO. in Osaka, which he did for several years. He was also a member of the Committee of the Osaka European Film Festival from 1998 to 2000.

The web site for the Short Shorts Film Festival is www.shortshorts.org.

Short Films in Japan

By Seigo Tono

As a director and an organizer of a short film festival in Japan, I am often asked two questions, each under different circumstances. Abroad, I am often asked, "Do you have short films of famous Japanese directors? Are there any shorts by Akira Kurosawa, Nagisa Oshima, or Yasujiro Ozu? We have never seen or heard of short films from them." In Japan, I'm often asked by everyone (including my parents), "It's great that you organize a short film festival . . . but what do you do for a living, really?" From these remarks and questions, you probably perceive a rough idea about the short film industry in Japan. It still does not exist, really.

Much like the Hollywood studio system in the fifties, most of the Japanese directors at the time that became world famous (including Akira Kurosawa) started their careers in Japanese motion picture companies. They were all employees of movie companies such as Toho, Shochiku, and Nikkatsu. All of them started as assistants in production, and if they got lucky, they became an apprentice to their "Senpai" or "older and experienced" directors. They assisted the director for many years before they finally became one. It was no surprise then, that they reached the age of more than 40 on their first feature film. Naturally, the young employed and apprentice directors did not have the luxury of making their films in their spare time. There weren't any film festivals in Japan or a tradition of screening a short film before a long feature. From the sixties to seventies, most of the well-known feature directors left the companies and became independent directors. And like in Hollywood, the companies stopped hiring the film directors. I personally have not seen any young Akira Kurosawa shorts or those from other worldly well-known Japanese directors.

Through repeated invasions by enemy countries, European countries suffered from an identity crisis. Many European countries used films as propaganda, not only for political reasons but also to promote their culture (and goods) in the world market. France is a good example of how the influence of French cinema has contributed to the consumption of French goods in Japan. Japanese people buy French wine, eat French cuisine, and consume expensive clothes and bags surely because of the influence of French images that we see in their films. The Japanese government, although it has now started to realize it more seriously, has been reluctant to accept that film exports are as important as exporting automobiles. For a very long time, the government has seen Japanese films as purely "entertainment" that is to be appreciated by the Japanese audience.

Whereas European countries have developed their own national film schools and short film festivals, Japan still did not see the importance of the future of cinema. Suddenly, in the eighties, the people in general started to realize that the famous directors were aging, and that there weren't many new talented directors coming out in the industry. There were film classes in some of the Japanese arts universities, but still, there weren't any pedagogic strategies to educate and grow new film directors. In many European schools, they established national film schools so that young elite filmmakers could lead the industry and eventually promote their culture overseas.

Europe has also established many short film festivals such as Oberhausen, Tampere, and Clermont-Ferrand, originating 20 to 50 years ago. Japan did not have any major short film festivals, except the Pia Film Festival, which was established in the eighties by an information magazine publisher. The Pia Film Fest has become the most famous film festival in Japan, showcasing both feature and short films as the hub of new Japanese young talent. Most of the crowned young filmmakers from this festival became freelance or employed directors for a production company making advertising commercials. They waited patiently for their chance to make a feature film, usually involving the capital of advertisement agencies and television companies. Many of the crowned directors from this festival have gone on to become famous directors. It is important to mention that the lack of educating the young (therefore, not having the opportunities for the young to show their student short films) is one of the major reasons that the Japanese film industry suffered a turmoil in business during the eighties and nineties.

So, where are the short films? That's where we, the Short Shorts Film Festival, come in. Established in 1999, the festival has been showing the works of young filmmakers both from abroad and Japan. The festival has asked prominent Japanese film producers and directors to be members of the jury, and they all became enchanted with the world of short films. Believe it or not, even established Japanese producers never had many opportunities to see short films before. After his festival participation as a jury member, a prominent Japanese producer developed the short films series called *Jam Films*, and its three installments were successful in both theatrical distribution and DVD sales. Each *Jam Films* installment had seven or eight short films directed by prominent Japanese film directors. With the success of *Jam Films* and the popularity of short films such as BMW films or on the Internet, many Japanese automobile, beer, and confectionary companies started to make longer versions of their commercial ads, or created a short film to be streamed on their web sites. However, Japanese consumers think that television and web sites are free for viewing, so people hesitate to spend money in order to watch something. Our company,

Pacific Voice, Inc., which produces SSFF, has considered the web site business, but we have been prudent and decided that it is not yet the time to do so.

To this day, to my knowledge, there aren't any Japanese web sites or cable channels that are successful with PPV for short film content. What the Internet has contributed to short films in Japan, though, is familiarizing its name to the Internet users. Before the Internet came along, people in general (including myself) had the image of the words "short film" or "tampen," in Japanese, as a kind of boring experimental film that we had to sit and watch at school as kids, during the "Morality in Society" class. Because of the Internet, people started to use "short film" as something "cooler" than its "dark and boring" film image.

There are still few opportunities for short films at this moment in Japan, but with the growth of new mobile technologies, short films are becoming a popular content. Not all short films are made to fit the small screen of mobile phones, but many content producers are now strategizing to specialize in making short films exclusively for mobile phones. Our festival, SSFF, tries to let young Japanese filmmakers and content creators understand that our festival is not the only place for them to win a prize or find producers of their future film ideas. Their short films or "content" can be sold to mobile or Internet companies and they can make a living. SSFF believes that short films will be a new kind of entertainment for a new kind of lifestyle. That is, short films as bedtime stories for kids, short films for older people in their homes, short films for students in education, short films for busy business people for relaxation, etc.

Although short films are not yet a major form of entertainment in Japan, they are indeed becoming popular. Fortunately, the growing popularity of short films keeps my job alive. You may still wonder what I do for a living besides organizing a short film festival. Actually, it is my full-time job. Two years ago, the Tokyo Metropolitan Government decided to become part of the festival, supporting us financially. Their participation has provided us with the stable budget to hire some year-round staff, including myself. The festival takes place every June in Tokyo, and the rest of the year, we look for sponsors because the government's funding is not enough. We also try to find ways to finance the festival ourselves, collaborating with the participating filmmakers for the use of content outside the festival. All these efforts take a great deal of time and energy. It needs to be a full-time job, and I admit that my profession is still a one of kind in Japan.

MARGARET VON SCHILLER was born in 1956 in southern Germany as the youngest of six children. After she completed college, her parents emigrated to Spain, and she had an apprenticeship in cabinetmaking, which resulted in her unusual craftsmanship and independence at a young age. She spent four years in the UK, France, and Spain, and her travels to the United States and South America furthered her interest in art, language, and culture.

After returning to Germany in 1983 she created programs about the experience abroad in radio broadcasting, which explored a new talent, while she continued her small antique furniture restoration workshop. Soon thereafter she began freelance festival coordination and served as an assistant director on international film productions, which drew her interest increasingly toward producing and directing film.

In 1990 the director of the Panorama section of the Berlin Film Festival invited her to join his team, where she remained for 16 years, until 2006. Seven months per year were dedicated to helping grow the reputation of the Panorama section and included deputy responsibilities. As programmer, she selected from among thousands of short films to curate the short film programs and presented the filmmakers at the festival.

Her small independent production company joined the postproduction group of Florian Koehler to form Mingusfilm Berlin, which focuses not only on film, but also on media art and photography.

Magic Little Differences: The European Audience Loves Short Films

By Margaret von Schiller

What young filmmaker doesn't dream of traveling the world with his newborn baby—the short film? Simply receiving an invitation to a festival brings forth the opportunity to meet other filmmakers from around the world, including those from your own country. You might even experience how close you are to others in your thought process when you finally meet the audience and feel their excitement. After all the hard work, when your film finally reaches that audience, you can soak in their comments and bathe in their understanding. (You may also be compared with other films and filmmakers, which is nothing to be afraid of.)

But where do you start in order to get there?

There are a million ways to make your dream become a reality. Bring forth your concept with a smile on your face and they will buy the idea—one might think. As long as it comes from the bottom of your heart—one might believe. Just stick to what your own truth is in order to get around the difficult periods. Inventing your story on your own, creating your images, and the lonely stretch of writing often are some of the hardest periods for a filmmaker. Certainly everyone who has gone through the production of a film knows the "Schmerz" (German for "pain") one goes through making a million decisions while trying to be 100% certain that each decision is the right one. It's a lonely job.

Why not become a writer or a photographer or a painter or a carpenter instead? After all, a filmmaker is as a little bit of everything. The format of short films allows you to bend this everything into all or nothing. There is no need to be correct, linear, continuous, or straight in the short form, which, by the way, doesn't make it any easier.

How do you convince someone with your style and form, then?

Short film cannot only be taught at school. The short format has an incredible ability to allow the filmmaker the chance to experiment. Still, the main ingredients are the classic all-time film language tools. You do not have to reinvent everything. This craft can be compared to the fine art of baking and patisserie. It is not only the quality of each ingredient but the matching and mixing of them that makes the end result tasty. If a cake is blue and tastes fantastic, it might take a moment in order to convince somebody else to eat it, but then—why not? My uncle was a great art designer and left a lot of beautiful drawings and sketches of his work. In later life he continuously told everyone that his lifetime achievement was really only based on other people's brilliant ideas. This is an example that film is not made by only one person. However short and modest one might consider a film everyone who participates in it deserves recognition and plays a part in its success.

The audience decides

Funny enough, the audience can excuse a lot. They go straight for the heartfelt emotion. Even poor technical quality can somehow be excused if the filmmaker's point comes across. I have seen terrible technical screenings for whatever reason, but the audience carried the film on to become an award-winning piece, whereas some perfect cinematography and camera-driven pieces went down disappointingly unrecognized. It is rare to find that every bit of a film is perfect—whether short or long, actually. If it grabs the audience, it is pure love.

The first 30 seconds

We are living in a fast world where somehow patience has been reduced to a minimum, but this surprisingly also allows for the opposite to take place. The success of extremely slow-paced films is also captivating. It's the feeling for rhythm and the right timing in the actors, the camera, and, last but not least, the editing that is crucial to the audience. If you allow me to add, the audience response is also influenced by the programmer's choice in which order the short films are presented. Only some 10 years ago we still accepted complicated, sad, and depressing short films that exhibited deep hurt feelings and themes that reflected our souls as sort of "rebels of the cause." Today we lean towards more soft-spoken tactics. Despite the trends the audience embraces all kinds of short film. They love filmmakers that portray personality, carry culture, preserve the almost-lost, or go over the top with their fantasies. We might change our taste once every so often but we cannot change our desire to be moved by something and to be entertained.

The global point of view

As a programmer I have observed that some subjects and themes come in incredible waves from all over the world. Our societies are portrayed in the past as much as in recent times or in futuristic settings, and have become more and more a reflection of our global perspective. Filmmakers create a very similar atmosphere, but each does so in their individual filmic world and using their specific way of storytelling. From Peru to France and from Oslo to Kapstadt, the man that kills his alarm clock half asleep in the first 20 seconds of the film is equally feasible. All those filmmakers do not follow a trend—since it also takes a year to make a film, if not two or three. They convey the concerns of a generation. This is a reason to become very precise in the development of the idea for your film. Only when you reach the final result can you discover whether the film is strong enough to stand out.

Every film costs money, no matter how short or simple it seems. Those who give money know this best, especially the parents, grandparents, and friends that contributed to its financing. Full of hope, they expect a special piece and become part of the excited crowd of a film premiere. The most prevalent way to get a return back on the investment is via a functioning short film market.

LITTLE FISH, BIG POND: THINKING GLOBALLY

In Europe this isn't as difficult, since a great deal of filmmaking is funded and the filmmakers develop good skills by completing funding applications. Perhaps this would be a better place if there was no commercial market at all, but this is unrealistic as long as the world doesn't fully recognize film as "the" art of the 20th century. Certainly as long as filmmakers want to see their future income in this world of filmmaking and film marketing, the quest for funding becomes ongoing.

We do need more TV channels to buy shorts and short film markets connected to festivals with acceptable fees paid to the participating filmmaker and not the other way around, especially since short filmmakers are the talent of the future, and many go on to make features. Unfortunately, the markets don't seem to adapt quickly enough to the new technology world we seem to be already living in, referring to the Internet, game world, mobile, micro features, MPEG-4, and whatever platform comes next. There are always new opportunities that should be investigated by filmmakers.

Let's be inventive, then, and share our experience.

If someone is good at telling stories adaptable to various formats, he or she still might be unable to put it out there. Well yes, one can find an agent, that's one way, but another way is to find allies. All the "Great Masters of Cinema" had or have their team of people to work with that they treat like a family. If we suppose that in many cases a young short filmmaker is a first-time filmmaker, he or she will have to find his own "family." Awards and invitations to festivals around the world (even the smaller ones) are perfect for this. Some of the film festivals are intimidating, but that doesn't matter. Soak it in, show them your film, attend all your screenings, stand up for it, and try to get as much from the audience as you can. Carry your promotional materials with you at all times. Make good records of whom you meet by listening carefully, remembering names, and putting on your nicest smile. It becomes part of your overall experience only much later. The festival world is one small circuit around the globe that deals with films and if you participate with a clear head and an open mind you will learn quickly.

The best thing in festivals is to watch all those brilliant films.

It is certainly very important to present your film in its best light, but the most beautiful part of all those film festivals is watching the films. It is a wonderful experience to have such a wide range of films being shown, and take advantage of that, especially if you have free access with your filmmaker pass, due to the invitation of your beloved short film. It's heaven. You will see the cinema in a different light. The large screens, the original versions, and the film prints in their different qualities and formats, each contains the personal handwriting of every filmmaker. Never expect anything, go for the given.

It's an inspiring trip around the world. Most of the time it feels "just right" to be part of this big experience, and it feels politically grown-up and important. Never forget to observe the audience carefully because this is the audience that will also come to see your film.

Europe and the European audience

In Europe we developed a fair deal of individualism over many centuries. All those small nations with their differences in culture and climate have gone through many circumstances about tolerance as well as misunderstandings and emotional clashes. Film is the medium that shows the many facets of our societies, whether past or present. Europe therefore might have a greater variety of films, and larger film nations like the United States have developed more of the commercial aspect due to a larger overall English-speaking market. The audience loves the variety and considers the filmmaker to be the eye and the film to be the window through which they are allowed to see the world. This experience comes primarily at the festivals and not at the box office, which is an altogether completely different experience, particularly when it comes to independent long feature films.

Maybe short films bloom like flowers

Short films are like bouquets picked in Granny's garden, bought in a posh flower shop, or stolen in a public park. The audience reflects this. And they are unpredictable, but reliable, and really very interested. They like to be taken seriously, they like to learn, and they can even take a lot of violence, but only if in the right context.

The audience in Europe is not so different from the audience in the rest of the world. I have seen shorts in Asia, Mexico, Russia, and Macedonia. I cannot see much difference with relation to the audience. People who come to see short films love shorts and every time the lights go down in the theater we expect to see the greatest piece of all times. If it is not, no problem—as long as it comes from the bottom of your heart.

ELLIOT GROVE was mesmerized by the moving image from a young age, but unable to watch TV or films until his early teens due to the constraints of his Amish background. Canadian-born Mr. Grove followed up formal art school training with a series of jobs behind the scenes in the film industry. Working as a scenic artist on 68 feature films and over 700 commercials in his native Toronto, he developed a distaste for the wasted resources on set and the union red tape that prevented filmmaker wannabes like him from getting their own features off the ground.

Mr. Grove moved to London in 1986 and in 1992, when the British film industry was drowning in self-pity, launched the Raindance Film Festival and, in 1998, the British Independent Film Awards. He has produced three feature films and over 150 short films. In 2001 Focal Press published his book *Raindance Writers Lab: How to Write and Sell the Hot Script*. His second book, *Raindance Producer's Lab Lo-To-No Budget Filmmaking*, was published by Focal Press in July 2004. His novel *The Bandit Queen* is being illustrated by Dave McKean and is scheduled for publication in 2008.

His production company operates under the Raindance banner and is currently developing a slate of ten features, the first of which premiered at the Rotterdam Film Festival in January 2006. He has three other features currently shooting in London.

How to Make It with a Short Film in the UK and Europe

By Elliot Grove

Filmmakers in Britain have always considered short form narratives and documentaries as a viable step into filmmaking. The BBC and Channel 4 in particular have commissioned and purchased shorts for broadcast on terrestrial television—often as a way to test new talent before awarding the filmmakers a more substantial contract to produce a feature film or documentary. However, since 2003, the landscape has changed. In the current climate the terrestrial television channels have scaled back their commissioned shorts programs and rarely acquire shorts for broadcast. This has left filmmakers with relying on festivals as the main alternative to getting their work seen.

Shorts typically have punchier story lines, are often shot on very low budgets, giving them a gritty look that, combined with sharp short stories, makes compelling viewing. Filmmakers have been shooting movies on their mobiles since 2003 when Nokia introduced the first camera phone. The haunting images on television after the 7/7 terrorist attacks in London demonstrated their news ability. This groundbreaking moment paved the way to the present BBC practice of issuing quality mobile handsets such as the Nokia N93 to home-based journalists, who then email in their footage for quick assembly, edit, and broadcast in the studio.

Using a short film, or a series of short films, has always been considered a viable and useful way to demonstrate one talent to the industry powers-that-be en route to building a career in features, or in commercials and pop promos. Here are the routes novice filmmakers are using in Europe. Many of these techniques are applicable universally.

1. Film festivals

A festival screening allows you to screen your film in front of total strangers, and often, in Europe at least, to people of whom English is not their mother tongue. Until you have sat in a screening room full of strangers watching your film you do not really know how the film "plays." Do they laugh at the right place, for example.

Getting your film accepted into a film festival is not easy. Firstly, you research the festival world (there are nearly 3000 film festivals around the world), download a submission form, and send it, along with an application fee and a copy of your film. Then you wait to hear if you have been selected. If you are selected, you then need to send the festival a screening copy of the film, usually on digibeta, along with a picture of yourself, or a still from the movie that they can use in their festival catalogue. Try and book your holiday around a festival screening. Get there a few days earlier and pass out postcards with a good strong image of your film on one side, and the screening dates and times on the reverse. Festival organizers should also be able to help you with a list of local distributors and sales agents who might be interested in acquiring short films (i.e., buying a license to screen your film). Contact these people by email and telephone.

Screenings at certain film festivals almost certainly guarantee other festival invites. Many festivals rely on bellwether festivals such as Raindance to act as a filter to whittle down the huge number of films to a manageable lot of a certain quality.

Remember that each festival has different taste, and to be rejected by one festival is not to be taken personally.

The best way to research film festivals is to look at these two sites: www.filmfestivals.com, an English-speaking company based in Paris, and www.withoutabox.com, an American company with a subsidiary office in London.

Top European film festivals for shorts

There are at least nine European short film festivals which show shorts only. Other festivals, such as Raindance, have dynamic short film strands. Research the festivals and try to ascertain which ones have videotechs, such as Rotterdam. At those festivals, even if you are not selected, industry scouts will be able to see your film.

International Short Film Festival Leuven — January: www.shortfilmfestival.org
International Film Festival Rotterdam — January: www.filmfestivalrotterdam.com
Clermont-Ferrand Short Film Festival — February: www.clermont-filmfest.com
Tampere Short Film Festival — March: www.tamperefilmfestival.fi
International Short Film Festival Oberhausen — May: www.kurzfilmtage.de
Cannes International Film Festival — May: www.festival-cannes.org
Cinema Jove International Film Festival — June: www.cinemajovefilmfest.com
Vila do Conde International Short Film Festival — July: www.curtasmetragens.pt/festival
Raindance Film Festival — October: www.raindance.co.uk
Kinofilm Manchester International Film Festival — November: www.kinofilm.org.uk
Encounters International Short Film Festival — November: www.encounters-festivals.org.uk

Sales agents
Hamburg ShortFilmAgency: www.shortfilmsales.com/
Future Shorts: www.futureshorts.com/
Dazzle Films: www.dazzlefilms.co.uk/

2. Internet self-distribution
The explosion of YouTube and MySpace means that you don't need to rely on the whims of a festival programmer (the job title of the person at a film festival who decides which submissions are selected for screening). You can simply upload your masterpiece yourself to one of the www2 sites, send an email to everyone in your address book with the link, and hope that enough people watch and love your movie and tell so many friends that your film becomes a viral hit leading to your discovery as the next Spielberg.

3. Internet distribution
Sites like AtomFilms, iTunes, and the Australian channel NICEFILM specialize in shorts and offer different forms of revenue recoupment,

either in the form of a one-off license fee or a revenue participation model based on the number of people who see your film (and see the ads on their site). Each of these sites has different adjudication processes.

4. Mobile telephone

Cell phones are fast becoming the "fourth screen" medium, after television, cinema, and computers. Mobile telephone operators are trying to encourage their clients to use their telephones for nontalking activity, specifically to watch films. The European mobile networks now purchase content for their users to download or MMS, either on an exclusive or nonexclusive basis (depending on the content). On one hand, they pay huge sums for the right to MMS their subscribers goals and key plays from the top sporting events, to small amounts to filmmakers who have created short films, typically under 40 seconds (for G2.5 users) to 120 seconds (G3 users). Filmmakers receive a few pennies per download from the €0.50–€0.75 charge they make to their customers.

Content aggregators such as Crucible Media and Raindance present packages to the European mobile networks. These collections of short films are discovered at film festivals or are the result of competitions like the now defunct Nokia 15 Second Shorts competition (www.nokiashorts.com). Filmmakers can make over $1000 a film, depending on the deal, and depending on how many people see their film or forward it to a friend. The Sundance film festival now distributes their festival's shorts and joined forces with the GSM Association, whose members serve more than 2 billion mobile phone customers across the globe, to create the *Sundance Film Festival: Global Short Film Project*, a groundbreaking pilot project to showcase and extend the reach of the independent short film genre to mobile users worldwide.

5. Competitions

There are currently so many film competitions that a reasonably talented debutante filmmaker should be able to get the latest cameras, editing software, and even first class trips around the world on the strength of their successful submissions. Before submitting to a competition, it is important to research the organization or company sponsoring the venture to see if you can determine the reason why. Sometimes they are created solely to promote a product or service. In such cases the benefit to you as a filmmaker is solely the value of the prize. The best competitions are the ones where the promoter is seeking content for their web site or broadcast channel, be it web-based, television, or mobile. In these cases, usually by submitting you will be included as part of their content and the possibility will exist to earn extra revenue or exposure. It is up to you to decide which will suit your career best.

BAFTA—the UK equivalent of the Oscars—held its 60 Seconds of Fame short filmmaking competition in 2007 and reserves the exclusive right to use the entrant's short film to market the competition or showcase the work of BAFTA within the license period. This is a good example of how the competition host gets the benefits of free or cheap content, and the filmmaker gets publicity and hopefully a career boost.

A Raindance tradition has developed where the winner of the Diesel Film of the Festival, sponsored by Diesel, gets the opportunity to create a 60-second festival identity for the coming year, which is screened in 150 cinemas for six weeks prior to the festival, on a 35 mm print. In 2005 the winner was the Japanese filmmaker Kosai Sekine, whose brilliant short film won, and his identity called *Daughter* went on to win three gold awards at the prestigious Cannes Advertising Festival in 2006, thereby launching Kosai into the world of the super commercial.

6. Airlines
Cathay Pacific and Virgin are the only remaining airlines who license shorts for their airlines. Filmmakers typically receive $500 for a six-month short. The best length for these shorts is about 10–15 minutes each, and soft romantic comedies are the topics the airlines like the most. The best agent to deal with is Dazzle Films in London. Owned and operated by Dawn Sharpless, it has been acquiring and selling shorts since the late 1990s (www.dazzlefilms.com).

7. Advertising agencies
Ad agencies are always on the lookout for hot new talent. If your work is very short (under one or two minutes) then an ad agency might consider you for a commercial. Make sure you invite the relevant executives from ad agencies in the cities that you play in. Obviously, London, Paris, and New York have the most agencies, but don't discount agencies in smaller cities.

Some agencies, like Saatchi & Saatchi, have in-house intranet sites (theirs is called Sushi & Sushi) where new work is put up for the exclusive use of their employees. The career advantages of this are obvious.

8. Compilation DVDs
Certain festivals like Raindance, organizations like Shootingpeople, and others, publish annual collections of DVDs which showcase shorts.

As part of their marketing campaign, these DVDs are generally given to journalists, ad agency creatives, and agents as a way of inducing filmmakers to allow their shorts to be placed on the DVD. From this platform, Raindance has noticed that the filmmakers included on our DVD receive many festival invites and offers of work.

FAQs

Should I put all my films on YouTube, or not?

YouTube is a great way to get your showreel up, but it ruins the premiere status of your films for festivals, other web distributors, and television. Be very careful about what and when you include your films on YouTube.

What is the most common reason filmmakers fail to sell their films?

Either they fail to tell a story or they fail to clear music rights. Or both.

Does it matter what I shoot my film on?

Absolutely not. The story you're telling is far more important. Just make sure you are able to deliver your film in the correct format and resolution required by whichever festival or broadcaster you are targeting.

What happens if I sign an exclusive agreement?

It means that you are unable to give your work to anyone else, sometimes even other film festivals. Consider the repercussions carefully before you agree to such a deal. Sometimes the commercial benefits will sway you, and other times it will be the exposure.

I've heard that Joost.com plays shorts. How do I get on there?

In order to play on Joost, you need to be accepted by a channel that is playing there, such as Raindance.tv.

Get more info from www.raindance.co.uk.

No Lifeguard on Duty: Internet and New Technology

Content.

Devices.

Platforms.

Users.

Seemingly overnight filmmakers are faced with a new vocabulary and no road map to navigate the new information superhighways. Cell phones have become mobile communication devices, and web sites have become content providers. The audience has become a group of users, and distribution now has many platforms. What does this all mean for the short filmmaker? Opportunities have become widespread if filmmakers understand how best to position their work and use the new technology to their advantage.

At the moment I am writing this, the Internet is the place where filmmakers can infiltrate interest communities, get feedback, and have their films exposed to a global audience with little expense beyond the production itself. What is critical, however, is understanding how to use the Internet and where to put that film to begin with.

My immersion into watching short films on the Internet began when I asked the 50 students in my producing course how long they are on their computers daily and where they troll in the World Wide Web. I wasn't surprised by the response that they spend substantially more hours per day on the Internet than they do watching television, but I was fascinated by how huge an audience a filmmaker can reach through these sites and if, and how, the new technology has affected the overall distribution platform for short films. I handed out index cards to my students and asked them to write down the web sites they frequented most, and I would then investigate them. I decided to wander through the web sites they wrote down to discover what's out there and what the viewing experience is like. I still "go to the movies" and see television as my primary viewing portal, but it was time to get with the program.

Many of my students mentioned familiar sites such as MySpace, Facebook, and YouTube, but a majority of the web sites they wrote down I had never even heard of, and I was surprised that, as film and television students, they weren't glued to sites like AtomFilms to watch product. I suggest to all aspiring filmmakers that they spend time watching short films on the web. It's so important to see what is being made in order to understand how your film fits in with the universe at large. Watching other filmmakers' work will inspire you and challenge you to create your own.

But I digress. The biggest adjustment for me as a viewer was sitting at my computer, which to me is "work" rather than "play." The web sites in general were pretty easy to navigate, with clearly defined tabs and search engines. I had difficulty with some sites at which the shorts started playing automatically, which was annoying since I wanted to read about them first and kept having to click the stop tab, but downloads occurred rather quickly and uneventfully. The physical aspect of viewing was not a problem, and it was easy to "browse" different films and categories.

The first site I went to was YouTube, primarily because it generates a great deal of water cooler conversation and has exploded in mainstream popularity. I personally attribute this popularity partly due to the reality show phenomenon, in which the "average Joe" has his/her 15 minutes of fame. Filmmakers upload their work directly to the site, with no prior review or submission criteria. The popularity of a piece is dictated by "the people" in that it is determined by the number of views. Democracy rules the Internet. Additionally, there are viewer ratings by stars, and various ways of sorting, so YouTube viewers can spot the newest work easily, for example.

My immersion prompted me to ponder what exactly a short film is today, and if we, as an industry, even have standards anymore. Can anyone pick up a video camera and make a personal masterpiece? And after doing so, how and why would over 1 million people watch it in one day? What appealed to me initially about YouTube was its ability to expose new talent without the constraints of a formal distribution network, but maybe that is its biggest problem for me. There are no gatekeepers.

What I encountered was an avalanche of gag jokes, offensive humor, and an inability to locate what I consider a "short film." It's a cra-palanche. And let me say up front that this is where I (and everyone else who feels the same way) need to look a little deeper beyond the superficial aspects of the work that is uploaded on YouTube. Yes, it is a little like looking for a needle in a haystack, but that haystack is filled to the brim with raw talent, and if the industry has the patience to sift through it, I'm certain it is a lucrative discovery ground for that new talent.

I don't prejudge films for their amateur filmmaking quality, but there are things I look for in what I consider a "good short." Well-developed characters: check. A story that sucks me in: check. An ending that's not a letdown: check. Many of the shorts I watched on some of the established short film web sites had all three, and I presume it is due to the expertise of acquisitions executives.

On one particular web site, I looked at a short that has been online since 2001, and to date this short has over 5 million views. I stared at the screen incredulously and my mouth dropped open. Five million views. How long would it take for a short film to reach 10 million eyes outside of the Internet? I'd be dead and buried long before that. Seeing large numbers like these made me realize that web sites have extended the life of a short film incredibly, to the filmmaker's advantage.

In the end, what made me think most about this experience was what the filmmaker gets out of it (since that's kind of the point of this book) and depending on the site, that may be a very different result. YouTube attracts eyes, and it would be virtually impossible to obtain that much exposure anywhere else in such a short time. Some career filmmakers are drawn to the more established short film web sites because there can be the rare opportunity for revenue, commissioned content, or syndication on one of the parent company's other platforms.

I was at an event recently and watched one of the funniest shorts I had seen in a long time. My friend approached the filmmaker and asked him what his experience was with the short film. He responded that he put it up on YouTube and it received a huge number of views. He was thrilled. I was perplexed. The guy obviously had talent, and spent the time and money to create this short, but because he had selected YouTube as its "distributor" per se, not only would he not make any revenue from it, but that really became the start and end of its life cycle.

His strategy was basic. He simply wanted people to see his work, and he felt he could never achieve that through traditional distribution goals. He didn't care about the money. I realized, albeit sheepishly, that this was indeed his choice. As a filmmaker, he had one goal in mind—eyes on his work—and this was just the place to do that. It's always the filmmaker's choice.

New technology is a conducive environment for short form content. Can you create a piece under seven minutes that is crisp, clean, and to the point? Now, can you do it in three minutes? Mobile technology and the iPod revolution have created increased opportunities for short films to get "out there." And we're only on the brink of this.

As I walked home yesterday there were people in a line that stretched several blocks. They were waiting for the Apple iPhone to go on sale. Some had been there for days. They had chairs, were playing cards, and chatting amiably. The last time I saw a line like this was for some rock concert farewell tour at Tower Records. All these people weren't waiting to buy tickets for a live performance, they were waiting for a piece of new technology. Some of the initial estimates say that 200,000 iPhones were purchased, at a price point of $500 each, minimum. Yep, clearly things have changed.

This chapter is not really about looking into a crystal ball and predicting the future of the Internet and new technology. It's about understanding what options are available now, and how aspiring filmmakers can best utilize the technology to further their careers and creatively position themselves for the future.

MEGAN O'NEILL is Vice President of Acquisitions and Production for AtomFilms, a leading entertainment provider of short content via Internet, broadband services, and mobile devices. Her acquisition of JibJab's *This Land* resulted in traffic of over 80 million plays. Besides acquisitions, she oversees the development and production of original series for AtomFilms's Studio. Prior to joining AtomFilms, she was the cofounder of Forefront Films, a 10-year-old distributor of award-winning shorts worldwide. In 1998, she coproduced Forefront's first feature film, *Relax ... It's Just Sex*, which premiered at the Sundance Film Festival and has been released in over 35 countries worldwide.

Ms. O'Neill has been a panelist or juror at numerous festivals, including the Sundance Film Festival, Ottawa Animation, the Galway Film Fleadh, the Cork International Film Festival, Aspen Shortsfest, Tribeca@IFP, Palm Springs International Short, Toronto Worldwide Shorts, and South by Southwest. She has been in the film business since 1988.

Conversation with Megan O'Neill

SB: What makes a film work for online as opposed to a festival, for example?

MO: There is nothing more thrilling for me as an acquisitions executive than the realization that I have just discovered somebody talented. Whether sitting in a film festival theater or leaning into my computer watching shorts online, I still get excited when I watch a short that really works. I can't wait to sign it and see how our audience reacts. If a short can elicit that thrill of discovery for its audience, on some level it will work everywhere—at festivals, online, on television, mobile phones, etc. However, generally shorter films work better online. An online audience is looking for short bursts of entertainment. Films that rely on character development and plots that are more intricate generally do not work online. Often films that are selected for festivals and television are fitting certain programming requirements. Sometimes shorts are selected thematically or for their running time in order to play with a feature. Many television stations will attempt to keep running times to 15 minutes and under so that they can program a film in either a compilation or in order to fill time. In the end, if a film is great it will be programmed. Adam Elliot's *Harvie Krumpet* ran almost 30 minutes and was hugely successful on television, online, and on the festival circuit. While winning an Oscar certainly helped attract audiences, the animation was successful due to storytelling.

SB: What do you look for when selecting a film?

MO: At AtomFilms, we pride ourselves in featuring some of the best up-and-coming creators in the business. We actively seek out work by filmmakers and animators who we think are going to be the next cutting-edge creators. We are looking for artists with unique visual styles who can craft compelling stories. Whether it's Flash animators who create popular, viral pieces, or festival filmmakers who move on to successful feature careers, we are always looking for directors whose shorts resonate with our audience. The ability to successfully tell a story in under five minutes is a critical test for most of the filmmakers we feature.

SB: How do you find short films?

MO: We source shorts at film festivals, animation schools, film schools, private screenings, comedy clubs, and increasingly online at a variety of web sites. We also encourage submissions via upload on our site— www.atomfilms.com. Some of our best shorts also come from referrals from our own Atom filmmakers.

SB: Do the shorter shorts (five minutes) work best or have longer ones worked too?

MO: Generally, online audiences tend to gravitate towards watching shorter films. While many of our most popular shorts are 5 minutes or under, we still acquire shorts up to 15 minutes in length, and sometimes longer. As is true for all shorts, the bar is set higher the longer the film runs. While some shorts play wonderfully in a film festival setting, it is a different environment than watching films on your computer.

However, there are still longer shorts that can be successful online. Generally, those tend to be comedies and animations—the two most popular categories on Atom. An excellent example of a popular, longer, short film—via the festival circuit, online, on television, and airlines— is Steffen Schaffler's *The Periwig Maker*. Steffen's perennial favorite short has had over a half a million plays on Atom.

SB: Do certain genres work better for online?

MO: People want to be entertained—particularly when watching films online. It's why comedy and animation tend to be the most popular categories, along with topical spoofs and music-driven pieces. If an animator is able to execute a comedy with a catchy song that can be tied to a topical event, it can prove to be wildly successful. An excellent example of one such short is *Star Wars Gangsta Rap*, which was a user-generated Flash animation created for Atom's Star Wars Fan Film Contest. It has been seen millions of times. Another great example may be the most watched online short film of all time—JibJab's *This Land*. This ingenious political spoof of the 2004 presidential election seamlessly blended funny lyrics and arresting cutouts to create a viral parody. The short was seen tens of millions of times, on both AtomFilms and JibJab's own site, resulting in international press and exposure.

SB: What about "offensive" or "mature" subject matter?

MO: Extreme or mature content can drive lots of plays online. Often, just the use of a sexy image or photo can prompt a viewer to click on the link. Many times, the films themselves are fairly tame or even funny. A suggestive title can certainly help a film stand out in an ever-crowded online video marketplace. An excellent example of a strong title in the extreme category would be the animated short *Roof Sex*. An international film festival winner featuring amorous pieces of furniture, *Roof Sex* was also a big online hit. Besides being an entertaining and wonderfully animated stop-motion short, it was a piece that had a terrific title.

SB: What are some of the general common problems you've encountered with films that you liked but that didn't have proper rights or clearances?

MO: As an acquisitions executive who has worked in the short form business since the early nineties, I can't think of anything more disappointing than finding a fabulous short and realizing that I can't acquire it due to a lack of clearances. In the past decade, both on the festival circuit and now online and on mobile devices, short form's popularity has only grown. But I still see many filmmakers who use unlicensed music in their films. Or, who cast actors but don't get them to sign talent releases. I am not a lawyer, and I can't give legal advice. But common sense should tell you that you should only use elements in your film that you actually have the legal right to use.

SB: What should filmmakers be aware of in terms of paperwork they need or deliverables?

MO: At a minimum, filmmakers will need their music and talent releases, a music cue sheet, and proof of ownership—generally some form of copyright registration.

SB: How do you develop ongoing relationships with filmmakers and what opportunities might exist for them?

MO: I am always looking to work with talented people. I watch short films to discover new voices. One of the most exciting aspects of my job is the thrill of discovering new talent. I love finding innovative creators to work with, both from an acquisitions point of view and from an original production perspective. AtomFilms is a site that is loaded with discoveries. Our audience comes to AF to see the next wave of talented creators. We feature Oscar winners and up-and-coming Flash animators, amateur UGC artists, and work from major animation production houses such as Aardman. When we find talented filmmakers, we try to forge ongoing relationships with them. Sometimes that means we acquire multiple titles from them as they continue to create short films. Sometimes it means helping promote their features as they continue on in their careers. More recently, we launched AtomFilms Studios, our online original production initiative which funds shorts and series. We have signed almost 20 deals, mostly with AtomFilms short filmmakers. Some of our AF Studio creators include PES, Oscar nominee Peter Peake of Aardman, the askaninja.com creators, Kyle Rankin and Efram Potelle (winners of Project Greenlight), and film festival favorite Amy Talkington. We encourage our filmmakers to send us pitches for original series that they think will appeal to our AtomFilms audience.

SB: I'm not sure how much in depth you can address the deal— exclusive or nonexclusive, time period, the fact that the filmmaker receives revenue, what that revenue is based on, etc.

MO: While there are many, many sites to showcase your work online, AtomFilms's is one of the oldest and most selective. We were one of the first companies to share advertising revenue with our creators. AtomFilms creators earn a share of the advertising royalties every time their film is played. It's a very democratic system. The more popular your film, the more royalties you earn. We have paid millions of dollars to filmmakers. AtomFilms is also very selective. We screen thousands of shorts a year and only acquire several hundred for the site. Our filmmakers are on the cusp of discovery. As an AtomFilms filmmaker, you also have an opportunity to pitch us for production funds via AtomFilms Studio. Most of the projects we have funded to date have been with filmmakers whose work we first acquired for broadcast on Atom. A good number of our filmmakers have been scouted by the industry via our web site and have ended up getting meetings and jobs via the exposure they have received on the site.

SB: What makes a film "ineligible" for acquisition for Atom?

MO: From a content point of view, we do not acquire films that encourage hate crimes, are incredibly violent, or show anything considered pornographic in nature. From a technical point of view, we do have to disqualify films with poor sound. Although we have acquired some foreign language films, it is incredibly hard to attract an audience when a film is subtitled.

SB: What advice would you give to an aspiring filmmaker?

MO:

- Make shorts, not longs. It's always better to leave your audience wanting more.
- Evoke emotion in your audience. Make them laugh, cry, be scared, etc. Give them a reason to stay tuned.
- Unless Brad Pitt stars in your film, leave the credits until the end. Engage them in your story, and they will be happy to read the end credits.
- Only use music that you actually have the legal right to use. There are plenty of talented composers trying to break into the film business who want to work with young talent and are affordable.
- Don't make period pieces. They are difficult to pull off, even for studio features. Plus, there have been enough shorts based on dead Southern novelists for a lifetime of viewing.
- Be honest with yourself about why you are making the short. Do you want to use it as a calling card to get future work? If so, do you have a game plan for getting the work seen by the industry? Do you want to license it to as many buyers as possible and earn revenue? If so, do you have your clearances?
- Be honest with yourself about what you have created. If you have shot a 30-minute short film, you shouldn't expect the piece to be a viral hit online. Most online hits are 5 minutes or under.
- At the end of the day, try to tell a story that actually means something to you, so that it will resonate with your audience, too. Some of my favorite short films are long, dramatic pieces, but they are executed so well that they stay with you forever.

- Watch some of the classics of short cinema to immerse yourself in technique and get a sense of what works, especially from a film festival perspective. Foreign standouts like *The Bloody Olive* and Oscar winner *Wasp* are two shorts that should be required screening in film school.
- Take risks. Short filmmaking should push the envelope. As film-makers, you have the freedom to experiment in shorts. There is far less room to do so once you work in television and features, when the budgets and the stakes go up.
- Finally, enjoy! Being a creative filmmaker is the best gig in the world.

ROBIN CHAN is Director of Broadband and Mobile Video at Verizon, where he is responsible for multiplatform video strategy.

Previously, Mr. Chan was Associate Director of Entertainment Programming at Verizon Wireless, where he helped grow VCAST into the leading mobile video service. He helped launch VCAST Mobile TV, the country's first multicast mobile TV service, and expanded content partnerships to include leaders from broadband, broadcast, and cable.

He was also Director of Sales and Strategic Distribution at HandsOn and ran wireless business development at Zagat Survey. He began his career in the Corporate Strategy group at Time Warner.

Robin earned his B.A. in economics from Columbia University, with intensive coursework in film.

Demystifying Mobile Video: The Market Opportunity

By Robin Chan

Mobile forces us to rethink the concept of a mass medium. The cellular industry took 20 years to reach 1 billion connections, 3 years to reach 2 billion connections, and is on target to reach its third billion by the end of 2007, according to Wireless Intelligence. China Mobile, the world's largest mobile operator, has more subscribers than the entire population of the United States. Both China and India average over 4.5 million new subscribers every month and are poised to be the largest mobile markets by 2010. Yet, only 25% of their population has a handset, so many years of growth lie ahead.

Informa forecasts worldwide revenue from mobile TV and video services will rise from $2.46 billion in 2006 to $8.35 billion in 2011. By 2010, 291 million people worldwide will use mobile video services, up from about 53 million this year. As a film producer, these forecasts suggest the formation of a whole new audience, with new expectations on how a story should be told.

Two years ago, we launched a service called V CAST, which was one of the world's first video services for 3G phones. The original strategy was to seek large partners with strong incumbent television and cable brands and sell the concept of entertainment on the go. We partnered with companies such as FOX, NBC, or MTV to communicate to mass audiences. Over time, once we had subscriber momentum, our full intention was to support the broadest spectrum of content and have more content providers empowered to bring their content to mobile audiences.

Fast forward two years and we've learned quite a bit what works and what doesn't. Broadband and youth brands appeal strongest to our early adopter audience. YouTube, Comedy Central, MTV, and Maxim are among our top VCAST channels. Over time, as our subscriber base has widened, we have seen our audience pool diversify. But significant migration to mass appeal will take time. In the present, videos that trend young feed the largest audience.

Original programming is happening, and the best path is broadband to mobile. Broadband and mobile are sister platforms of a web-oriented new generation, and some of the best short form broadband video will work great as snack-sized entertainment on a phone. The broadband video audience far exceeds the mobile video audience for the foreseeable future and enjoys the benefits of over 15 years of video infrastructure to ensure content discovery and sharing. More importantly, creators are also able to monetize their work through advertising and can market to viewers directly.

Creatively, broadband content is cheap to produce and is not regulated by government, which enables considerable experimentation. Some of the best stuff is being made by people who never learned the rules of traditional video production and originated as a video podcast or YouTube channel. An explosion of creativity is happening online, where entertainers are building audiences from scratch. They don't need a studio system to find an audience and monetize their content.

Genres will expand. What has worked particularly well at this stage appears to be comedy, broadband, and sports, as previously mentioned. When technology improves and then stabilizes, storytellers can focus users on the story, rather than the underlying device or technology. People will consume episodic programming once it's tied into the fabric of their daily lives.

New genres will also emerge. The unprecedented wave of user-generated content will take on a new velocity once billions of multimedia phones are harnessed for media creation. Imagine billions of people streaming and uploading videos around the world.

Cutting-edge storytellers around the world are going multiplatform with their storytelling. The idea is that you have a story that can migrate from any point of origin. It could start at your cell phone when you wake up in the morning. It could evolve towards your PC when you're at work and the story could end at your television late at night. Or it could be the opposite. You could be watching a trailer on YouTube and it goes to your cell phone as you keep going throughout your day; you can complete the experience on television. The entertainment industry will coax stories out of each platform in new ways.

But while this market holds plenty of promise, there are significant challenges ahead. The industry needs to work together to ensure market adoption through standards. Mobile operators play a significant role in making this medium successful, but we need partnerships across the entire value chain to make the pie a lot bigger. Mobile operators should have the same minimum network speeds in order to ensure a consistent viewing experience. Handset manufacturers need standard codecs like 3GPP or MPEG-4 so content providers can focus on one video format. Content programmers have to develop original programming that makes the best use of this new medium.

Interfaces need to improve. When you are at home, you forget how easy it is to watch television. You push your remote or you push the power button and voilà, you have TV. If you're online you go to a URL and voilà, you have YouTube. On a mobile phone we are rapidly transforming this device from a voice-centric device into a data-centric device. It's going from your ear to your eyes, and the interface needs to change in order to make that happen. The current hardware is designed so that you can dial phone numbers. In order to discover content, you have to toggle into a shopping cart or some sort of service site and find the content and it's not as intuitive as what you have with TV and online.

That is changing rapidly. You're seeing landmark developments happening now, including the Apple iPhone and the Prada phone, both of which have touch-screen interfaces. Verizon Wireless was the first to launch live, simulcast TV on cell phones. These new phones have a hard-coded button for one-button TV access.

In addition to interface improvements, the whole architecture of mobile data will be predominantly client-server, facilitated through features such as search and voice recognition. The mobile phone will also be optimized to control other devices, rather than be controlled, like a PC. It will be known for its upload, rather than download, capabilities.

To conclude, I encourage filmmakers to look at mobile not as a derivative of any platform we currently understand, but rather something entirely new. Mobile video seeks its own destiny and identity. It will actively negotiate its seat on the table, alongside television, film, and broadband video. For storytellers seeking a new path of expression, this is the opportunity.

JIM BANKOFF is an experienced and accomplished executive in the consumer Internet business and advises companies big and small on their online media strategies: how to appeal to customers and advertisers alike with innovative and intuitive web services. He left his post in January 2007 as EVP, Programming and Products of AOL, in which he led a global team of content programmers, designers, and web developers that developed web sites and applications for an audience of over 100 million.

Under Jim's leadership, AOL's broadcast of *Live 8* made history as the first nontraditional program to win an Emmy Award. Mr. Bankoff spearheaded product development of the new AOL.com, which launched in July 2005, and has led the development of web sites such as TMZ.com, the number one entertainment news web site, with Warner Bros. Telepictures division. He presided over dozens of world-class consumer web sites ranging from Moviefone to AOL Music to Engadget. Mr. Bankoff also oversaw AOL's industry-leading instant messaging services, AIM and ICQ, and new social networking and community applications, including Netscape.com.

Over the years, Jim has served as President of AOL Web Properties, responsible for Netscape, CompuServe, Moviefone, MapQuest, ICQ, and AOL instant messenger services, and where he coordinated the integration of online properties across Time Warner.

In addition, Mr. Bankoff serves on the board of Network for Good. He received a master of business administration degree from The Wharton School at the University of Pennsylvania and a bachelor of arts from Emory University.

Conversation with Jim Bankoff

SB: I'd like to begin by talking about the whole aspect of indie film-making and online content. What advice do you have for filmmakers to best utilize the Internet environment, what tools should they have, and how can they take advantage of what's available to them?

JB: Taking it from the top, the technology has changed and a lot of what we focus on is how technology has changed the creation process and the cost coming down in terms of production cost. Hopefully that lowers the barriers to aspiring filmmakers. So with production coming down the next question is, "What's distribution?" And just as technology is transforming production, technology is also changing distribution, and of course technology is changing consumption as well. Where we go to see movies, how we see movies, how those movies get into people's hands or in their eyes is really something else that I think people focus less on.

We know it intuitively, so we all know about YouTube and the other sites. But something I think people don't stress enough is how you build a following and an audience for yourself. It's one thing to put in on the Internet. It's another thing to get people to understand more about you and to keep people coming back so you can build an audience. I always encourage people to think beyond the film as well. Think of yourself as your own distributor and your own marketer. So if you were a big movie studio, you would have a department for production and a department for marketing. As an independent filmmaker you're a one-person studio so you have to really think through all those functions. In the one woman/one man marketing department there are a number of tools at your disposal and they're all about forming that relationship and beginning that conversation with your audience.

Think beyond the actual film itself. Think about how you create that conversation. There are tools that you can use. I think we all know what the tools are, we can make a list: you can keep a blog, you can offer up a feed to your content, you can create a dialog with your audience. AOL offers a lot of different tools to do that. One of them, that you want to think of, is your buddy list. Your buddy list is probably on your desktop, and you have all your friends, colleagues, and classmates on there. Not only does the buddy list tell you when your friends are online, but it is also something that you can use to share your content with them. Every time you create a new scene, or even if you have a thought that you haven't introduced yet, and you want people to share in that thought with you, it's a simple mechanism to alert everyone on your buddy list. Those that want to participate can, and those who don't are not bothered by it because it's an unobtrusive thing. That's one mechanism. Another mechanism is keeping a blog and talking about thoughts that go into the process. Get people engaged in the process. If you're casting, use that as an opportunity to market your film and market yourself by talking about the process and soliciting cast members.

SB: For example, if the filmmaker has a rough cut of a trailer, they can get feedback. The point is to get some interaction and get people aligned with you.

JB: Absolutely, that's a great example. My overall point is that we tend to think too much about just the finished product. Obviously that's the goal line, that's the center of the universe, but in order to get attention to your film, in order for the film to get distribution you have to grasp onto every part of the process and use that to your advantage to build an audience. Whether that's the making of the trailer, whether it's casting, whether it's a decision that you're tying to make around a plotline or a script line—involve people in that. Pick and choose and do what's right for your project. The idea is that every single part of the process should be open to engage the audience, and that way you give more people the opportunity to get themselves out there using the various tools at their disposal.

SB: Do you think filmmakers should have a web site for themselves as well as a MySpace page, or should they decide on one path or another?

JB: I'm careful about saying there's one rule that applies to every project. I think the real power comes in understanding what your project is about and making sure that the medium aligns with the message. I think if you do that well you can be very powerful. Having said that, there is something to be said for ubiquity. So you want to be careful to not be overexposed, but I don't think that's the problem with independent filmmakers. I wouldn't obsess too much about having too many entry points. The default should be to create all those places, whether it's a MySpace page, putting your stuff on UnCut or up on YouTube or Yahoo. Use everything at your disposal to get yourself out there as much as possible. If I can create a short film about the subject matter just as a teaser for the ultimate finished product—I can get that out there, every step along the way across all those distribution points that are part of the web. Since you can't do everything, do the things that are going to get the widest possible audience to align with the message that you tell.

SB: Younger filmmakers have difficulty thinking beyond their demographic, even if their audience is not their 18–24 demographic. What are ways to reach out beyond their peer group to their potential audience?

JB: That's an interesting thought. We have an expression, "You don't want to build for the building," or in this case produce for your own demographic. You can temper that with producing what you know. The web obviously can be a great tool to expand beyond your core audience, beyond your circle of friends. I think it's important not only to leverage your extended web friends, but go to web sites, pockets of communities where they align with the subject matter of your film. If there's a theme to your film, or a character in your film that has a particular trait or cares about a certain issue, whether it's dramatic, comedic, or documentary, there's likely going to be a topic in your film that aligns with a community that's already established on the web.

SB: With the Internet, now you have to think globally, so that's also an important thing to remember.

JB: It's all about the communities. You may say, "Mine isn't an issue film, mine is a funny short I put together." Well, I bet even those funny shorts have a theme, or a character that will have some appeal to a targeted community, and you should try to figure out what that is.

SB: A lot of online content is very offensive, and would be, if it were in the movie theater, rated R or NC-17 or X. I'm not saying "don't make it" but I'm saying maybe filmmakers need to think about offensive content or subject matter. What does the future hold for this kind of content?

JB: Well, you know, let me answer your question from a different angle and talk about what I think is driving that. Media is fragmented. It used to be that you had to go watch whatever was in the movie theater, or you had to watch whatever was on your four channels of television, and then your four channels rapidly became 500 channels, your movie theater rapidly became video on demand, and then the Internet just further fragmented it. So now you have literally millions of media options: millions of short films, millions of big films, and television shows to choose from. There's a lot of stuff out there. I think the reason you see the stuff you label as offensive I view as people trying to outshock one another. You saw it in radio, when shock jocks emerged because there are so many options on the radio dial that someone had to stand out, and frankly, that's kind of an easy way to do it. It seems to be bubbling up into the daily zeitgeist. What our friends share with us in our emailboxes or on our MySpace pages is whatever the most shocking thing of the day is. We see that reflected in popular culture, whether it's the *Jackass* movies, whether it's *Punk'd*, whether it's TMZ finding Michael Richards going on a racial tirade. Those things break through because there's so much to choose from that, unfortunately, that's what gets our attention on a day-to-day basis.

That, however, should not be confused with what is lasting and meaningful and substantive culture and creation. It's important to draw the distinction between the two. Ask yourself, "What do you want to be?" Personally, or even speaking for the largest distributor of content, we don't seek to judge one better than the other. I think that's up to the artist to judge. Ask yourself what kind of creator do you want to be? Do you want to be someone who kind of creates that flash for the day, and that's nice because you get a lot of attention, but have you really created something of substance that's going to last or have you just created the flavor of the second on the Internet? If you aspire to do something bigger, change the world, change people's perspectives on things, doing something for the shock value isn't going to be a sustainable thing. That would be my argument from the creator's perspective.

SB: Can you comment on serious filmmakers feeling safer on traditional short film web sites rather than the mainstream sites because their films get lost in all the shock value videos?

JB: I would imagine like with any growth of any medium and with any kind of creative pursuit there is innovative work and there is derivative work, I think what you see now is, frankly, a lot of derivative work, because so many people have been empowered with these tools doesn't necessarily mean that they're all good. The democratization of content creation is great. I'm all for it. I've got a camera and I use it and film my kids, but do other people want to see films of my kids? Probably not. And I think when you open up the creative process to everyone you lower the barriers and you do get some derivative work. You're talking about a younger demographic and they're seeing this, and they think, "OK, how do I do that?" as opposed to thinking, "What can I do that's original?" That takes talent, and not everyone has talent just because they have a camera.

SB: That's also why I like to encourage filmmakers to seek out competitions, particularly on the web, so they can get feedback.

JB: That's another thing when we talk about uses of the web and how to build an audience. I think you have to be fearless about getting peer review and just getting reviews from all corners. And the people

I find who are putting content on the web are the people who put themselves out there and are very vocal themselves, but who also can take what they dish out and embrace it. They want to hear criticism and the feedback because it makes them stronger. Competitions are a way of showcasing that work and getting that feedback.

SB: When I think about sites like TMZ for potential documentary filmmakers, that's a great way to practice. Look and find something. If you want to be a journalistic filmmaker, that's a great opportunity to get your feet wet.

JB: I was one of the people who started TMZ, and that was a lot of our thinking behind it. There's all this low-cost video being produced and I thought about how we could tap into it in a way that's relevant. I would say there are two ways: one, if you find something newsworthy, in terms of an anonymous tip box, they'll take your film as long as it's "real." But, if you really have a talent for this stuff, they'll hire you. You can be a stringer and go out there and have a beat, and it's a new kind of newsroom for the new media in the new century as opposed to a whole formal traditional news-gathering organization. This is quick, it's scrappy, it tends to be younger people because they're a little more fearless and they're not afraid of getting it. So I agree with you, that's a new way. There are a lot of new outlets.

If you're really creative and a marketer and use the tools to distribute the content you can build an audience. And from there, that can be a business in and of itself at some point, but it also is a mechanism for you to be discovered and find people who can finance material and bring you better projects as well.

SB: How do you see the kind of crossover platforms—mobisodes, etc.?

JB: In the United States, as we sit here today for this interview, the Internet is continuing to go like gangbusters, and mobile as well, though mobile from a much lower base, and the infrastructure reminds me of 10–12 years ago, when I was first getting involved in the online industry. Everyone was on dial-up, so while you knew you could do all this cool video stuff, and a lot companies were being formed in the first bubble to put videos on the Internet, there were some fundamentals that were missing. First of all, no one had the bandwidth. No one had broadband connections, so people couldn't enjoy that content.

Here we are, 10 years later, and this time it's for real because most of us have broadband connections and can enjoy the content. And by the way, there's a business model there too. We can sell advertising against it and charge for it, so there's a way for people to make money and a way for people to view the content. Mobile will get there too. Mobile as we speak right now, in terms of streaming content, is not as penetrative, but as networks expand in the U.S., and as devices become more video enabled, it's going to happen. It's a matter of time, so I think people who can create content and start to experiment with this new medium should make sure the content is right for that medium. Not all content is meant to be enjoyed on a two-inch screen six inches from your face, but a lot of it is, and it's probably better for that environment—short, crisp, interesting things. I would say people who can get out in front of it without being too far ahead of the curve but can figure out what works best in that environment will be really well-positioned for the years where mobile video is as ubiquitous as online video is today.

SB: Does this expand any potential for revenue for the filmmaker or is it just potential expanded exposure?

JB: The answer ultimately is yes, of course; however, immediately that may not be the case. Like anything else, there has to be some critical mass before that's going to happen. Ultimately, people are going to pay for good content. And they'll either pay for it by licensing it, selling advertising, sponsoring, or by buying it if they're a consumer. So I hold a lot of faith that quality content will find a way to make money. The fact that there are so many options now just makes that even more so. Sites, mobile providers, will and are competing for content. The quality creator will be well positioned.

Now anyone can come out of the blue and take off and it's much more penetrable and much more accessible. I used to have to go to Fox or Warner Bros. just to be able to afford to shoot a film or to be able to get it into a movie theater or get onto network television. Well, I don't have to do that anymore. In order to get a lot of promotion for it and in order be able to grow my audience much more rapidly I still would like to align with one of those entities because they will help me get my work in front of an audience, but they are not essential for me to create and be discovered initially. And that's great—that's democratization.

SB: I'd like to talk a little about *Live 8*, since it was such an achievement.

JB: I was the executive producer for *Live 8*. That was definitely a breakthrough moment for online media. It's not as though no one had ever tried something like that, although clearly there had never been a six-city multiple screen show, so that was innovative in and of itself.

What was most important about it was that it was the tipping point. There had been video on the web prior to it (I had produced a lot of it) but you knew at that moment, for the first time, it crept into the mainstream consciousness that hey, this is an alternative method to consume video. I knew going back to my hotel room, logging on, and seeing the experience, the blogs, and what the people who were viewing it were saying. It had been happening before then but that was definitely the moment that we flipped the switch from interesting novelty to mass market media. From there, it just skyrocketed. From there, YouTube came on strong, from there everyone was showing concerts, every network was putting their shows, nightly news broadcasts, and every single music video on the Internet for free. That just opened up the floodgates and that's why it was such an important event from a media perspective.

From a human perspective, it also did a lot of good in raising awareness of the plight in Africa; it actually was a political event that encouraged the G8 to give money. So it had a lot of important and lasting ramifications, but from a media perspective, it really was that tipping point that took what was an early phenomenon of watching video on a device that wasn't a television and moved it into the mainstream.

SB: I read about so many millions of downloads in a specific period of time after the concert, so that longevity, that extension of time for the event, changed things as well.

JF: You bring up an important point—time shifting, and video on demand, and music is an interesting one because a music concert is a piece of content that once the performer puts down the microphone it vanishes into the air. We're in New York City right now—how many clubs are there tonight where there are going to be performances, where there are so many talented people creating content and creating special moments? There's only been one window historically for that special moment—sitting in that club and listening. Once the lights went on, it was all over. Well, now all that can be captured and archived. What you saw with *Live* 8 was that for every one person streaming the content during the event, there were 20 who viewed it in the next two months. That's not just the case with *Live* 8 but with performances in general, the ability for the consumer to view the content when he or she wants, on demand, and shift the time. You see it happening all over the place. Consumers are getting control, with their TiVos, with their iPods, and with their broadband connections. It's a wonderful time not only to be a creator with all those low-cost production mechanisms, but to be a consumer. You should think about that when you create. Think about the fact that consumers have this control and you should cater to it.

SB: Do you think that people have to really think when they create content that they are creating for a specific medium? Should they think about that?

JB: Certain things are universal, whether it's a computer screen or a television, and those are things that engage you. Is there a story? Is there an emotional attachment? Are there characters that one can identify with emotionally or otherwise? Those are universal themes of storytelling or human emotions, things like that don't change because of the device you're creating for. Having said that, this medium provides what I'll say is a more expansive palette for storytelling. It provides interactivity, it provides community building, so yes, you can think definitely about it. You can think, "All right, how do I engage the community, how do I get people talking about this, how do I provide the mechanism to do that, how do I perhaps be more provocative and encourage conversation and how does my work take on a life of its own? It's more than just what I film, it's about a whole community that can emerge from what I film." Therefore, you have more tools in your kit in order to tell your story and create something larger. I think people should think about it from that perspective.

There's never been a more exciting time to be a content creator. There's never been a more exciting time to be a consumer. Go forth, create, think about the new tools that you have at your disposal, and be your own person. Be your own storyteller, don't try to rip something off, that never really works in a lasting way. If something isn't working you can change it. You can take the feedback and you can work and keep on going until you get it right.

JON GRIGGS is what you'd call an Englishman in New York. Chased out of school by his headmaster; several years spent in the service of Her Majesty and a couple more spent flying choppers to offshore rigs. And then, finally, to America and a rekindling of a lost desire — film — and a gravitation toward storytelling through the art of directing, writing, and editing.

Airspeed, a documentary on the U.S. national skydiving team that aired on national cable, was his first work. His other credits include the feature films *Choking Man* (editor), directed by Steve Barron; *I'll Believe You* (editor), directed by Paul Sullivan; and *The Skeptic* (associate producer/post-supervisor), directed by Tennyson Bardwell. Short film credits for editing include *Apple's Cherry* (SXSW 2006), directed by Jesse Scolaro, and *Missionary Impossible,* directed by Glen Brackenridge and Curtis Brien.

He feels a degree of responsibility for the corruption of children's minds through his editing work at Nickelodeon, and he is also known for his propensity to argue politics and religion (especially after a beer or two)—something that seems to be much frowned upon in polite society.

Deviation marks his first narrative film as writer/director.

Brave New Virtual World

By Jon Griggs

Endless. Limitless. The possibilities are.

The means by which to have a voice heard, to tell a story to the world, have never been greater or more accessible. As short filmmakers, we are riding the wave of new media convergence, new narrative paradigms, and a multitude of new distribution models.

Peachy, huh? "Hurrah for us!" I hear you cry. Well, yes, it IS a phenomenal time to be a short filmmaker, but above the glorious silver lining lurks a soggy cloud that is well worth being aware of. Just so you can make sure you put on your overcoat and galoshes when you go out. And in case you are starting to worry that somehow this book has mysteriously morphed into a "How-to Guide for Wannabe Meteorologists," let me hasten to introduce myself.

I am not a weatherman. A filmmaker from New York City, an ex-pat Brit and part-time geek with most of my work entailing freelancing as an editor for clients such as MTV, Nickelodeon, and a plethora of indie feature films and documentaries. And, occasionally, I cease my procrastinations and write and direct my own work. *Deviation,* the story of an online-game character's attempt to break out of the cycle of futile violence that has been his sole existence, premiered at the 2006 Tribeca Film Festival as part of the Tropfest@Tribeca competition, picked up two awards at the Academy of Machinima Arts & Sciences' Machinima Festival, and played at the Clermont-Ferrand Short Film Festival. It is the first Machinima film ever to play in competition at a major film festival. And through the process of creating and distributing *Deviation* I got to discover what that drab cloud I alluded to earlier was made of.

"Now, hold on!" I hear you cry, "What the hell is Machinima?" and, "Why does he keep banging on about this weird cloud—isn't this book supposed to be a guide to swimming upstream?! One elemental analogy is enough, surely?"

Ahh, but it's all liquid, my friend. It's all liquid. I beg your patience and assure you that all will be revealed in due course.

Allow me to take you back to January 2006, to Fiddlesticks, an Irish pub in Greenwich Village, New York City. A birthday bash and a mix of friends, one being the marvelous collator, curator, and instigator of this splendid book you hold in your hands, Sharon Badal. Liquor content up, defenses down, the lovely Ms. Badal suggested that I make and enter a short film into the inaugural United States chapter of Tropfest, Aussie John Polson's brainchild (not the one eaten by dingoes), which was to be a part of the 2006 Tribeca Film Festival. I already had a feature film in Tribeca, writer/director Steve Barron's gem, *Choking Man*, which I had coedited and was currently post-supervising, and I felt I had more than enough on my plate.

But as a New Yorker, I am unabashed in saying that Tribeca holds a place dear in my heart, not only because I worked the first festival but because of what the festival has meant to the spiritual and practical recovery of the downtown area in the aftermath of September 11, 2001. The Tribeca Film Festival embodies the indomitable spirit of New York City. And also, when Sharon Badal *suggests* something, that's a bit like having Don Vito Corleone asking if you are free for a spot of high tea on Sunday afternoon. You go. And you take extra cucumber sandwiches.

After feverishly rubbing my two brain cells together I came up with several ideas, most of which were "pooh-poohed" outside a smelly downtown coffee shop by La Badal. But one caught a spark. The idea, to use an online computer game to tell the story of one man's questioning of the status quo—a short, darkly comedic, subtle political statement about choice and the need for individual questioning. The virtual world of the game environment and characters would not only be the setting for the story, it would also serve as a central conceit, and act as the studio sound stage on which to create the film. Inexpensive and novel, a brave new virtual world of filmmaking.

Repurposing other media and mediums to make films has always been on the fringes of the filmmaking mainstream and in that grand tradition, the convergence of filmmaking, animation, and game development over the past couple of decades has led to the creation of a new creative medium: Machinima (muh-sheen-eh-mah). (Told you we'd get there.) Only in the last few years, though, have the techniques

205

and software and hardware platforms become sophisticated and, at the same time, simple enough to allow the average filmmaker to access them as filmmaking tools.

But here comes the cloud. Repurposing other media to create a new medium opens up two Pandora's boxes (she actually had a whole collection, not just the one you usually hear about); the first is Intellectual Property and the second is Commercialization. And what I mean by these two things is, who owns the rights to a film that has been created by the repurposing of another medium? And, who can legally recoup the financial benefit of distributing said film? The former point is particular to Machinima films, but the latter point is relevant to ALL short filmmakers, no matter how they created their films. Consider this—YouTube.com sold for 1.65 BILLION dollars and other media corporations have been shelling out big bucks to grab a stake in the emerging world of online short format distribution and the advertising revenue that it generates. Massive change is occurring right now in the world of new media and with that change comes great opportunity, but also a great desire by the established media entities to control that change.

And so, there I was, happily sailing along with the success of *Deviation*, not realizing that the storm cloud of Intellectual Property and Commercialization was steadily building on the horizon. . . .

I created *Deviation* using the popular multiplayer online game Counter-Strike, a first-person shooter (which I had been playing for years). I took a minimalist Machinima approach to creating the film— that is, I used the visual elements of the game without too much recoding or manipulation to create the scenes. I don't want to slog into too much technical detail, but here is what I did, as concisely as I can put it.

Online multiplayer games are conducted through a host server that coordinates the data transfer so that each game player logged onto that server gets to see the actions of the other players. Think of it like this—imagine a simple room with one door and two characters standing in the room, a muscle-bound Barbarian wearing little but a soiled loincloth and a rather petite Fairy, wearing nothing but flowers and sporting a fine set of iridescent wings. The Barbarian character is being controlled by a kid sitting at his computer in Los Angeles and the Fairy character is being controlled by a mother of six sitting at her computer in New York City. Using his keyboard, the LA kid moves the Barbarian across the room and towards the door. The game server extrapolates this changing positional information and sends data to each of the players' computers so that what they each see on their respective computer monitors correlates to what is happening in real time. The mother of six "sees" from her character's first-person perspective the Barbarian walk across the room to the door; the LA kid "sees" the first-person perspective of his character approaching the door, except that he doesn't quite get there. The mother of six's Fairy character pulls out an AK-47 assault rifle and fires a burst at the Barbarian as he reaches the door. The server extrapolates the action of both characters, including the physics of the bullet trajectories in the virtual time and space and relays this data to the computer of the kid, who is somewhat surprised to find his Barbarian is now resting in a pool of blood on the floor of the room. He got "pwned." So where does the filmmaking come in?

Well, imagine that a third character, controlled by a filmmaker, was also in that room, tucked in a corner. The server would be relaying the data to the filmmaker's computer so he would also see the action that happens, from his character's first-person perspective. Using a screen-capturing program or even a conventional camera shooting the monitor, the filmmaker could record the action from his perspective. If the action was repeated, he could also capture the scene from a different angle, by moving his own character to another part of the room.

This is essentially what I did—I had four players scattered across the United States who were logged onto the same game server as me. We were talking to each other using headsets and a third-party voice communication application so that I could direct the action and setup of the shots. One of the complexities of the shoot was that instead of having a character in the virtual space, I was in control of a "virtual camera," which meant I could position my viewpoint anywhere in the environment that I wanted to record the action from. This was hugely flexible from a filmmaking perspective but it meant that I had to be very precise with my direction since it becomes somewhat tricky to block a scene when the director is just a disembodied voice! The four players delivered the lines to script for timing purposes and to allow me to match facial animations to dialog. We blocked each scene and rehearsed and did multiple takes of multiple angles—just like a regular film shoot. I captured it all direct from the computer monitor with a Panasonic DVX100 shooting at 24p with some of the settings tweaked to eliminate artifacting from the screen.

Prior to putting all of this in motion though, and being a responsible kind of chap and having a good understanding about licensing requirements for film, I made strenuous efforts to contact Valve Corporation, the company that developed Counter-Strike, to ask their permission, to make sure I credited the right departments and to get their support.

Not one of my emails or phone calls was returned. Hmmmm, curious, I thought. But nonetheless, I forged on, figuring I would hear from Valve in due course, and recruited the cast to play the physical roles of the characters from the online gaming community. After several weeks of planning and script writing, we shot the scenes in one day in my home office.

The next few weeks were spent editing, voicing the parts with professional actors, and recording the sound design and score. Several sweaty-palmed weeks later, after I submitted *Deviation* to the festival submissions department, I received a phone call and to my great delight, the film had been accepted into the Tropfest@Tribeca competition. I called and emailed Valve with the news that I was in a major festival and that I really needed to hear from them. I received a reply within the hour. (I guess "Tribeca" translates in computer code into "open sesame.") And, joy of joys, Valve was cool with the film going to the festival. (Let's face it—it was going to be free marketing and PR for the game and the company.) All was right with the world!

Deviation screened in front of an audience of 4000+. And just as exciting, John Polson, the creator of Tropfest, asked to use a couple of shots from *Deviation* in a new feature he was directing entitled *Tenderness*, starring Russell Crowe.

Again, I contacted Valve to make sure they were OK with this and the blessing was given. But the first strands of a knot were growing in my stomach—I kept asking for a formal agreement letter to be signed between us, but nothing was forthcoming. After the festival I wanted to keep the buzz going and posted the film on my own web site and by using some discrete viral marketing techniques, I received over 250,000 viewings in 5 days. I was blowing through bandwidth charges like Imelda Marcos in an Italian shoe shop.

The publicity caught the eye of AtomFilms, who offered to distribute *Deviation* on Atomfilms.com. Now, I can't say enough good things about AtomFilms—the business model they have for the distribution of existing films and for the development of new ones should be the standard. Short films, individually, rarely generate huge amounts of revenue. We all know that and that's not why we make them, but having your film distributed by a company that gives you a share of the advertising revenue and that has a vested interest in supporting and nurturing short format films and filmmakers gets my vote, any day of the week.

So here I am, a distribution deal in hand, a good relationship with the game company, I am sitting pretty, right? More free marketing for Valve Corporation when *Deviation* goes online, AtomFilms's advertisers get eyeballs on product messages, and I get valuable exposure as a filmmaker and perhaps some small revenue returns to help offset the costs of the production. Alas, were that so.

At the mention of the AtomFilms, Valve became very avian-like. Avian of the flightless variety. Ostrich, in fact. With head buried in the sand. There was hesitation on the other end of the line and a vague statement about not wanting to commercialize Valve's intellectual property. Curiouser and curiouser. Valve did offer to distribute *Deviation* on its own online platform, but of course it would be, in their words, for noncommercial purposes. Taking my lead from MacIntyre, the questioning central character of *Deviation*, I felt it only right to point out that the Valve platform also served as an online store for the purchase of computer games (millions of dollars worth) and that hosting my film would benefit their sales and marketing. The Valve business would benefit commercially, the viewers and users of the Valve site would benefit experientially, and I, as the filmmaker, would in essence be paying for Valve to benefit from my hard work. Not particularly fair.

This point didn't seem to go down too well with the Valve representative I was talking to.

And herein lies my fundamental point about new media; when a short film is released online, someone somewhere is making money off that, be it advertising revenue, network charges, or subscriptions. Case in point—at the 2006 Academy of Machinima Arts & Sciences' Machinima Festival the film that won the award for best writing was *Male Restroom Etiquette*, a witty and beautifully gross short created by Phil Rice. The film was released on YouTube and at the time of writing it has received over 3,400,000 views. The founders of YouTube, Chad Hurley and Steve Chen, would like to thank Phil for his kind donation, but unfortunately they are somewhat busy quaffing cocktails and sunbathing on a small South Pacific island. Which they own.

It is my contention that as short filmmakers it is our responsibility to voice our opinions and to put a value on our creativity, because if we don't, no one else will, to make sure that some of that revenue flows back to sustain the creation of more innovative, intelligent, witty, and insightful films.

OK, back to the story at hand. From this point on and despite many calls and emails to the Valve offices in an attempt to figure out a solution, I heard nothing, Valve went into stonewall mode. What the hell was I going to do? I had an acquisition agreement sitting on my desk from AtomFilms, but there was no way I could sign it as the Atom lawyers would have just thrown it out when they found out the games company were not on board.

"Publish and be damned!" I hear you cry. And I would have loved to be able to do that, but unfortunately, this is where things get a little bit hairy. Valve was acting as if they and they alone had rights over my film. I think they were mistaken—it was my script, my actors, my music, my characters, my sound design—in fact the only aspects of the game that I used were the game engine, the environment, and the physical form of the characters within that environment. In film terms, this would amount to the set and the wardrobe for the actors.

I wanted to fight. I wasn't going to lie down and let this corporation tell me what I could do and couldn't do with my film. It was time to get me some lawyer muscle.

Step forward the Electronic Frontier Foundation (EFF) and the resolute Fred von Lohmann, Senior Staff Attorney. One of the country's leading advocacy groups, I learned about the EFF whilst editing a documentary about computer hackers. I naturally turned to them for help. Fred was a wealth of information and a great support (and still is). We tried all sorts of approaches and overtures but at the end of the day even Fred was being ignored by Valve Corporation—I guess they REALLY didn't want to speak with any lawyer that wasn't one of their own! It came down to this: even if AtomFilms were prepared to distribute *Deviation* without Valve being onboard, or if I had distributed it any other way, then I was at risk of being sued, to the tune of six figures. Yes, that's right … six. You see, Valve has a line in all their EULAs (End User License Agreement)—those pesky things you NEVER read but always click on when you install software—and that EULA stated that in the case of legal action, the losing party would be liable for Valve's legal costs. All of them. Ouch!

So, here I was caught between hell and high water. I couldn't just walk away from my film, so I came up with a last-ditch plan. I was going to take it to the people. If Valve wouldn't give me permission, then I would reedit the film to remove what they considered their intellectual property. I created a "protest video" stripping away the picture, leaving my sound design, score, dialog, and story, and replacing the picture with simple titles that documented my struggle with Valve. One of the final title cards listed the emails of the key people at Valve Corporation and called upon the viewer to write in and voice his or her opinion. The plan was to do a viral release, with simultaneous postings to multiple video-hosting sites worldwide. I started to leak out information as to what was happening, getting ready for a massive release, and through my contacts in the Machinima world, word apparently got to Valve as to what was going down. After months of being nonresponsive to phone calls and emails from either myself or Fred von Lohmann, I suddenly received an email from Valve saying that they would like to "chat" with me!

I stepped away from launch pad. T minus 4 hours and holding.

OK—I thought, this is going to go one of two ways. It's either that we were finally going to be able to figure something out, to everyone's benefit, or Valve was going to pat me on the head and try to stall me from releasing my protest video. I was hopeful of the former.

The conversation went something like this:

They told me that Valve was a big corporation and I was not. That they would not give me permission and that they were sorry but there was nothing they could do. And that more importantly, there was nothing I could do.

OK—so they didn't say that exactly, but that's pretty much how I heard it. And so I told them about my cunning plan—I told them I was sorry to hear that they wouldn't give me permission and that I was being left no alternative. I said I wasn't being allowed to tell my story and that, as a filmmaker, I had been backed into a corner. I informed them that I had created another video documenting my struggle to get *Deviation* released and that I intended to release it shortly.

There was a deafening silence from the other end of the phone line, apart from what I swear was a muffled choking sound. Then finally they asked to be given until the end of the week, to see what they could do.

I got my permission. *Deviation* is currently playing on AtomFilms. Word.

Sadly, despite this success, the cloud has still doggedly refused to go where clouds should go when their time is up. The issue is still ongoing. I recently returned from the Clermont-Ferrand Short Film Festival in France and now have offers from a French public television channel for national broadcast and from a Canadian distribution company that wants to distribute *Deviation* internationally. I am brainstorming ideas of how to make this happen—do I go for the publish-and-be-damned approach? (Fred von Lohmann and the EFF are advising me that this is a very treacherous path.) Do I make a new film to try and get around the legal aspects, perhaps a documentary of my experience with *Deviation* playing as part of the larger piece? Do I play the protest video card again? Or do I fly out to the West Coast to Valve and turn up on the doorstep, hoping to talk some sense into them?

I honestly do not know which way to go right now. But at the time of writing I have already placed a couple of calls to Valve to explore the options. Both have been ignored. . . .

In the world of short filmmaking, no one can hear you scream . . .

. . . which is most definitely a very good thing, since the sound of a frustrated filmmaker slamming his or her head off the nearest, hardest surface, whilst emitting the piercing shrieks of a castrated banshee, is a sound that only the mad should be privy to. So, in summary, what to tell the filmmaker bravely crawling his or her way up the Class V rapids? Hang tough. Persevere. Value your work, so others will do likewise. Be aware of the issues of rights and do your utmost to resolve them before you spend valuable time, energy, and assets in production. It's a brave new virtual world out there. Go forth and multiply.

BAHMAN NARAGHI is head of Red Envelope Entertainment, the newly established original content division of Netflix, Inc., and overseen by Chief Content Officer Ted Sarandos. Mr. Naraghi is responsible for leading the acquisition and funding of dozens of original titles each year for the Beverly Hills-based division, focusing on independent films, foreign-language projects, and documentaries.

Mr. Naraghi segues to Netflix from Intermedia, where he served as Chief Operating Officer since 2002. Previously, he was Corporate Executive Vice President of Finance and Operations at Miramax Films. This followed five years with Universal Studios where, after coheading the newly created Strategic Planning and Corporate Development unit, he was appointed Chief Financial Officer of Universal Pictures. Mr. Naraghi was subsequently promoted to Executive Vice President in charge of integrating all of Polygram's film operations into Universal and supervising all aspects of operations, finance, and general management for Universal Pictures International.

After receiving his MBA equivalent from the École des Hautes Études Commerciales in Paris and a baccalaureate degree from the Lycée Henri IV, Mr. Naraghi began his career in entertainment in 1990, appointed by the French bank Crédit Lyonnais as its representative at MGM during a period when the studio faced serious financial difficulties. He supervised the rebuilding of the studio, including the hiring of a new management team led by Frank Mancuso; the sale of some of the company's noncore assets; and the buildup of its new business plan, readying it again for sale in late 1995.

Conversation with Bahman Naraghi

SB: Can you discuss the original content initiative and what it means in terms of opportunities for the independent filmmaker?

BN: Let me give you the genesis of why Netflix got into the original content initiative in the first place. Netflix has been in existence since 1999 and has been growing exponentially. We have 6 million subscribers, over 70,000 titles that we offer for distribution on our site, and we expect to reach up to 10 million subscribers, hopefully, by 2008 and 20 million, hopefully, by 2010. Its sheer existence and model has revolutionized and brought a breath of really fresh air into the distribution of film content. What I mean by that is that I think Netflix has the capability through the recommendation system (the volume of rating data that the company has in its system) of over 1.6 billion ratings in our possession. It allows a very pointed, very specific recommendation system and a very sophisticated algorithm to recommend titles to people and thereby really expand the reach of a whole bunch of films with new or library titles that people would not have a chance of seeing or know about.

SB: Do you think it reinvigorates the traditional distribution platform?

BN: Absolutely. And to the testament of the service, we're doing 70% of our business by and large on what we call catalog titles, which are titles over 12 weeks old, and only 30% of our business on new releases, which is effectively the exact diametrical opposite of the traditional rental model. Every month over 95% of our 70,000 titles get rented at least once.

SB: That is a particularly huge number because that is indicative of the power of word-of-mouth.

BN: It is indicative of the capability of the system to really dig deep into the product offering and be able to offer to each subscriber a select group of titles that are best adapted to their taste and what they've seen before, and rated before, and all of that directed of course at expanding the reach of these films, but also maintaining and even increasing the satisfaction of our customers with the quality of the service.

It's the cornerstone of what we need to do, and that's what brings me to the content initiative. The first goal of the company, connecting people to movies they love, is to maintain and perpetuate a high level of customer satisfaction because that's our reason for being and that's our chance for success. Our customers don't pay every time they rent, they pay a monthly fee as opposed to paying per view. As a consequence it's very important to us to maintain a level of satisfaction of service for the customer so they accept this idea of continuously paying every month for a service, which they may use sometimes more and sometimes less depending on their viewing habits.

The original content idea came up about two years ago in the company under the leadership of Ted Sarandos (who is the Chief Content Officer and is basically running all the content and acquisition activity of the company). We started getting into the idea of offering certain types of films, of buying outright, and offering them to the subscribers, not necessarily on an exclusive basis, because we thought that those films have the particular elements that would be uniquely pleasing to a certain group of subscribers that we have. At the time, the company was obviously smaller and its subscriber core was much more of a "film buff" audience, and, interestingly enough, even though the company has been growing pretty substantially in the past several years, we still are noticing that those categories of films that were identified a couple of years ago are still the films that continue to outperform on the service vs any other platform. These are by and large original independent films that have a unique voice, documentaries that have a social content or a political content, and foreign-language films. These are the three categories that really can outperform on our service.

SB: Those are the types of films that really have the toughest path in the traditional distribution arena.

BN: These are the films for which we really have the tools to identify immediately a core audience to recommend these films to. Very often we are the only place where that core audience can really find those films. Our shelf space is unlimited. We don't have the physical limitations of traditional retail and we have control of data on our subscribers that really allows us to pinpoint every time a group of subscribers that we know will be extremely pleased to see any given film.

There's also an economic reality to all this. We do not receive payment on a per-view basis, but on the other hand when we acquire titles for distribution we either buy a certain volume of DVDs outright at wholesale prices, and we own them outright and put them out for rent, or we do revenue sharing models whereby we pay the licensor a certain amount every time the title gets rented. Both of these models are kind of unrelated to the monthly fee revenue system that we have, so there's a dichotomy between our cost structure and our revenue structure.

The company has been very shrewd at actually managing that in a very scientific and analytical way to make sure we don't buy too many units on a given title and we always measure the volume that we put through the system with what we expect to be the demand for that title. On the revenue-sharing side, which is where we pay every time a title is viewed, there are those type of titles that have a tendency to outperform, and we observe that sometimes it is much more beneficial to us to acquire that given film outright, lay the money out up front, acquire the film over multiple distribution system models, be able to advertise an acquisition price by selling the TV license, sublicensing traditional DVD distribution, etc., and retain domestic rights for that amount. That could be a fraction of what we would pay if we were just inheriting that title for traditional distribution.

That was the premise behind the original content. So for the titles that outperform, we're much better off acquiring them. We would then have the flexibility of releasing these titles however we choose. It's the best way to cross promote the titles across multiple platforms and not be tied to windowing restrictions that third-party distributors may impose on us.

SB: How are you going to find these projects?

BN: The third leg of that whole issue is the ability to build a library and feed our nascent electronic distribution model with topical titles, where we would not have any right restrictions and could freely put on the electronic distribution system without having to go though pay-TV licenses and restrictions imposed by third-party licenses. The way we're finding these titles is that I came here nine months ago to restructure the group and get it into real shape with a certain amount of capital that the company made available to us. We have an acquisition team, whereby we canvass the market on a regular basis. Our head of acquisitions and distribution, Liesl Copland, comes from Cinetic, which kind of gives you an idea of the profile I'm seeking for this group. Liesl not only understands distribution and ancillary markets, but also has a unique and very high-quality relationship with filmmakers of strength. Therefore, she can direct product to us at a much earlier stage than if we had to wait for festivals. Our acquisition model is still fairly traditional. We have received a lot of submissions ever since this initiative was publicized and started, I would say 100 submissions a month. We obviously also cover film festivals—all of the major festivals and some of the minor ones, like South by Southwest, and I'm interested in covering Miami because I want to give a voice to really quality Latin films and expand our reach to the Latin audience. We look for original content with a very unique voice that really contributes something to the viewers.

SB: Will you own that original content?

BN: Yes, we will buy the distribution rights outright for an extended period, an average of 15 years. We also do some production but in a very limited way. When I started this job I thought I would be doing more production because I wasn't sure how much free product there was in the marketplace that would match the need that we have. Frankly, having been here nine months, and having covered big festivals pretty substantially, I very rapidly came to the conclusion that we really do not need to get into the production business in any meaningful extent. Coming from a studio background I know the pitfalls of production and frankly, if I can avoid taking too much production exposure, I'm much better off because there is so much product available out there.

SB: Filmmakers are hungry, and the number of features being made because of the ease of technology has been overwhelming.

BN: That's what we observed. There is a lot of quality product out there. Sundance this year was absolutely crazy, first of all because of the prices that the people were willing to pay for a lot of films, but also because of the depth of quality of a lot of the product that's out there, whether it's documentary, narrative, or foreign language. I was impressed by the diversity and the originality of the product, and that's a testament to the programmers. A lot of people are complaining that there was no "big hit." Yes, there was no *Little Miss Sunshine*, that's true, but for one *Little Miss Sunshine* I thought there were 20 or 30 films that did not have distribution when they reached the festival and all got picked up and are really good films.

SB: That's hopeful. Companies like Netflix seem a hopeful alternative to the sometimes antiquated theatrical distribution environment.

BN: Absolutely. Frankly, the efficiency that we provide is in distribution, the flexibility that we have in expanding the reach of the product in whatever means possible, and the cross-promotional effort that we put into Red Envelope, where we are not scared of premiering on television before we put the movie out on Netflix. Theatrical is kind of like a necessary evil. It's the least efficient form of distribution in my view, but it's a necessary passage for a lot of the films to create a certain level of credibility and awareness. I'm hopeful that in time we can come up with alternative models that will show the filmmakers and the audience that there are other ways to recognize a film's quality and to make the audience aware of certain films.

SB: The current generation is very open to receiving information and entertainment in ways that prior generations were not. It was so gratifying to me to see so many independent films and short film collections available on Netflix because there is an outlet, not just for people who live in New York or San Francisco or Boston to have access to these kinds of films.

BN: You would be amazed how many of these "quirky" films we actually put in the system in some of the most removed areas of the country. Do you know how happy it makes me that people in Kansas City are renting *An Inconvenient Truth?*

SB: What can you say to that first-time filmmaker who is getting battered against the wall with people saying nothing is ever going to happen with his/her film?

BN: I would say, if in your inner core as a filmmaker you feel that you have something really unique and original to say, go ahead and make your film. With the explosion of distribution channels, and we're just one of them, you will have ways (if you have that original voice and the capability to translate that original voice into compelling images) to find distribution.

We're not in the model of theatrical and television and traditional DVD and Wal-Mart anymore. We're in the universe where you have a Netflix, a YouTube, a MySpace, plus all these other services that we don't even know the name of but that hundreds of thousands of people are already using—blogging systems, community services, college tours that can be done now in a much more efficient way. You don't need to spend a quarter of a million dollars. I can go on and on about distribution platforms that are not hip driven or driven by the most common denominator in terms of consumers and can differentiate product based on the subscriber's taste. But the success always relies on the originality and sincerity of the film.

DAVID STRAUS is Chief Executive Officer of Withoutabox, Inc., the market-leading network for independent filmmakers that he cofounded with Joe Neulight in 2000.

Mr. Straus met Mr. Neulight at UCLA and approached him about starting a small side business buying and renting out Avid systems to Hollywood productions in the early days of nonlinear editing. Working as producers, directors, and writers, Mr. Straus and Mr. Neulight made a number of short films that played widely and successfully on the international film festival circuit. Mr. Straus was also a producer on *Amy's Orgasm*, a feature that secured domestic distribution and was voted the audience prize at the Santa Barbara International Film Festival.

In 1999, Mr. Straus began talking with Mr. Neulight about partnering in a new endeavor. Mr. Neulight, who possesses a knack for systems and invention, conceived of the International Film Submission System as a point of entry, and together they spearheaded the idea.

Starting with just a handful of filmmakers, Withoutabox has now grown to nearly 100,000 film rights holders in more than 200 countries, and more than 600 festivals utilize it. Withoutabox has the largest database of independent films and film rights in the world. In the past year, the company has expanded its offerings to include services that enable independent filmmakers to market and self-distribute their films. With the new Audience by Withoutabox, the company has become a player in the growing social networking phenomenon that the Internet enables.

The Power of Distribution, in the Hands of Filmmakers

By David Straus

Remember what it felt like before you made your first film? You probably did what most first-time filmmakers do—you asked for permission. You asked if you could make the film, get financing for your film, et cetera, et cetera. Then one day you realized that the only way to make your film was to just go ahead and make it and to stop asking for permission. At that moment you went from wannabe to director, caterer, grip, and producer. You became a filmmaker.

Once the film is made, however, most filmmakers seem to forget about their power and once again begin to ask permission—this time to market and distribute their films.

Imagine if you kept the power.

Bypassing traditional channels of distribution or working with them differently, filmmakers are controlling their own destiny more and more in a digital age.

We created Withoutabox to help filmmakers break down the walls that prevent independent artists from seeing a return on their work. We're democratizing the process of distribution and empowering individual rights-owners to find their audiences. Withoutabox uses new technology to make it possible for filmmakers to offer their work directly to consumers at every level, from theatrical screenings to television broadcast to a DVD, or online.

Through our company, filmmakers can manage their professional lives with a system that allows them to identify a fan base, anywhere in the world. It will connect them with filmmakers who have a similar base and give them the opportunity to cross-pollinate and market their films to a larger overall audience, much as film festivals have done to date. The opportunity increases as the model is multiplied out to thousands of other independent filmmakers who are doing the same thing—each contributing to one other's fan base while building their own. Through the same system, filmmakers can set up screenings at theaters, museums, coffee houses, or living rooms, wherever their fan base resides, and then sell tickets to the screenings or offer the opportunity to buy the film online or on DVD. It is our goal to empower filmmakers to monetize their wares without asking for permission, without worrying if someone else will allow them to market their films.

Technological and financial barriers to self-distribution have finally fallen, and filmmakers like Lance Weiler (*Head Trauma*), Mike Shiley (*Inside Iraq: The Untold Stories*), Tiffany Shlain (*The Tribe*), Arin Crumley and Susan Buice (*Four Eyed Monsters*), along with many others, are discovering and evolving the art of DIY filmmaking and hybrid distribution.

As a filmmaker, you too can green light and release your own films or simultaneously work through existing channels. If you want to partake in traditional distribution you no longer need to choose between self-distribution or traditional. It is becoming increasingly clear that studios no longer exercise all control over content, and filmmakers can now better determine how to showcase their work. Traditional business models for film are not the only ones available.

New models for profit, marketing, and consumption of media are increasingly driven and aided by better access to information about what audiences want. New sites, like MySpace, Revver, and others, along with DVD on-demand, digital downloads, and cell phones, have brought about an explosion of screening opportunities, and there is greater access to information on independent film than ever before. As these and other social networking sites have found, audiences enjoy getting involved in the process and being asked to participate. Withoutabox adds to this dynamic, by enabling filmmakers to access even more information and feedback from their audiences, while the audiences can connect with other fans and discover films they would never have known about if limited to traditional distribution channels.

The next era of distribution is about you as a indie filmmaker finding a way to harness the power of all the thousands of sites like MySpace, YouTube, Revver of the world and to find those ways that you can use those sights to be able to build demand and book your own theaters or sell DVDs and downloads, all to your own benefit.

Films with budgets from $10 to $10 million are now in a greater position of power than ever before. And with the arrival of digital film distribution, independents and emerging talent are now able to access major opportunities for profit. Advertising and product placement dollars are moving to the web, and opportunities for corporate sponsorship have proliferated for online media like film.

If you are not sure how to begin, or where to start, here are some easy steps you can begin to do the moment you've decided to make a film:

1. Log onto all the social networking sites you can, including MySpace and Audience by Withoutabox, and begin to build your fan base.
2. Make your blogs personal so that the members of your fan base feel connected to you. Encourage questions, and try to bring people into your process throughout the production.
3. As your film is shot and edited, keep the interaction with your fan base going, and update everyone on all latest developments. Set expectations about when your film will be ready to screen, and possibly let them know about the festivals you are applying to.
4. Enroll your family and friends to sign up on your social networks and be active. New fans that are just getting to know you will learn more about you by the interaction you are having with those friends and family members who also participate on your network.
5. Once the film is complete, look for the festivals that would best suit your film. You can find many if not most of them through the search engines at Withoutabox and you can use your Withoutabox listing to quickly and easily apply to festivals around the world, augmenting your existing fan base.
6. Don't give up on the festival circuit. Getting your film out to festivals is often the best first step in the distribution process. All the films that have been successful at DIY (do-it-yourself) distribution have first been successful on the festival circuit. This does not mean that every film gets into one of the larger festivals—it

means they were all submitted and had screenings at festivals of all shapes and sizes. Remember, every audience member counts because every one person who sees your film and enjoys it can recommend it to someone else, and that's becoming more and more important in an Internet age.

7. If your film gets into a festival, use it as an opportunity to have the fan base you built to help you market your film at the festival. Designate a "street team" where the film is playing and encourage them to all buy tickets, and get others to buy tickets. After your screening encourage the audience to log on to your Audience account at Withoutabox and give you feedback on the film.

8. Once you are done with the festival circuit, you can use the Digital Dashboard on Withoutabox, a product to be launched in 2007 that allows self-distribution and syndication from a single location, with perpetual reporting on where and how the film is being watched. Maybe your film will break out with a company like Amazon, or Google, or one of a hundred other companies seeking films so that they can leverage their technology and allow you to monetize your film. Or perhaps you'll find that you can profit more by offering the film for sale yourself, selling DVDs and downloads with products we offer directly to filmmakers in cooperation with our partners like the ones at Customflix.

9. You will also be able to identify where in the United States you might want to screen your film theatrically, or maybe share a theatrical screening with another filmmaker or several short filmmakers. At Withoutabox, you will be able to presell tickets to such screenings and use those advance ticket sales to book your theatrical venues.

Throughout this entire process it will be up to you to keep in contact with your ever-growing fan base and not to despair if your fan base starts out small. It will surely grow and as you move from your first film to your second, through your career as an indie filmmaker, the fan base you begin to bring together will become those people that help you promote and market your films.

At Withoutabox, we work to build systems that organize and connect various film communities into one network, allowing film creators to manage their lives and plug into the film lovers who wish to discover, buy, and share unique films. By leveraging new technological tools, you can begin to realize profit from your work and create a lucrative career that you design yourself.

Swimming Lesson #7

Navigate the Rapids:
Film Festivals

Film festivals are the most likely first baby step a filmmaker will make out into the universe after completing a short film, and also the most likely place where the film will find its first audience. It is therefore very important not to take this foray lightly. Navigating the film festival circuit takes organization and strategy as well as an understanding of how festivals work.

The first thing to understand is the difference between a "festival" and a "market." In a general sense, festivals showcase films, and there is commonly a competitive element to them, that being awards that are bestowed at the conclusion of the festival, decided upon by a jury comprising industry professionals. Some festivals have noncompetitive categories as well, for those films that don't fit the competitive parameters; some have special student film categories and some have awards for narratives, documentaries, and shorts. Festivals get you exposure.

The phrase "market" refers to a component of the festival that is specifically geared to distributors and film buyers. Some festivals have "libraries" where buyers can go and view work privately. Cannes, Berlin, and AFI/AFM have markets associated with them. Markets are designed to assist the filmmaker in making his or her work available to buyers for potential distribution.

There are thousands of festivals from which to select, and they range from Sundance to Slamdance to Raindance. How do you decide? One way to help you is by categorizing the types of film festivals that exist.

The Big Guns—I use this phrase to refer to the large, prestigious festivals that show both features and shorts. In my opinion these are Berlin, Cannes, Sundance, and Tribeca. For most filmmakers, acceptance into Sundance represents the "brass ring" of independent filmmaking. (I have excluded Toronto from this list because it accepts only Canadian-made shorts.) The Big Guns naturally receive a huge quantity of submissions for a limited number of short film slots, so the competition is fierce.

Major Festivals—These are the other festivals that have a good following and reputation, and there are many of them, including Ft. Lauderdale, IFFM, LAFF, London, Miami, Montreal, Rotterdam, Santa Barbara, San Francisco, Seattle, and Telluride. *Variety* publishes a film festival guide annually that is also available online and is a must-have tool for filmmakers.

Short Film Festivals—Clermont-Ferrand is the granddaddy of all short film festivals, and many international buyers attend this festival. The other major shorts-only film festivals are Aspen, Palm Springs, and Toronto Worldwide. A filmmaker should submit to each of these festivals. Unlike those for feature films, these short film festivals do not have premiere requirements, so the short can "run the circuit" and theoretically play at all of them. They accept many shorts and create numerous programs, so the odds of being accepted are greater.

Regional Film Festivals—These are "small town" types of festivals that attract a local population, and a limited number of distributors might attend them. If you come from one of these regions, or your film's subject might appeal to a geographic area, you might consider these.

Specialty Film Festivals—There are ethnic festivals, gay/lesbian festivals, political festivals, festivals dedicated to animation or Machinima or documentaries or a variety of special subjects. Depending on how your film's subject fits in with their focus, these festivals may represent a viable option for you.

You must critically evaluate your film and decide how you want to approach the festival circuit. That is, which festivals you are going to apply to and in what order, keeping in mind the following considerations:

225

Running Time

While your short film is in the script stage, you should have a strong sense of what the final running time will be. Running time impacts the festival potential. Many people will tell you that the ideal running time for a short film is under 10–12 minutes, and this theory is based on maximum opportunity because at this length, the programmer has the option of considering the film as part of a short program as well as for it to be shown before a feature that "matches" well in subject, tone, etc. However, not all short films need be this length. Longer shorts that run from 12–25 minutes are perfectly acceptable for short program consideration, and with short film festivals, the desire to create a wide variety of offerings means that a program's "recipe" includes both shorter and longer pieces.

Short narratives over 25 minutes are always a challenge to program, especially those filmmakers who push the envelope of "under 40 minutes" and submit something that runs 37–39 minutes long. Understand that a short film program is designed to offer a pupu platter of films to its audience, and for a longer short to have the ability to "anchor" a program, it has to be great. Even if it's great, programmers normally do not create a program in which one piece is the center of attention—it's all about being able to expose new work and to have a good selection of pieces in the program. A long short means that there are fewer "slots" available in that program. I dare say that if you create a 37- to 39-minute short it will be an uphill battle, if not impossible, for film festivals to program it. I'm not saying don't make it, I'm saying that if you do, have realistic expectations about what's going to happen to it in the festival context.

Premiere Requirement

While most festivals have strict premiere requirements for features, in that they may not have been shown prior to that festival, short films have much more freedom since they rarely have to follow that stipulation. You should think about which festival you want to have your first showing at—that would be your short film's "premiere." That decision is partly based on when your film is finished and available to submit. For example, if it's May and you've just finished your film, I don't really think you're going to wait until the following January for Sundance; that would be sitting idle for months, and acceptance into another festival prior to Sundance does not preclude you from being accepted into Sundance.

Be cognizant of not submitting to another festival in the same city as your dream festival. For example, if you want to be in the Tribeca Film Festival, don't show at Harlem, Brooklyn, Coney Island, etc., because your film has already been exposed regionally and thus there is no newness or promotable element for the programmer. If your short is "overscreened" it means that it has played in far too many festivals for it to have much value, especially to the Big Guns. Even though there is no strict premiere requirement, programmers like to tout how many world premieres they have in their program, so be alert to that.

Completion Date

I'm going to make an unusual comparison here to online dating, since I think it works. When someone initially posts their profile and photo on one of these sites, it is flagged as "new" so anyone looking knows that this is a new person. Newness attracts attention. That is part of the appeal of a short film. Programmers are looking for new projects. Your short film has an active lifespan of one to two years after its completion date. Festivals do not normally program films that are older than that, unless it is for a specifically designed or retrospective type program. That's why you need to start planning your festival attack when you are in postproduction or earlier. The workbook chapter at the end of this book will help you to strategize, but you should keep in mind that you don't have "forever" to get your film out into the marketplace, and the longer you wait, the more competition you will face from the newer, recently completed films.

Exhibition Format

With so many different shooting formats today, from mobile to video to HD to film, there is no prejudice. It doesn't matter what you shoot on, but it does matter what you show on. Each festival has specific exhibition formats. In their applications, they will state that if you are accepted, you must supply them with a print or copy of your short in one of their exhibition formats. If, for example, a festival will only show in 35 mm film or HD, you must provide a copy in one of these formats. If you can't do that, don't apply to that festival. Although this book is not about making a short film, a good piece of advice here is to say that when you create your initial budget you should have a line item for festival expenses. These expenses include blow-up or transfer expenses, travel and lodging expenses, and publicity material expenses. It would be a shame to be accepted into a festival and then not to show because you can't afford to make the format they need for exhibition or to go to that festival.

The first phase of festival submissions is "Call for Entries." This is when the festival announces when it will be "open for business" to accept submissions for the next edition of the festival. Many festivals have several tiers of submission deadlines, the first being the early submission deadline. I cannot stress enough that if your film is ready in time, you should make every effort to get the film in under the early submission deadline. Why? First of all, the programmers are fresh and ready to go for the next edition. Most of them have had a good long break from watching shorts and are now excited to begin again. The percentage of submissions received is relatively low compared to the regular deadline. Financially, early deadline submission is usually a less expensive fee, so you save some money as well. Early submissions, similar to early admissions in a college application, tend to set the bar for the year, so the later your film comes in, theoretically the programmers already have selected some film, so the available slots lessen.

Should you decide to wait until the regular or late submission deadline, not only will you pay more, but your film will be part of the avalanche of film. Consequently, by this time the programmers have watched hundreds of shorts, are utilizing screeners to plow through the avalanche, and are bleary eyed and brain weary.

You should not rush maniacally to complete your film for the early deadline. You only get one shot, and the film should be in the best condition possible before you submit it. Festivals do accept works-in-progress, but if you are sending in a total rough cut, devoid of final picture, sound, mix, etc., that is a very tough film to review, since the programmer has no idea how to evaluate what the final project may be and therefore would be unable to render a final decision until the film is in more of a final state. Another mistake filmmakers make is that they submit something nonfinal, then keep calling the festival to "replace" that copy with a newer version. First of all, this swapping out is a problem for the festival because if they have already reviewed your film, you're essentially asking them to do it again, and again, which is literally not possible given the massive quantity of short films they are reviewing. The bottom line is—if your film isn't ready, do not submit it.

The following essays and interviews are by, and with, some of the key programmers in the festival arena. They should help you further strategize how your project fits in and provide a "behind-the-scenes" peek at the men and women behind the curtain.

KATHLEEN MCINNIS is a film festival veteran, independent film publicist and producer, and Loyola Marymount University School of Film and Television's Film Festival Specialist. She recently served as Festival Director for the 11th Slamdance Film Festival in Park City, Utah, January 2005, as well as Director of Programming for the 2005 and 2007 Palm Springs International Short Film Festival.

Long associated with the Seattle International Film Festival, where she held the positions of Lead Film Programmer, Director of Industry Programming, and Director of Publicity/Promotion during her 12-year tenure, Ms. McInnis was also responsible for creating the "Seattle Summit," a vital trade and media-only conference on the global state of independent film, cohosted by Screen International.

In addition, Ms. McInnis cofounded the popular SIFF Fly Filmmaking Challenge in 1996, producing nearly three dozen unique short films with such diverse directors as Adrienne Shelly, Julia Sweeney, Sherman Alexie, and Guinevere Turner.

A respected film journalist early in her career for such publications as *MovieMaker Magazine* and *The Seattle Times* and for KCMU

(KEXP) Radio, Ms. McInnis was also Vice President of Festival and Filmmaker Relations at FilmFestivals.com in 2000.

She has served on juries and panels at Toronto, Sundance, Galway, Seattle, Anchorage, Slamdance, Palm Springs, Miami, and SXSW film festivals. Ms. McInnis has a B.F.A. in acting from the University of Washington.

A Briefing on Shorts

By Kathleen McInnis

I'm lucky enough to on occasion be asked to come speak at a university or be on a festival panel about film festival strategies for filmmakers. Most often, it's for filmmakers of short films. (I learned long ago not to call them short filmmakers lest they be vertically challenged and thus offended. It was at the same time I learned the hard way not all filmmakers of queer cinema are queer themselves, but that seems far less intuitive.) I've been blessed with an extraordinary career, one that led to me being entitled a "film festival specialist" at Loyola Marymount University School of Film and Television, where I'm currently on staff. The job is great—barely five weeks into the New Year and I write this from my third major festival. The job is also great because every spring I'm faced with a few hundred newly emerging filmmakers who all have the same question: What festival should my short play in?

When I was traveling the festival lecture circuit, as it were, I would offer up a three-hour show of sorts, charting out A- and B-list festivals, deconstructing words like "deliverables" and "press kits," mapping links and highways between festivals and goals such as "industry profile," "publicity," "cash awards," and "next project money" or just "desirable location." I always allowed for question time at the end of each talk and inevitably the first hand raised would ask: So what festival should my short play in?

I've been in the festival biz for over 15 years. I've been a lead programmer (Seattle International Film Festival), program director (Palm Springs ShortFest), festival director (Slamdance), and festival producer (Cinerama Festival). I've produced shorts that have played Sundance (twice), Rotterdam, Aspen, Cairo, Slamdance (years before I worked there), Seattle (okay, *while* I worked there), Tribeca, New Zealand, on TV, online, and on the phone. I've covered festivals as a journalist and worked them as a film's world premiere publicist and now am even a film festival specialist at Loyola Marymount University.

And the only thing I know for sure when you ask me what festival your short should play in is, I have absolutely no idea.

But I do have some ideas on how you can figure it out.

Step 1: What's the real question?

Instead of asking me what festival your short should play in, I want to challenge filmmakers to ask the real question: What do I want this short to do for me? Short films get made for dozens of reasons. Some of the more popular ones include: "It's a calling card for a feature" (which only works if you have a feature script in hand, by the way), "I'm satisfying school requirements," "It's all the money we could raise," "I want someone who can hire me to notice my work," and/or "My friend sold his film to Canal + for $20,000 and got a three-picture deal at Fox."

If we make some critical assumptions here, say for example, (1) you've made the very best short you could and told the story you wanted to tell exactly the way you wanted to tell it; (2) you were a responsible filmmaker and cut every extraneous thing out of the film possible, leaving a clean, lean storyline full of your creative risk and vision; and (3) you actually let talented people like cinematographers and editors and especially sound designers do their jobs to help you make the project better than it could be with just you alone; then you have a get out of jail free card and might as well collect your $200 now and move past Go. You get to look at the over 2000 global festivals and make strategic decisions based on what you want the film to do for you. Looking for an agent or manager? You'll choose festivals where they go to scout new talent (not a big list by the way— it's industry-heavy festivals and destination markets like Sundance, Tribeca, Cannes, Clermont-Ferrand, Aspen, Palm Springs, Quebec, Toronto World Wide Shorts, Annecy). Looking for high profile awards and big audiences? Try Seattle, LA, AFI, Hamptons, Sao Paulo, or Tampere. Want to get big prize money? Munich International Festival of Film Schools awarded 5000 euros (currently about $6400) to their winning short. The grandfather of short film festivals, Oberhausen, awards a cash prize of 7500 euros. St. Kilda Film Festival declares their $10,000 prize the largest in the country. Never heard of it? You would have if you lived in Australia, as it's been around for 24 years.

Step 2: But . . .

Yeah, it's really never that easy, is it? Here are some of the top "But—" I hear all time.

"But I never cleared that Nirvana song I cut to."

"But I spent all my money on glossy press kits."

"But I already have it playing on four online sites."

"But it has the guy from Texas Walker Ranger in it. No, not that
guy. The other guy."

"But I shot it on film/on HD/with my mom's video camera."

"But everybody worked for free."

"But I want to wait for Sundance."

Step 3: Go back to the beginning
Let's dispel some myths right at the very beginning.

You do not have to "know someone" to get your film programmed at a festival.

If you made a film that falls into that 1% lightening-in-a-bottle category, it doesn't matter if you know someone or not, your film will be
programmed by every festival that sees it. If, however, you made a film
that falls into the top 5% it's-really-good-but-so-are-the-other-250-films-
it's-competing-with category, you don't need to know a programmer
because you will rise to the top of their viewing list.

But, if you made a film that falls into the 94% it's-good-but category,
you might need to know someone who can get your film past the
prescreeners. That doesn't mean you're on a short list to festival play, it
just means you have a chance to bypass the early filter and make sure
you're seen by the people making decisions. WARNING: This does not
mean you get to start haranguing programmers! Programmers faced
with watching thousands of films cannot, should not, and mostly will
not take filmmakers' calls. If they do end up speaking with someone
on the phone, you run a very real risk of just pissing them off. This
also applies to program coordinators, whom you usually can get to on
the phone, as they get paid to take your call. Remember this, you may
only have one of them but they have 4000 of you. Your best bet is to
get to people who can champion your film to programmers for you.
Let them see your film and decide if they can recommend it.

You do not have to have a famous person in it or a famous person directing the short to get programmed into a festival.

Famous people do not guarantee festival play, especially if they are cast
only because they have some modicum of fame and not because they
are right for the role. Same for famous directors . . . unless of course
they're famous because they're great directors. So, just because you
let K-Fed direct or star in your film it doesn't mean your film will

automatically be programmed. It might mean you need some therapy as a producer but that's another chapter. (In years to come, all of you for whom pop culture references will be fleeting should just look up K-Fed to get my point.)

You do not have to have a film print.
There are still film-centric festivals out there, but as the majority of festivals play some form of digital, you can realize your potential without ever having gone to print. WARNING: Some festivals, however, still only play BetaSP, as that deck is quite a bit cheaper to own (yes, we know your film looks better on DigiBeta; you'll probably have to get over that). To be prepared, have BetaSP, DigiBeta, Minicam, and even a DVD backup version of your film.

You do not, as a rule, have to worry as much about premiere status.
As filmmakers of short films, you're in a unique position regarding premiere status. Yes, some festivals will still like to be able to claim you as "their" filmmaker and so will want to premiere your film. Yes, some programmers will think you don't need their help if they've seen that you have already won a dozen awards and played hundreds of festivals. However, most programmers at most of the big festivals believe the same thing: there are far too few venues for short film play and therefore they should play as often and as widely as possible. This does not, however, include playing online.

You do have to realize the odds.
In 2007, Sundance programmers cut over 4500 short film submissions down to approximately 270 and then down again to the approximately 70 shorts played in packages. Festivals like Seattle, Slamdance, LA, and AFI easily receive 2000–3000 short film submissions for anywhere from 50 to 100 slots. Quite often, being rejected at this level has nothing to do with your film. Palm Springs ShortFest and Clermont-Ferrand (as well as others) put every film submitted into their market whether it gets into the festival or not because they know many good films just won't get festival time and yet still deserve to be seen.

You do have to read the application and follow the rules.
Think of it as a litmus test. Think of it as being in an audit with the IRS. Think of it as being on the witness stand. DON'T give them anything they didn't ask for; DO give them everything they ask for. That means be prepared. Take set photos while shooting. Write a brief director's statement. Get your technical information together correctly.

(No, really. No fooling. If you don't know if you have a mono or stereo sound mix, or if your aspect ratio is 1:85 or 1:35, or if you shot on digital but up-res'd to HD or vice versa, then find out and put it down correctly on the form from the very beginning.) Spell the names on your cast/credit list correctly. If you are submitting through your school or producer, **make sure the contact person's phone number is one which gets answered on weekends.** (How many times have I needed confirmation at the final hour on a weekend when school offices aren't open? And how many times, not getting an answer, have I simply moved on. . . .) Whatever you do, don't make it hard for them to program you. Assume your paperwork will get separated from the submission disc. Make sure your disc will play any DVD deck or computer, especially if it was generated on a Mac. Know that in the festival office, no one cares if you have glossy press kits or not.

233

You do have to know your film and the festival you're applying to.

Figure out what kind of film you made. Don't ask your friends or your mother or someone's golfing buddies. Put ten people you don't know together in a room, show them the film, and ask them to write down words they think describe it. Don't challenge them, defend the film, or tell them they are cinematically challenged. Ask for their opinions after you gathered their notes. Then, look at what your favorite festivals play. Go to the festival if at all possible and watch the films programmed. Do they gravitate towards long or short? Dramatic or comedic? Edgy or slick? Apply it to your film and figure out if there is a fit. And then, next time you make a movie, know what your peers are doing. Be challenged creatively. Push some limits, take some risks. Immerse yourself in the culture of your industry.

You do have to think ahead.

Unless you're making a movie only you will watch in your living room by yourself. WARNING: Thinking ahead means more today than it used to. It means getting set photos, of course, and cast/crew releases, and having deal memos. But it also means making sure all rights are cleared (music, logo, geographical sites, names), having a distinct line of ownership (a paper trail that establishes you as the undisputable and rightful owner), and possibly even having E&O insurance (errors and omissions insurance, which many content providers are now asking for because their parent companies, like Viacom or GE, require it).

Step 4: Reassess. Realistically.

Now, armed with a little knowledge, ask yourself the following questions again.

1. What do you want the film to do for you?

Make a list in order of importance: Awards—cash, jury, or audience? Industry attention? Press attention? Audience attention? Or do you just want to be invited to a really nice location for a few days (a very valid desire sometimes)?

2. How much money, time, and effort can you devote to achieving your goals?

Assume it will cost you between $25 and $50 each time you submit to a festival. Overseas festivals generally have no submission fee (thank you to the support of a national cinema), but you still have to pay postage. Submission to 20 festivals could be $1000, which could be a whole extra day of shooting. No matter how organized you are, each month it will take you a full day to put together the submission packages for that month's deadlines. Even if you use a service like Withoutabox, you'll want to back up materials. How many times can you do this?

3. What kind of film do you have, really?

What is its reality? Should you focus on genre-based festivals? Should you try for the lowest hanging festival fruit or aim at the brass ring? Should you rent a screen, show it to your cast/crew/family, and then move on to the next one?

4. Can you travel with the film?

Sometimes the hassle of constantly submitting can fade when given airfare, hotel, dinners, and big name industry attention in Bozeman, Montana, at the Hatch Film Festival.

5. How long do you have it in you to stay with the film?

What else is going on in your life? Are you moving on to other films? Thinking about your mortgage? Starting a family? Or are you just desperate to get away from the Sturm und Drang of endless submission paperwork?

Step 5: Never stop making movies

Because if you could have been a dental hygienist, you would have been a dental hygienist. You are a filmmaker for a reason. Don't stop. Don't give up. Do it again. And again. And again. And every time you do it, learn something new. Because I, and 600 of your soon-to-be best friends, will be in the front row seats, anxiously awaiting your latest work and ready to cheer you on.

JAMIE WHITE is Executive Director and Founder of the Colorado Film Foundation, a nonprofit organization, and its label, the Film Festival Collection. He has over 20 years experience in the film and video industry.

In 1998 Mr. White was hired to help launch a video/DVD label in Los Angeles, overseeing the acquisition of the majority of its initial catalog. Previously, he founded and managed a laserdisc company for 10 years as President and CEO, Lumivision Corporation, building up an exclusive catalog of over 225 high-quality titles on laserdisc (feature film, documentary, animation, classic television, education, fine arts, and music). He was a producer and executive producer on a number of projects, spearheading the preservation and film-to-video restoration of several important silent films in collaboration with the International Museum of Photography at the George Eastman House, which garnered high marks and awards from the press, including *Entertainment Tonight*, *LA Times*, and *Siskel & Ebert*. Under his leadership, Lumivision itself garnered numerous awards from the Laserdisc Association, ASIFA, and *Video Magazine*. He negotiated successful bundling agreements for video CD and DVDs with Apple, IBM, Pioneer, Samsung, Hewlett–Packard, and Compaq.

Most recently Mr. White was asked to be an expert on a panel about short film distribution at Palm Springs ShortFest and served on a jury at the Digital Arts Festival for the Boys & Girls Club. He is a fourth-generation Coloradoan and a graduate of Bennington College in Vermont.

Show 'Em Your Shorts!

By Jamie White

There is little I enjoy more at a film festival than sitting in a theater watching short films and taking in the audience's reactions around me. I wish more people could enjoy the same experience. Directors of these short films have a challenging time not only getting into a festival, but finding distribution so their work can be seen. A need exists for other ways to see and also learn about well-crafted short films. One of the best ways to understand this artistic process is by hearing from the filmmakers themselves about their work. With all these thoughts in mind, the nonprofit Colorado Film Foundation decided to launch the Film Festival Collection label, creating another way for short films to be seen by an audience and providing both a showcase for the filmmaker's work and a learning tool for students, emerging filmmakers, and film lovers.

Our *shorts!* DVDs, released under the Film Festival Collection, are compilations of award-winning short films, with filmmaker commentary, from all over the world. It is very hard to see good shorts outside of a festival—our DVDs provide another avenue for short films to be seen by a wider audience. The *shorts!* volumes, released every year since 2003, each contain around three hours of short films and six hours of filmmaker commentaries. Our plan is to increase the number of releases and even the format on which to view these short films. Look for our Film Festival Collection channel online. We want to provide as many quality platforms for our filmmakers' shorts to be viewed as possible.

shorts! DVDs are available from our web site, filmfestivalcollection.com, through retail outlets, online rental, and some libraries. They can even be found at certain film festivals—we offer a discount to our fellow nonprofits running film festivals as another way of helping them increase their revenue while offering unique merchandise. Because of the diversity of the short films and the exclusive audio commentaries by filmmakers, the DVDs also serve as a perfect educational tool. Some schools have used the DVDs as a "textbook" for film class.

Every short film we license must have at least one, but usually two audio commentaries created by the filmmakers themselves for the film to be included. These exclusive commentaries are valuable for those wanting to learn more about how a film was made—gaining further insight into the creation of the work. We ask each filmmaker to include two different commentaries, creative and technical. The creative one is more conceptual and might go into detail on the story, how the short came together, or the filmmaker's influences. The technical commentary will have more of a focus on topics including format choices and why, cinematography, camera type, lighting, animation technique, editing, or even issues obtaining story or music rights.

To help promote the filmmakers and their work, the DVDs are given to "guests of the festival" at a number of festivals and events in North America, from New York's Tribeca Film Festival and Colorado's Starz Denver Film Festival to California for the Los Angeles Film Festival and the Independent Spirit Awards. This ensures that many filmmakers and others in the industry get the chance to view the short films on *shorts!* It is also our way of supporting these film festivals and events by adding something unique and film-focused to the "gift bags" given to filmmakers and guests as a "thank you." We've heard from a number of filmmakers that our *shorts!* DVDs were one of the items they most enjoyed receiving.

There are many wonderful short films created by students and emerging filmmakers to seasoned directors. We have purposefully chosen to keep a broad programming focus and include a wide variety of titles from all over the world. In the volumes of *shorts!* you will see all types of titles, from animation and drama to documentary, and varying source materials, from video to 35 mm film.

When programming for our *shorts!* we seek out films a number of ways. As programmer, I attend the top film festivals, including the best festivals dedicated to the short film format: Aspen ShortsFest, Palm Springs ShortFest, and the Worldwide Short Film Festival in Toronto. I keep a list of favorites from all the short films presented at these different festivals and others that have been sent to me directly from filmmakers, film schools, and short film distributors around the world. This ends up totaling a few thousand each year, so I'm constantly taking notes to help me keep track of them all. I always recommend that filmmakers send along their short film as soon as copies are available. If we sign up a short film, we often don't release it until near the end of its film festival run—many festivals won't show a film that has had a commercial release. Friends and colleagues in the film festival world who like our nonprofit's approach helping promote filmmakers, their short films, and the short film format pass along their ideas as well.

We currently choose from award-winning short films for our collections, which does help narrow the selection from the amazingly large number of short films produced each year. This does mean any type of award from acting or cinematography to an audience selection.

Although the only requirement for acceptance is that the film has won an award, we do have some suggestions based upon the most successful short films we have viewed. Ideally, a short film should be only as long as it takes to express the story or statement. Too often a film loses the viewer's attention because it is just too long. We do not have limitations on running times for the films we choose and have included short films from 30 seconds to 35 minutes. However, in general short films are often more marketable if they are under 10 minutes in length. The introduction and credits should be kept to a minimum so the focus is on the film itself. Seek out the best available cast you can, as the wrong casting choice can make or break the film. Make sure you have all the necessary rights for your short from the story to the music used. Too often the music is thought of last and a short has little chance of an after-festival life. If you only clear film festival rights, then you might run into trouble if someone like us wants to expand your audience somehow and offer your short on DVD, cable, streaming, or for download. It is always better to clear all rights for all these uses beforehand, or at least negotiate and have in writing exactly how much you will need later. It is usually less expensive working out a music rights deal before than trying to clear the rights after the fact. If you find it is too expensive to license the music you really want, you might look for someone willing to compose something similar for much less—they might like the extra exposure—or do some homework online and find public domain music that would work.

All of our contracts with filmmakers are nonexclusive—we want the filmmakers to get as much exposure for their films as they wish and not have their rights tied up. In most cases, the more places their short can be seen, the more chances it will be seen, and that's a good thing! We pay our filmmakers a royalty on gross sales, so any royalty monies coming in from sales of the DVDs are divided between the filmmakers included in each volume of *shorts!* In this way, we also create a vehicle for filmmakers to be paid some money for their efforts.

My hope is that hardworking filmmakers included in our *shorts!* volumes or Film Festival Collection online channel will have their work seen, have future successes, and even move on to feature films if they desire.

GEORGE ELDRED is Program Director for Aspen ShortsFest, in Aspen, Colorado, one of the most highly regarded showcases for short cinema in North America. He is one of the shorts programmers for Sundance Film Festival and serves on juries, on professional panels, and as guest curator at several major international shorts festivals. A University of Wisconsin–Madison graduate in art, Mr. Eldred worked in film and video production and at the San Francisco International Film Festival before joining Aspen Film in 1996.

Conversation with George Eldred

SB: Let's start by telling everyone a little bit about Aspen ShortsFest and the vision of that festival.

GE: Aspen is a community-based organization that holds a number of festivals and film series year-round for the local members of Aspen as well as for the international tourists and visitors that we receive. Our shorts festival is held the first or second week in April. Over the past few years we have received 2000 entries every winter and we winnow that down to a list of about 60 finalists that we screen in our competition. The competitive series has awards in four or five different genres. We are one of the festivals that qualifies a film for the Academy Award, so we go by their definition of a short film, which is 40 minutes or less.

SB: Can you talk a little bit about your background and your experience as a programmer?

GE: I have a degree in art and have always been interested in film. In my final semesters of school I started making Super 8 movies and shorts. After graduating I moved to San Francisco and worked in the independent and commercial video production scene there for several years, as well as on several other shorts for myself and for friends in the film business. I worked on features, music videos, and commercials. I started volunteering for the San Francisco International Film Festival, and gradually I got more involved and eventually wound up being part of the staff there. I worked with them seasonally for several years, and for one or two years as Programming Assistant. I had the opportunity to move to Aspen and took the position with the Aspen Film Festival, now called Aspen Film, and have been working here since 1996.

SB: When do you actually start watching films?

GE: It's getting more and more a year-round endeavor. As part of the outreach, I go to other events around the world. I attend the Clermont-Ferrand Short Film Festival, and I have also gone to festivals in Toronto, Australia, Palm Springs, and others depending on budget and time.

SB: Unlike with features, a short film can play "the circuit," and world premiere status is not as critical.

GE: That's right, there are more and more opportunities, either to self-publish on the Internet or through DVD. Shorts, of course, do not receive the kind of attention that feature films do and they don't hit the threshold of awareness for a larger audience that feature films can achieve, so there is minimal opportunity for the average viewer to not only see short films but to be aware of them. Festivals, particularly short film festivals, are a great way to draw people in. It's hard to describe to someone who hasn't seen a shorts program what exactly it is without bringing them in, and that's one of the great functions a festival can do, not just for individual short filmmakers but for shorts in general.

SB: What do you look for as you go through this massive quantity of short films? What strikes you? What's your take and how do you put the programs together?

GE: Every programmer who understands what he or she is doing is aware that there are different styles of programming. There are programmers who program just for their own taste and really don't care if the general audience likes what they're showing. That style of programming is really great for adventurous types of programming, such as an underground film festival or the kind of showcases that you tend to find in specialty screening venues in New York, or LA, or around campuses. Those are a lot of fun.

Generally, most of us are trying to match an appropriate film to an appropriate audience so we try to be as familiar as we can with the range of taste that our particular audience would appreciate. We can bring, not necessarily good films, but films that would be best appreciated by our audience. We're not looking for crowd-pleasers but films that we feel, from our experience, that our audience would get the most out of. For my audience here in Aspen, I don't necessarily program as many pieces of intensely challenging work that a programmer in New York or LA or Sundance might. I do program things that have a classic art-cinema or American independent feel to them, things that I feel like an average audience would enjoy or feel connected to the story or the content.

SB: How do you eventually get them into a program?

GE: That's a lot of fun, and part of the enjoyment of putting together a shorts program as opposed to programming features. Unlike the extended mosaic of a feature program, with features spread out over days and weeks, each individual shorts program is a little bouquet or puzzle of several different individual pieces. It's a lot of fun to try to match a little cluster of works together in each program, and then to arrange those programs over the flow of a festival.

SB: Are there any particular genres that you have found more prevalent this year?

GE: There's a perennial ample supply of dramas, that's always sometimes as many as two-thirds or three-fifths of the number of entries we look at in Aspen. We're always looking for works that have other ranges of tones, things that have a little humor in them, and works like animation and experimental shorts that bring a different kind of approach and flavor to the artistry of moviemaking. We appreciate the fact that filmmakers who make drama have something that they want to say, and in many cases it's a serious intent, so I spend a lot of time watching dramas.

SB: When you go into the process, do you have a goal in terms of percentage of the pie that you'd like international vs domestic or is it, in the end, what films work the best?

GE: We're looking for the best collection of really strong, very affecting works that I think our audience will appreciate. We don't have a quota at all in terms of films from one country or another, or a particular content. We sometimes wind up with more films from the United States than international, and some years it's the other way around.

SB: I notice that a lot of the comedies just aren't funny.

GE: I can agree with that. I was on a panel in the summer and we talked about the impact of the Internet and of digital moviemaking and accessibility and how many more people have access to making movies now. One of the things I've noticed is not so much technical proficiency, although that definitely can be all over the map (as it always has been), but in this do-it-yourself-TV and do-it-yourself-Internet work, there's a very exaggerated sense of the lowest common denominator and really short gag movies—"the exploding gerbil" as someone called it. Those things don't necessarily translate to the appreciation of a general audience in a theater. One of the things that's actually been a treat this year, as opposed to the last two or three years, has been the effect of world events and national/regional events that are reflected almost instantaneously through each year's product in short filmmaking. The turnaround, the expense, and the immediacy of shorts is of a completely different scale from features. It can take years for a feature project to make it through the preproduction mill. On the other hand, a short filmmaker can go out with a small crew and make something on a weekend. The effect of the world climate in terms of the war in Iraq, post 9/11, the regional problems like the hurricane, were all things that weighed heavily on people's minds and showed up in their work, particularly artwork. For whatever reason, it was a little lighter this year with more variety of tone. Another thing that helps lighten us up is that there are a lot of things that are categorized as dramas but some are lighter in tone than others, some that are very serious, and some that you could call comedic.

SB: Would you talk a little bit about some consistent problems or common mistakes that you see?

GE: Filmmakers need to be able to work with the tools that they have at hand and the resources they have available to them. The nice thing about the wonderful wide world of festivals is that there are people out there that can appreciate those challenges that independent and short filmmakers face. Filmmakers shouldn't necessarily worry that perhaps they don't have everything that a Spielberg has to accomplish something, but it is very important to be able to have the skills and the resources available to effectively communicate what the filmmaker's vision or passion or subject is in making their movie. Outside of certain basic rudiments of moviemaking, it's not so much the skill set as being able to try to garner the best resources. If there's a fiction film that filmmaker wants to make and it rests very heavily on the emotional nuance of performance, then they need to find the best actors they can who fill those roles and the ones that are most appropriate for those parts. Quite often I see very effective performances from people who are not professional actors, but the filmmakers had the ability or good luck to pick the right person for their characters. The flip side of that is a poorly cast person for a particular role can really kill the effectiveness for the general audience. It's being able to use the resources to "match" the filmmaker's vision to the story idea.

SB: What advice would you give to a brand new filmmaker thinking about creating a short film but has not gone to film school?

GE: That's a bit of a challenge, and one of the things I've noticed a lot with moviemaking around the world, both shorts and features, is that the opportunities for learning the craft of moviemaking are really widespread now. You don't have to go to an A-list film school to be able to get some hands-on and practical schooled experience in a workshop or an internship and see how movies are made. That practical real-world experience is really valuable just to get you through the frustrations to not have to reinvent the wheel and to learn the mechanics of moviemaking. That said, the best method for learning in any of the arts is to actually do it. The great thing about video and desktop computer editing is that the barriers to having access to the tools and being able to afford to play with them is so much different than it has been in the past. I think a really important key to it is "play." I encourage anyone who wants to make movies to make them and not worry with their first projects whether they're going to be fit for viewing by anyone other than their friends and mother. Just finish one and make another one and keep making as many as you can and setting goals with what you want to learn in each of the cycles the production goes through.

Not only should a young filmmaker make as many shorts as they possibly can, but they should educate their "eye" to shorts by taking every opportunity to see well-made work. Most peoples' experience of cinema and video is formed from watching hours of episodic 30-minutes television and 90-plus-minute features. The short form is a unique cinematic genre, like poetry or short stories or short essays, and most of us still don't have enough opportunity to see and learn from really outstanding examples of the full range of the art and craft of short cinema. As enjoyable as they are, Saturday-morning cartoons, MTV videos, and now self-posted online videos are not the most expressive and creative examples of all that can be done with shorts.

An excellent place for seeing a broader range of such creative work is at festivals, and a final bit of advice would be that aspiring filmmakers take every opportunity to attend screenings at short festivals or the shorts programs at major feature festivals in their area. They should see as much as they can to get a better sense of the amazingly diverse and imaginative works that can be created in the short form.

One of the things the short medium is really great for is as a learning medium as well as an expressive one. You don't have to spend eight years to get the project funded and in the can. You can go out on a weekend and make something. If you think of an appropriate and exciting subject, the most limited means can be used to create something really imaginative and quite wonderful and something that other people would be excited to share.

KEVIN HAASARUD is Founder and Director of the Film Program for HBO's U.S. Comedy Arts Festival, the nation's premiere forum for comedy held annually in Aspen, Colorado, that has shown such pictures as *Napoleon Dynamite; Garden State; Super Size Me; Good Bye, Lenin! Human Nature; Thank You for Smoking;* and *Dave Chappelle's Block Party,* to name a few.

Prior to this, he spent six years with HBO Original Programming in the development of Emmy Award-winning comedy specials and series (*The Larry Sanders Show, Tracey Takes On, Def Comedy Jam, Mambo Mouth,* and *The Ben Stiller Show,* among others). He got his start working with Roger Corman at Concorde/New Horizons and is a graduate of St. Olaf College, with additional studies in philosophy and psychology at Oxford University. When not absorbed in all things film and comedy, Mr. Haasarud becomes an enthusiastic focus group member for his wife, Kim Haasarud, a professional mixologist.

Some Serious Funny Business

By Kevin Haasarud

Comedy is serious funny business

It's perceived to be the most difficult of genres. When comedies work, they provide audiences collective catharsis. When they don't, the silence is deafening. And for their troubles, comedies rarely get a fair shake at awards time. The Academy has only awarded five comedies "Best Picture" since its inception: *The Apartment* in 1960, *Annie Hall* in '77, *Driving Miss Daisy* in '89, *Forrest Gump* in '94, and *Shakespeare in Love* in '98. By the same token, comedies often provide the greatest return on box-office gross relative to negative cost. The best rely on character and story. No need for big special effects. The laughs are the thing, and with a strong story, production value can be a supporter rather than a driver.

So you want to make a comedic short?

Brilliant! We can use more of them. But what is funny? I should point out how I define comedy. In my opinion, if a picture uses *humor with intent* it qualifies. What I mean is, if the characters use humor to push a storyline forward at significant moments, they're in the club. *Life Is Beautiful*, for example. A movie about the Holocaust a comedy? Yes, because the humor is used to push through a painful storyline. What is it someone said? "Humor is the sharpest form of social commentary." I think that's true. I enjoy the Farrelly brothers, but I also love Gilliam and Jean-Pierre Jeunet. I think comedy can be the antidote to the travails of the age. Just watch what happens to a room full of people laughing . . . it's great catharsis, it's great social binding, it's the way to talk about things that might be too painful to consider otherwise.

So you love comedies, and you want to make a comedic short. Some advice?

A great story

First of all, let's talk story for a second. Your story is your bedrock, and it sounds tired and trite, but it can't be restated enough. A great story will overcome almost all of your production pitfalls. The story creation phase is the only place where you're probably not spending money (it's rare to pay or be paid for a short film script). And if it's not on the page, it's probably not going to be on the screen. As you work on the script realize this is the only part of the process where time is free. Do readings for friends, have fun with it, try different things. With comedy if you're not getting laughs, you're not getting anywhere. Take the time to hone the dialog and finesse the story beats so they do your story justice. And speaking of stories, I implore you: please, no more movies about movies. You may not be able to help yourself, but stories about the entertainment business are a dime a dozen, and unless you can improve on Altman's *The Player*, you're fighting an uphill battle. It's a big world out there, and the entertainment business has been documented to death. Find a story that is set in a world the audience finds fresh and different. You come from a unique background that (most likely) has not been steeped in Hollywood since birth. You have a distinct lens through which you view the world. Polish that lens, show us that world.

Next: Get good sound

Don't underestimate the power of sound. Substandard sound will blemish your project from the very first frame. Grainy images and poor lighting can be excused as "artistic" choices. But in this era of good sound-recording devices, it's almost impossible to forgive subpar sound. If you're including location sound, learn how to use the gear or hire someone who does. It'll be the single best investment you'll make in your production.

Use good actors

Especially with comedy, if your actors don't ring true it's going to be a long slog. It's fun to use friends and family . . . and it's easy to throw someone in the mix because they're enthusiastic. But realize, they are what the audience is going to be watching (animation aside). You need them to be skilled. Spend some time with casting. Professional SAG actors will bring a degree of experience to the proceedings that may save you money in the long run (read: fewer takes). Speaking of SAG, don't be scared of the organization. They are there to help get their members an honest day's work. Don't ask your SAG actors to work without your project being a signatory; it preys on their passion to work and to be involved with you and your exciting project.

Film vs tape

Digital looks great these days if treated well with lighting and finessed in post. Cheap video looks and feels like what it is. Stories that are "reality-based" can benefit from being shot on handheld consumer cams. But mostly shorts that are shot on video look like someone wanted to take the cheap way out, and that hurts them. I'm not condoning spending zillions on production, or even saying not to shoot a project if it can't be shot on film. I'm just saying shoot on a format that supports your story, and if you're on the fence about digital vs film, shoot some tests and view them in the forum you hope to be showing them in (a theatrical venue, a computer screen, etc.). Make the decision at that point. If it really seems like film is the way to go, but you can't afford it . . . consider waiting until you can, and spend the extra time honing your script.

Short means short

A well-crafted 5-minute short is infinitely more satisfying than a 30-minute average one. There's no reason for a short film to be longer than, say, 20 minutes. If the story you want to tell is over 15 minutes . . . consider where you want to show it. If it's beyond family and friends, ask yourself some hard questions. Maybe you can tell the story more economically. I can tell you from a programmer's point of view, the longer it is the less likely there will be a slot for it at a festival. Typically, shorts play in festivals as collections, and if there is one that is 30 minutes, it means there probably needs to be another of equal length. And it eliminates the possibility of playing it in front of a feature. Especially with comedy. I've seen shorts where the final credits are longer than the story . . . and that's fine! At the end of the day, you want an entertaining piece that lots of people will see. Don't do yourself the disfavor of thinking a longer piece will somehow be taken more seriously. Economy is the key. Leave someone laughing and wanting more, and chances are they'll want to hear what else you would like to make. Ninety percent of the best shorts I've ever seen (and I've seen thousands) are 7 minutes or less.

Who is your audience?

Be clear on why you are making your short and who your audience is. Is it just for fun? Do you want to show it beyond the living room for family and friends? Is it for the web? Do you want to play the festival circuit? Do you have aspirations of selling it to cable? Is it a directing reel? All of these are viable audiences, and each has their own demands. These demands will directly relate to what makes sense for you in terms of the story and the budget.

The critics

Filmmaking is generally a communal experience in which your crew, actors, editors, and so forth all come together and end up making something greater than the sum of its individual parts. It's probably true that you'll be your own worst critic, and that if you make something that you like, there will probably be others that like it too. That said, the moment you show it to another person is the moment your realize people often have different likes and dislikes. And everyone will have advice. If you're one of the lucky filmmakers that have sensibilities that mirror your society's bulk of film viewers, you're on you way. Just hone your craft and be tenacious. On the other hand, if you're like the vast majority of filmmakers, your sensibilities are not going to be embraced by masses. They are going to embraced by more niche-oriented groups. The trick for you will be in identifying these groups, hearing their comments, and honing your project so that it appeals to them. Don't forget your story though . . . it's yours to tell, and do everything you can to stay true and make it manifest.

It's done. Now what?

Sales of shorts are tough. The good news for comedies is, everybody wants them. The festival circuit loves them. Broadband and wireless carriers love them. They are seen as the most viral of content, and they can be fun business cards for feature work. The bad news is, nobody wants to pay for them. There are a few domestic cable groups still buying, but most (HBO, for example) don't. You can do some foreign sales, and there are some good short film sales agents that can help you with that. And there are a few groups that compile short film DVDs . . . but they don't sell that well, unless they have some hook (animation, gay-themed, etc.). Broadband becomes the place for most. And interesting things are happening there. I've recently programmed a few animated shorts for a new HBO "virtual space" in the virtual world "Second Life," in which a select groups of "avatars" will be able to watch animations. Go figure. But once again, no cash for the creators. Just exposure. Short films are not generally money makers, they are a means to an end. Some broadband groups like Revver are figuring out revenue-sharing arrangements tied to advertising dollars. But generally you will be hard-pressed to make much dough. Be clear what your end goal is, and spend appropriately.

A final note: Funny wins

People love to laugh. And if you deliver laughs, you will find work. New digital production tools and new avenues of distribution make this an exciting time to be a filmmaker. If you have access to a camera and broadband, the world can be your audience. But filmmaking takes not only talent and inspiration, but an amount of chutzpah, organization, and economy. Millions of user-generated shorts are posted daily; the general quality is substandard. Easy access to production tools is taking away from time developing stories fully. Know that if you spend that time, what you create will (potentially) rise above the rest. At the end of the day, your story is your salvation, and your ability to tell it economically and with some artistry will be what elevates it from good to great. Have fun!

JOHN POLSON is the founder and Creative Director of Sony Tropfest and has played a pivotal role in the development of the festival since its inception in Sydney in 1993.

During the festival's infant years, Mr. Polson combined organizing it with his flourishing acting/directing career. His screen-acting career began in 1986, during which time his interest in film directing began to surface. With film stock given to him by Kennedy Miller, he made his first short film, *An Evening with Herman.*

He has received a myriad of acting accolades, including several Australian Film Institute nominations and Best Supporting Actor award, and is a recipient of their Byron Kennedy Award for his contribution to the Australian film industry as the director of Tropfest. Sony Tropfest is now considered to be the world's largest short film festival. In 2006, John Polson and Tribeca Film Festival founders Robert De Niro, Jane Rosenthal, and Craig Hatkoff created a new Tribeca Film Festival program, Tropfest@Tribeca.

Mr. Polson's first feature film was *Siam Sunset*, which was selected to screen at the 1999 Cannes Film Festival, where it won the Rail D'or award, or audience award. It also won prizes at several other festivals around the world, including Yubari (Japan), Puchon festival (Korea), and Hawaii (United States).

In 2000, he appeared in the blockbuster film *Mission Impossible II*, and in 2002 he directed his first U.S. feature film, *Swimfan*. 2005 saw the release of his third feature film, *Hide and Seek*. Mr. Polson's latest feature film is *Tenderness*, in which he directs Russell Crowe and Laura Dern.

Conversation with John Polson

SB: Tell me about the inception of Tropfest Australia and how that came into being.

JP: In 1993, I was in my twenties, I was an actor, but really my secret ambition (and it wasn't that secret) was to make films. From early on, almost as soon as I started acting, I would save up my money as an actor and I would make 16 mm short films on the weekend. I made my very first film on video called *Surray Hills 902 Springroll*. It was obviously a mockumentary that spoofed the television show. It followed this food delivery guy around. It was ridiculous, but the point was in the delivery guy's spare time he went to this café called the Tropicana, so a lot of the film ended up being shot there. The film was probably 11 minutes long.

When it came time to screen it for the cast and crew (about 15–20 people), I decided it might be a nice idea to show it at the Tropicana. So I asked the owner of the café, and borrowed a television and video player. I showed up that night with the tape, and there were 200 people there. People had a great time seeing themselves on the screen, seeing the streets, and seeing the café they were sitting in on the screen, which was kind of novel.

At the end of the night I got up and said, "We're going to have a festival. It's going to be in one month and we're all going to make films. I don't want people digging out their old film school films, it's not about people showing stuff that you made years ago. It's about making films, getting off your ass, really, and making films."

A month later I borrowed my dad's van and rented four television screens, figuring there would probably be more than 200 people this time. Nine people gave me tapes and 1000 people showed up, trying to be in this café that only holds 100, and so 900 people were on the street. I had to turn the TVs out towards the street against the glass so that people outside could see what they'd come to see. Meanwhile, people were spilling out onto the street blocking traffic and the police showed up. I'm trying to explain the history of this thing and how important it is to all these people who've made these films. At one point these two cops told me to shut it down. They didn't want to do it themselves because they could see a lot of people were focused on these movies.

The turning point for me, and to this day for Tropfest, was, when one of these cops, the older guy, started to watch one of the films. Meanwhile, the younger guy started giving me a hard time insisting that I shut it down. The older guy got swept up in the story seeing his own streets and his beat, so he tells the younger guy to shush up while he watches this movie. They let me play out the rest of the night. The traffic went around and that was the beginning of Tropfest. That was the very first actual festival.

SB: So suddenly you're in charge of this film festival?

JP: It's like this idea happened by accident. For the first two or three years, I was very much a reluctant leader of this festival. I wanted to be an actor and a filmmaker and suddenly I had this baby and it's wanting all this attention, and people would come up to me in the street and say, "Hey I was there last week in the street. Next year why don't you do this and this and this?" I remember thinking, "Why don't you do it? Why am I this guy who has to do this festival?"

So now it's this big deal, on the night itself there are probably 200–300 people who work on it, there's a live audience of 150,000 on one night. We get 800 entries, we choose 16. We have a brand new initiative called the regional digital screening network. We send our satellite signal digitally to rural areas around Australia, there are about eight of them, and people will come to one of those cinemas from their farms and watch the whole event. They will watch not just the films but the arrivals, the judging, and the celebrities as it happens live, so it's truly a national event.

It occurred to me early on, this was not some bizarre business plan, thank God, because in the early days all I did was lose money on it. What it came out of was a love of short films.

My earliest experience with a short film, strangely enough, was not watching one, but somebody telling me about one, and it stayed with me to this day. It was probably 10 years before Tropfest started. Somebody described to me a story they had seen in a short film and it just struck me in such a profound way. I found out many, many years later, after searching online when Google finally came about, and I put in key words since I didn't know the name of it. It was a film that I now own called *An Occurrence at Owl Creek Bridge*, which is a 20-minute short film. It's a story about the split second before death and what can happen. Somebody told me that at a dinner one night and it just stayed with me, and I thought, "Wow, what a powerful medium short film can be."

I'd never seen a short film but something about the story stuck with me forever. It was really because of that that I became fascinated with short films. Not as a sort of "poorer cousin" to what a feature film is, but a beautiful art form in its own right. In the same way a short story is not a short novel. In truth you can examine an idea in a short film that you could never examine in a feature film, ever, because you have two hours you have to worry about, you have subplots.

With short films you can take one simple very minute detail of an idea and examine it from all directions and really look into it. You can experiment as you can never experiment as a feature filmmaker with the camera moves, the sound, and the music. It's an incredibly important part of our culture. I've seen over the years literally thousands of films that have come in to Tropfest, and can honestly say that many of the biggest revelations I've had have been watching short films or animation, so it's been pretty impressive.

SB: How did you come up with the signature item?

JP: The TSI (Tropfest signature item) came about because I realized, probably the second or third year, that as much as I wanted this festival to be about production (because that was always my goal), it was about people sitting about believing that somebody else had to tell them they could go out and make a film rather than realizing that it was really up to them to get out there and do it.

What happened in the early years was that people would find a film that they had already made a couple years ago and they'd just hand in that, hoping that it would get in, then they'd get a little second hit of glory from the same film. That wasn't the point. The point was new fresh ideas. I figured the only way to police that was to dictate that it has to have a certain item. It turned out to be a great marketing tool. It's great fun for the audience and very fun for the filmmakers. Many times a filmmaker wants to make a short, and may be really talented, but they need a little bit of inspiration about what it might be.

SB: You want to see how they creatively incorporate it.

JB: That's it. I've always encouraged people to put it in the background, it's not meant to be what your film's about or the theme. The theme to me is the heart and soul of the film. The TSI is not the theme, it's really meant to be a secondary idea that's there to show that you didn't dig something out of your bottom drawer, that you went and made this film.

SB: When people think about short films they think about comedy, and believe that you can't do a serious story in a short amount of time, that there's not enough time for plot or character development, and I disagree. Can you talk a little about genre?

JP: It's a good question because in the early days of Tropfest people made comedies because comedies work. When you have 100 people or 1000 people or 10,000 people in one place, there is something about comedy that feels as if it unites people. It's also an instant gauge of the film. With a drama, it's more difficult to understand if people are understanding or being impacted by a film. Honestly, we had a bit of an issue in the early days because people just started to almost belittle Tropfest as a "gag" film festival. We had not just comedies, but what you'd call a "gag" film, where something happens right at the end. It's a big laugh, and that's the end.

SB: It's the "punchline" film.

JP: Yes, the punchline film, right. And I was somewhat upset by that because I had a firm belief that this forum, this platform was much deeper than that. You didn't just have to have a little joke, and get a laugh, and everybody goes home and forgets about it. I had a couple of films get in that weren't comedies and I thought they went very well. Because there's no instant gratification, maybe people let it slip their minds, so I pretty publicly in the late nineties went out and said, "Look, we can show other films." People assumed if they weren't funny or if they weren't a comedy filmmaker they wouldn't enter. Audiences were thinking, "If I don't want comedy, then I'm not going to go to Tropfest." We made a kind of pretty public push that we thought it was deeper than that.

Fortunately for us, I think it was in 2000 or 2001, a film called *Lamb* came in; we'd already had a couple of dramas, but that was the first time a drama won. It was a big deal for us because it showed that there were some funny films that night, but this film about this blind boy with sheep actually won the night. The judges responded, and since then I feel like it's pretty balanced. Of course we get comedies, and I'm glad we get comedies, but I make a very real effort every year to make sure that out of those 800 entries, we find the best dramas and we put those in as well. There are many examples of films that didn't rely on the gag or the punchline, that were much more hard hitting. Not that they're better or worse; there's a place for them in the festival, as well.

SB: I want to encourage aspiring untrained filmmakers to seek out opportunities like Tropfest and to explore them and not to feel intimidated.

JP: That's what it's about. This is kind of a level playing field with Tropfest. It's not about where you went to film school, it's not about who your friends are, how much money your family has. Twenty years ago, even a short film cost $100,000, you had to get the camera and the film—the video camera did for short films what the cassette player did for garage bands. It gives access to anybody who has got half an idea that they think might work on a screen, and especially with digital editing systems, if you've got a computer you can edit a film. If you've got a video camera, or a friend with a video camera, you can shoot a film.

Personality is what matters. When I go to see a feature film I spend two hours with that director, really, about what their view of the world is. And if you've got a view of the world, and if you feel like you've got an idea for a film, stranger things have happened than making a film and getting an audience. In Australia, we've had many, many people over the years who have made short films, come really from nowhere, and have gone on to make feature films.

A film opened in Australia about a month ago, and it has become the top Australian film for the last few years; it's called *Kenny*, directed by a guy named Clayton Jacobson, who made a short at Tropfest three years ago called *Tickler*. He got in and he got a lot of attention. He's an actor and was in a film called *Buried*, which we had. Now he's directed the number one film in Australia and he's making a television series, he's a hit. Robert Connelly, who made a film called *The Bank*, has a film that's done really well in Australia. One of his short films along the way showed at Tropfest six or seven years ago. What we've tried to set up is a magnifying glass of talent. Usually the day after Tropfest people have agents who didn't have agents before.

One of the things an audience responds to in films is originality. Make your own way and figure out what you like and don't like and what your ideas are. Honestly, any way you can get to be a good filmmaker, you should grab it. There's a strong belief among many filmmakers I respect—make your own rules. That's what I try to do.

KIMBERLY YUTANI is a Los Angeles-based film programmer. She is Associate Director of Programming at Outfest: The Los Angeles Gay and Lesbian Film Festival, and a short film programmer for the Sundance Film Festival. She is also the programmer for Fusion, the Los Angeles LGBT People of Color Film Festival. She has served on juries at the Toronto International Film Festival for the Short Cuts Canada Award and the Berlin International Film Festival for the Teddy Award. Prior to her film festival work, Kimberly was a film critic and freelance journalist focusing on independent film.

Your Short Film and the LGBT (Lesbian/Gay/Bisexual/Transgender) Film Festival

By Kimberly Yutani

Why should you consider LGBT film festivals when making your film?

As a short film programmer for Outfest: The Los Angeles Lesbian and Gay Film Festival and the Sundance Film Festival, I end up seeing over 2000 short films a year. Regardless of the subject of your film, your odds of getting into Sundance are slim (about 0.02% these days)—that's the bad news. But the good news is, if you have gay themes or characters in your short, your chances of getting into an LGBT festival are significantly better (in Outfest 2006, about 130 shorts were programmed out of the 500 that were submitted; a little over 25%). At LGBT fests, the exposure and the networking opportunities are countless, and the audiences are some of the most die-hard, supportive, and enthusiastic film fans out there.

That said, a word of warning: Like any film project, your sensitivity and commitment to your subject and characters are vital. This isn't to say straight people can't make movies about gay people, or lesbians can't make movies about gay men, etc., but your insight into your subject and how you present that information is the key to your project's authenticity. No matter the length of your project (maybe barring the 10-second mobile short), you will be spending so much time working on it that you really have to be passionate about your film and know why you're making it.

How do I make a good LGBT short?
Watch other short films.

As a short filmmaker, it is important to see what other short filmmakers are doing. These days, LGBT-themed shorts are readily available. Go to LGBT festivals, buy or rent DVD compilations (Wolfe Video is a great resource for queer shorts and Strand Releasing has some strong gay shorts in their *Boys Life* series), watch Logo's Click List, download them off of iTunes, and search for them online. Whether a short is great, mediocre, or bad, it's essential to know what is getting submitted and accepted (or not) to festivals.

How long should my short film be?
You'll read this a million times in this book: A short film means a film is short. Kirsten Schaffer, Senior Director of Programming at Outfest, is only half-joking when she says, "A short should be under 5 minutes!" Jim Cashman's *Dinner Conversation* is a low-budget, no-frills project shot on video. The fact that it's 4 minutes *and* has smart and snappy writing and strong performances lends to its versatility to go into any program or before a feature. A longer short—over 20 minutes—decreases its chances of acceptance. There are always exceptions, like Pascale Simone's *You 2* (a delightful lesbian Dutch 25-minute short) and Carter Smith's *Bugcrush*—a beautiful, thrilling, and frightening 35-minute short. These shorts could not be more different, but for either sheer entertainment or artistic merit, these

are outstanding shorts that are worth the two slots they take up in a program. For the record, I'm happy when I see a short with a run time that's under 15 minutes.

Beware of clichés and hot topics

Whether you're making a documentary or narrative short, think unique, specific stories. Before you pick up a camera, seriously think about your story and why you want to make this film. If you're making a documentary about something in today's heated political climate, just know that you might be taking on a subject at least ten other filmmakers are probably working on too. At Outfest, we were barraged with gay marriage shorts after the San Francisco 2004 same-sex weddings. Quite a few of these submissions were shaky home video-style pieces, most of them simply documenting events and not giving us extraordinary insight into what we didn't already know via CNN. Right now, there is a surplus of the following in the queer documentary world: gays in the military, religious gays, gay parenting, and meth addicts. (Of course, if you find a gay Mormon couple in the military who are doing meth and have kids, now that's the doc I want to see!) If you're writing a narrative, once you have a script, put your ego aside and ask your cinephile friends for honest feedback on it—have they seen this story before? Do they think it's original? What's new about it? What isn't?

Case study: Family Reunion

Every LGBT programmer has seen thousands of coming-out films— often the story of a teenage boy/girl secretly in love with their best friend, only the best friend is straight, and at some point the gay character comes out to any combination of their object of desire, their parents, and themselves. Coming out is an important part of the LGBT identity and these stories are an essential story to LGBT filmmakers and audiences. There's nothing wrong in wanting to tell this story—your approach just needs to be creative.

Isold Uggadottir's *Family Reunion* is about a young woman living in New York City, whose family and friends don't know she's a lesbian when she returns to her native Iceland for a visit. In the first few minutes you might think it's a normal coming-out story. However, the way Uggadottir uses a specific setting, her very personal insight into Icelandic culture, combined with the fact that she has a clever twist to the coming-out aspect of her story (which actually makes it either a dual coming-out story or an anti-coming-out story), creates a truly unique film.

Uggadottir says her goal was to make a "complete film" (her scenes are filled with extras and her film is full of authenticity and spontaneity) with a "less-is-more story where you don't tell your audience everything and you let them figure it out" (interestingly, the audience is still one step ahead of her protagonist). Her hard work paid off and the success of *Family Reunion* is not surprising—it premiered at the Frameline San Francisco International LGBT Film Festival (Uggadottir was the recipient of one of the Frameline completion grants), then played Outfest, the Palm Springs Short Film Festival, and the Reykjavik Film Festival before it got into Sundance in 2007.

A few tips for your shoot and after

Use a tripod. Unless you're looking for the Blair Witch, odds are you're not going to be able to pull off your handheld footage.

Use actors. You think you can cut around bad performances, but it will make your editing process a nightmare and crappy actors are often hard for programmers and audiences to ignore.

Get a still photographer on set. When you get into festivals, good artwork is crucial. All fests rely on strong, sexy photos to market their programs. If you have a nice still, you might well find yourself representing an entire shorts program!

Seek out friends for advice. Much like the process with your script, once you have a rough cut, hold test screenings for your friends, classmates, or anybody else who will watch your film and will give you brutally honest feedback. Find out what works and what doesn't.

Applying to festivals

Almost every major city has an LGBT film festival. At Popcorn Q Movies (www.planetout.com) you will find listings of over 150 LGBT festivals around the world—start applying. The bigger fests in the United States are Frameline's San Francisco International LGBT Film Festival, Outfest in Los Angeles, Newfest in New York, and the Miami Gay and Lesbian Film Festival. Internationally there's Inside Out in Toronto, Verzaubert in Berlin, the London Lesbian and Gay Film Festival, and the Torino Gay and Lesbian Film Festival. Be sure to read each festival's submission guidelines carefully and follow the directions. This sounds obvious, but at Outfest I'm always surprised by the ways in which our directions are ignored. For instance we ask for submissions in industry-standard 5¼-inch by 7½-inch plastic safe cases and a great percentage arrive in other types of cases (and some in no case at all)!

Avoid DVD flair

Don't worry about making a fancy cover for your DVD—your information written in Sharpie on a DVD is all that's needed. DVD menus with outtakes, behind-the-scenes, etc., are not necessary either. I love when I pop a DVD in my player and the movie just starts right up.

You're in!

Go to the festival—not only will you have fun, but this is an investment in your career. Seeing your film on a big screen with an audience is valuable feedback—it will show you your strengths and weaknesses as a filmmaker. It's also important that you connect with other filmmakers—meet them and see their films. If you get into one festival, chances are you will get into other festivals, and you'll discover you will spend many of the next few months with the filmmakers. I've seen filmmakers in the same shorts program go on to form support/goal groups, collaborate on projects, and become good friends.

Also, LGBT-themed shorts are hot. Distributors are at LGBT festivals looking to buy shorts, and managers and agents are looking for exciting new talent. You need to be there to meet these people in person. This is a market that's exploding and the more exposure your film gets, the better. Though nothing has been set up for short filmmakers to make millions yet, some filmmakers are making some decent cash off of iTunes sales now, and you simply never know what the future holds.

If you get into one festival, be prepared—programmers read each other's catalogs and solicit films. Filmmakers often tell me how overwhelmed they are by requests for their film after they get into Outfest or Frameline.

Thanks, but no thanks

Being turned down from a festival is never fun, and the fact that we have to deny films is one of the crummier parts of our jobs as programmers. It's true that if your film is not of high quality, it is unlikely it will be accepted to many festivals. However, we also have to sometimes reject films that are extremely good. If you're confident about your film, don't take it personally—your film is turned down from a festival for so many reasons that shouldn't concern you. Easier said than done, but you do have to learn to detach yourself from the process. The important thing to remember is that you now have a complete film in your hands, and that is already your biggest accomplishment.

Some recommended viewing: *Looking for Langston* (d. Isaac Julien); *Came Out, It Rained, Went Back In Again* (d. Betsan Evans

Morris); *Trevor* (d. Peggy Rajski); *Uncle 'Bar' at Barbershop* (d. Kwon Jong-kwan); *Stag* (d. Ian Iqbal Rashid); *Two Cars, One Night* (d. Taika Waititi); *With What Shall I Wash It?* (d. Maria Trenor); *The Underminer* (d. Todd Downing); *Peace Talk* (d. Jenifer Malmqvist); *Hold Up* (d. Madeleine Olnek); *Doorman* (d. Etienne Kallos).

TREVOR GROTH is Senior Programmer for the Sundance Film Festival, where he has worked since 1993. He programs narrative and documentary features and is the head of the short film section of the festival.

He is also Director of Programming for CineVegas. In its sixth year under his guidance, CineVegas has emerged as one of the hottest film festivals in the United States.

He helped to conceive and produce the Sundance Online Film Festival, which marked the first time that one of the major international festivals showcased their short films online.

Mr. Groth has been a guest curator, panelist, and juror for numerous international festivals, as well as a consultant on a number of film productions and for IFILM.com.

He grew up in Salt Lake City, Utah, and started attending the U.S. Film Festival (which later became the Sundance Film Festival) while in high school. He began working for the Sundance Institute in their development department and at their filmmaker labs while in film school at the University of Utah. Upon his graduation in 1993 he moved to Los Angeles to join the programming staff.

Conversation with Trevor Groth

SB: You and I both know that for short filmmakers, Sundance is the "brass ring," and I really want to give them a sense of reality-base in terms of submissions vs acceptance and a little about that process.

TG: We have had a steady increase in the number of short film submissions since I've been doing this, and I started in 1993. Each year since then it climbed steadily and steadily, and then when digital technology became accessible to everyone there was a huge jump in the numbers of submissions. In fact, one year we climbed to 2000 and the next year we were closer to 4000. We didn't see that coming, necessarily, that massive of a jump but since then it has steadily increased, and we're up to about 4500 submissions. We narrow it down, and this past festival we only showed 71 short films so the competition is very tight. It's sort of a herculean task to get through all of those submissions in a very short amount of time. We start accepting submissions in August so it takes August, September, October, and into November to get through all those films.

SB: Do you advise people to submit under the early submission deadline?

TG: The advice I give is, "If the film is finished, send it in." We definitely try to make sure that every film that is submitted, no matter when it is submitted, is given the proper attention. For our own sanity, the more that comes in early the better so that there's not this huge glut at the submission deadline. That said, we also want to see films in as close to finished form as possible, so it's not worth getting the film in early if it's not finished yet.

259

SB: What is Sundance's position in terms of exposure of the short prior to it getting to you?

TG: That's a good question because it's one of the misconceptions out there in the world. With our feature films we definitely have a sort of premiere status expectation and rules accordingly, but for shorts we don't. In fact, any chance a short film has to find an audience, and especially a theatrical audience, we don't want to take that away from someone by saying we want some sort of premiere for this short film. It's a different business between features and shorts. With a feature film your world premiere is when all the press is going to see it, when all the buyers are going to see it, so you only have one shot at it, but for short films it doesn't work like that. So for us, we just look for the films that we feel make up the most interesting program for us, no matter where they have played prior to us.

SB: What about trends, have you seen any topical trends?

TG: The thing is, with 4500 shorts you manage to see a little bit of everything. I think there are sort of reactions to filmmaking styles that happen, such as when Quentin Tarantino first hit with *Reservoir Dogs* and then *Pulp Fiction*, there definitely were some imitators out there who were influenced by him in that style, and Kevin Smith had a similar kind of influence on filmmakers, so you definitely see some reaction to films that have success and try to copy that success. Recently, there has been a certain trend towards reaction to the political climate with all that's happening in the world right now, with the war and what's going on in the Middle East, and even with Katrina here at home and the government reaction to that. I definitely have seen people using film as a way of expressing political viewpoints and voices that maybe otherwise aren't being heard in the news or in the media. I think short films are great because they can truly be pure voices without the commercial constraints that you have in the feature form, so that's been a really interesting trend recently.

SB: I have noticed, and it's been one of my challenges programming, that there's really not a lot of comedies out there.

TG: It's a good point. The past couple of years I have noticed we've had some really interesting longer, narrative shorts where people are developing their craft and their storytelling styles in that realm, but I have seen a drop in the number of short, funny shorts that were always kind of a staple at a festival. Everyone kind of looked to see the films that were in front of the features that were kind of a quick burst of comedy. I don't know if people have just tapped out all of those good ideas, but I'm hoping now with the new wave of people looking for short content for mobile phones and for the Internet, there will be a new wave towards people coming up with those because I miss them.

With our short programs, we always try to have a balance and take people on a ride of ups and downs, but at times lately the better shorts have all been pretty heavy. It's always great to find that balance.

SB: Can you talk a little about putting the programs together?

TG: For us, we program as a collective group, we do everything as a team. Our process is having one of the programmers watch every short, and as you see things that you respond to, passing it on to the other programmers. Then, we narrow the 4500 down to about two or three hundred that we really all responded to and think would be good for festival consideration. As a group we start putting together programs that we think are a good representation of all the different voices and styles out there. It seems like we always agree on about 80% of them and those are sort of locked in there. The last 20%, one of the programmers has to fight passionately for a film even though the other people have some issues with it. You look at all the different factors such as regionality, where someone has come from, and if you have a gender balance between female and male directors. I've always thought of the films as little pieces to a puzzle and when it's all programmed you look at it and make sure that all those pieces add up to a whole that you feel represents everything that you want to.

Those battles for the last few spots are interesting because it usually comes down to someone's passion for a film vs a collective.

SB: It's interesting that you used the word "ride" earlier because that's the word I always use when I talk about what kind of "ride" the audience is going to have in that program, and I love that part. What do you love most about short films?

TG: A short film is really one of the purest forms of creation in the visual medium. I think the people that are making these shorts, for the most part, are doing it because they really have an unwavering passion to create and to tell these stories or to express these visions. There is so much freedom that comes in making a short film, that you can really discover some fascinating worlds and ideas that oftentimes get compromised in the feature form. I definitely think there are the people that make a short film as a calling card and that's a very real component in the short world, but oftentimes those aren't as interesting as the people who just constantly create in the short form. I also think the incredibly wide range of films that you see in watching all of these shorts is mind-blowing at times. I've always sort of championed them as long as I've been at Sundance because they are sort of the underdog, in a way, and especially in America. Overseas there are a lot more resources for people to tap into government funding, and television that actually pays money for them, but in the States it's the underdog. I think they can be just as powerful as features.

261

SB: Some people are adamant at saying a short should not exceed 15 minutes, period. I am not one of them. What are your thoughts about running time?

TG: I am totally with you. I think you just stay true to your vision. If it's 5 minutes then that's the film that you make. That said, I will say that after watching all of the submissions, the number one complaint that I have about many of them is that they could have been shorter. I do think it's important to not be afraid to lose some fat on these shorts. Some people forget that you're not looking at a feature and you don't have to do the sort of character development arcs that you would in a feature and it's OK to lose some things for the impact that the story can have. I agree, some of my favorite films that we've shown at the festival have been 35 minutes long.

SB: Let's address a little more those other opportunities such as the cell phone initiative, the arrangement with iTunes, and the Internet, especially with Sundance being a forerunner for these markets.

TG: We've always tried to figure out what the short film's place is in the industry and ways to support these filmmakers and these films. For a long time we've had our Sundance Online Festival, which has evolved over the years initially to showcase shorts that were specifically made to be seen on a computer but is now made up of the short films that are actually at the festival. It's such a great opportunity to showcase these filmmakers and films to such a massive audience. When you think about the number of people that can see these films at a film festival, it's a few hundred, but if you put them online they can be seen by billions of people. We embrace that because for a short film there is very limited opportunity to be seen. We didn't think it was a limiting experience but an expanding experience. We've met some resistance from other festivals and the Academy has issues with films being online and that's very real. Each individual filmmaker has to decide if it's worth it or not. For us, we feel that as short films are still struggling to find any avenue to be seen, that this is something that we don't want to limit. We have taken away our rules, we're still supporting work and a filmmaker.

Recently we had this initiative to produce short films for this mobile phone conference that happened in Barcelona and it was a really eye-opening world to have access to in terms of potential. More people have mobile phones than there are televisions in the world, than have Internet connection. The technology is such that the screen size is small but there's so much detail that it's a very viable format for short films. We are constantly looking for new outlets for these films and to find new exposure for these filmmakers, which is ultimately what we're trying to do.

SB: What advice would you give to a young aspiring filmmaker?

TG: The advice that I would give is fairly obvious but it's good to hear. Stay true to your vision. Don't compromise and don't try to guess what the market wants or emulate someone else's style. The films that I always respond to at Sundance are the ones that show me something that I've never seen before. It's really these intense bursts of originality; if you really are passionate about storytelling and filmmaking then just dig down deep inside and find something that's personal to you and stay true to it.

Swimming Lesson #8

Waterlogged: My Story

As one of only two Short Film Programmers of the Tribeca Film Festival, when people discover what I "do" for a living, it is usually followed by the question, "How many do you watch?" When I answer, "Oh, usually 1500," I notice a visceral and physical response on the part of the questioner. A slightly raised eyebrow, a step backward with hands upheld, or a blatant jaw drop. This is almost always followed by the question, "How do you do it?"

I answer this question a number of different ways, depending on my mood:

I'm a machine/alien.

I have no life.

The fast forward button.

Truth be told, how I do it is inexorably linked to why I do it. I do it because I love it. And speaking for film programmers and buyers everywhere, we couldn't do it unless we loved it. We love it because each year, each season, each time we watch a short we are on a mission. That mission is to find new talent. But internal motivation aside, people, especially the filmmakers themselves, are curious as to the process of watching and selecting these films, so I thought I would enlighten you on how I "do it." Every programmer "does it" his or her own way, but I'm going to share my way with you.

Starting on November 1, I put new batteries in my DVD remote, grind up a fresh bag of coffee beans, and bring home my first batch of short films. It's like Christmas morning to me and I am eager to unwrap these gifts. It is the start of months of living in my pj's and watching movies. It is a solitary world, one that requires patience, focus, and self-discipline. Make no mistake about it, this is work. During these several months, I have enormous responsibility. I am responsible to the festival. They trust that I will select the best films from this year's crop. I am responsible to each filmmaker that submits a film. They trust that I will watch their film with an open mind and clear head.

I used to get a lot more exercise in this job. Lugging home mailbags of VHSs, people on the subway would stare and wonder what's in that bag. My upper body strength increased over the past several years. Last year was the turning point in technology, with most short films being submitted on DVD. This made me more efficient. No need to rewind tapes, and I could now easily transport 100+ DVDs in a small portfolio.

After being on hiatus for months, I always look forward to starting again. Yes, I do talk to my television, aloud and sometimes loudly. My comments range from "you must be kidding me" to "that was great" and everything in between. I sometimes wonder what my neighbors think. Do they think I speak ten different languages, as Spanish, Polish, Russian, and Middle Eastern dialog filters through the walls? Do they hear me laughing out loud? (Rarely, but it happens.)

Even though I am physically alone, I am transported to each film's world. I have been around the world ten times at least, been aware of what the collective consciousness is out there. Inside, I am outside. I do not watch for more than two hours straight, because my attention starts to drift, and I owe all those people to whom I am responsible 100%. I take a break, eat a snack, check my email, leave the apartment to go to the gym, breathe in some fresh air, and see other humans.

My mother mocked me last year when I bought a senior citizen-like recliner. She offered to purchase the matching snack tray accessory. My back had started to bother me from all the up and down couch to television repetitive movement. Short film carpal tunnel, I think. I reorganized my living area, and the recliner became my office. When I sit in that chair, it's time to get to work. Like James T. Kirk on the Starship Enterprise, remotes by my side; beam me up.

Once I start, I get "in the zone" and it becomes almost obsessive–compulsive. "One more, I'll watch one more," I think to myself, and then watch five. If I'm not "in the zone" I know it right away, and I walk away. If I'm too distracted about something else going on in my life, or another task on my "to do" list, I can't focus on these films, so I can't say to you that every day I watch for a specific number of hours.

Sometimes it is difficult to keep my energy and enthusiasm up. If I've watched 15 shorts that day and selected zero, that 16th is a tough one to put in the DVD player. If number 16 rocks, I'm reenergized, and it gives me the will to go on. If not, time for a break.

While I'm on this tangent, let me share with you what my programming colleagues and I think are some tired and overused short film elements (in no particular order). That's not to say you should never use these elements, but know that we have seen them in hundreds of short films already:

A short that begins with a quote, usually by a deceased person or famous writer.

The first shot of an alarm clock going off, and someone waking up.

The pan-across-a-mantle of photographs under the main credits.

Watching someone shave, put on makeup, or brush their teeth in the bathroom mirror while staring intently at him/herself.

Shorts guided completely by voice-over narration. Try to "show, don't tell."

Use of repetitive footage/montage sequences, since we just saw this material several minutes ago.

WATERLOGGED: MY STORY

I usually hit the wall around 700 or so, when I look at my notes and, with utter disbelief, realize I am not even halfway though the crop. That's the toughest point in the process, the sheer numbers of it all. At this time, I feel like a runner in the New York City Marathon before crossing that 59th Street Bridge. Time to rally.

The first year I programmed Tribeca I was scared to death. In the Sally Field school of acceptance speeches, would they like me? Would they buy tickets? Would people see what I saw in these films? I had honed "my eye" during 10 years in film distribution and another 10 years teaching film, but this was a different thing. I gulped when I saw the Sundance short film announcement and they had chosen several that I didn't care for at all. I questioned myself constantly. That first year, I sat through every short film program like a mother at her child's violin recital. These were "my babies" after all. I sat in the back, gauging the audience response. Did they "get it"? They did, and that first year's initiation gave me the confidence to stand by my decisions. I don't second guess myself anymore.

I screen blindly. I don't read a synopsis or logline. I put that DVD in and watch. Sometimes I am so stunned by a film's brilliance that I hit the pause button during the end credits and take a moment to think. If it has made me cry, I sit and cry. If it has given me an unforgettable experience, I sit and relish that moment. It is those moments that I remember most about the experience of being a programmer. I am as passionate about discovering a new film as you are about making it.

When I began as a programmer, I wanted to do it creatively. My problem with many short film programs was that they were difficult to watch, jumping from serious to comedic; the films had no relationship to each other. We decided to group the films together with a thematic ribbon tied around them. Not a literal theme, but something that made sense, some common element that made them "fit" together as a group.

When my coprogrammer Maggie Kim and I are finished watching individually, and then watching each other's top choices, we hole up in the conference room and put it all together. We each have our favorites, which we champion. We start thinking about the films in context with one another. What will that "ride" be for the viewer? What short makes a good "transition" piece from serious to comedic or vice versa? How do we want to end the program and what feeling do we want for the audience when the lights come up? We don't go into it thinking about the thematic ribbon—that eventually reveals itself to us as we put the programs together. This part of the process is my favorite, because we are creating a whole out of its parts.

And finally, there's the festival itself and that first gathering where I get to meet the filmmakers. Up to that point, I have no communication with the filmmakers whatsoever. I love short filmmakers because they are in the moment with me. They are thrilled to be there, and I am thrilled to give them the opportunity. Like many of my colleagues, I crash after the festival. I am physically and emotionally exhausted, going into self-imposed exile for a couple of days. Then suddenly, I have all this free time.

What do I do with my days? I catch up on all those feature films that I haven't watched for six months.

It's the best job in the world. For me.

The Unfortunate Television Incident

I decided that before you get ready to tackle the workbook, I would conclude this book with an amusing and true tale of woe. Mine. Although entertaining, and at my own expense I might add, there's a lesson in this experience that I hope you'll think about during those moments when you question your career path, your decisions, and your sanity.

As I've said in this book before, I love my job. Not only do I get to experience all these short films, but I do so in my pj's at home during the dark winter months in Manhattan. While my friends and colleagues are concerned with inclement weather, subway delays, and getting to work on time, my major concern is making certain I have enough coffee to get me through the day.

Naturally, watching 1500 shorts means my television gets a great deal of use, and in order to get through that quantity, I have to strictly structure my day and allocate blocks of time for viewing. Sometimes things just don't go as planned.

Holiday time is a particularly difficult period to adhere to my self-imposed schedule, what with events, final grades at NYU, and shopping. Things get a little stressful. The Friday before Christmas I was deluged with out-of-town visitors, here for a couple of days to take in the sights and sounds of New York during Christmas. I was getting a little "antsy" sitting inside and blew off watching films to go have some fun with my friends. Yes, I'll admit that I met them for drinks and had two very fine glasses of Australian Shiraz and some great conversation.

I returned home around 10:00 P.M. and sighed as I looked at the pile of DVDs expectantly waiting for me. I changed my clothes, settled in to watch for a couple of hours and grabbed the television remote. I pressed the button and I heard, well, nothing. Not nothing exactly, more like a "puuuh" sound. Yes, it was the death rattle of my television. I jumped up, pressed the power button repeatedly, unplugged and plugged, and finally accepted that it was dead. Addressing the television directly, I yelled, "Not now, not this week. Don't do this to me." (Expletives deleted.) I had 200 shorts to plow through in the next week and the clock was ticking.

I realized with dread that I would be going to one of those large electronic stores (the one where the guys in the blue shirts follow you around and ask if you need help and when you do they can't answer your questions anyway) the day before Christmas Eve to buy a television. The Day Before Christmas Eve. In New York. Now, I'm one of those people who starts Christmas shopping after Thanksgiving and have it all wrapped up by Pearl Harbor Day, so the prospect of this was horrifying. It would be a nightmare.

Looking at the clock, I remembered the store had extended holiday hours and there was a slim chance that I could still get this done tonight. We'd had a relatively mild winter, so I threw my coat on over my pj's, stuffed my feet into my trail runners, and scurried to the store, which was a few blocks away. Half tanked up on Shiraz, with my pink bunny flannels poking out the bottom of my coat, I frantically entered the store.

"Televisions! Where are the televisions?" I interrupted the greeter's lethargic "Welcome to Joe's Electronics, how can I help you?" speech. He stuttered, "One flight down," and I was already halfway there. When I got to the television section, I said to the first blue shirt I saw, "I need a television right now." She began to inquire, "Plasma, LCD, HD, . . ." and again I interrupted, "Cheap, with a picture and sound. That's all I need." Incredulously, she simply pointed in the right direction. I bolted to the first reasonably sized and priced television I could find, and said, "I'll take this one." It was a whopping 76 bucks, made by a no-name company, I'm sure cannibalized with used parts in the Bronx, but I didn't care. She told me there were no delivery slots until after New Year, and I said, "I'm taking it with me." By this point I had heated up, and unzipped my coat, so my pink bunny pj's were quite visible, making me look, shall I say, a bit unstable.

I whipped out my credit card and ran up the escalator to pay. I said to the cashier, "Ya got any rope?" and made a makeshift "leash" on the box. I'm sure the employees talked about me when I left, dragging the television behind me like a dead baby seal.

There I am on Broadway. The Friday Before Christmas Eve. In New York. There wasn't a taxi to be found. I start heading home, schlepping the television like a Sherpa climbing Mt. Everest. I'm sweating, and swearing, and then I spot a homeless guy with a cup. "Hey buddy," I say, "I'll give ya ten bucks to help me carry this across Broadway." He snatches the bill, and with superhuman strength hoists the television up and across the wide avenue, then recrosses to his "post."

I'm moving very slowly now, huffing and puffing, still scouring the streets for a cab. An off-duty taxi pulls over, and the guy asks "Do you have a television in that box?" My first impulse is to respond with a snide remark, but I'm too tired to think of one, so I mumble, "Uh-huh." "Get in," he says, and this knight in shining yellow armor puts the box in the trunk, drives me home, and carries the box into the lobby. He won't turn on the meter, and he won't take the 20 bucks I offer as a tip. The Christmas spirit lives. In New York. Unbelievable. I felt like Jimmy Stewart in *It's a Wonderful Life*.

In a New York minute I have the new television set up and the dead one out the door and it's only 11:30, still time for a couple of shorts tonight. Catastrophe averted, I'm back on track. I put the first DVD in, and it's one of the best ones I've seen the entire screening season. Wow. So when people say programmers have the easiest job in the world, don't believe it.

The point is, I could have made any one of several decisions, each of which would have been easier than the one I chose. I could have behaved like Scarlett O'Hara and dealt with it "tomorrow." I could have packed up my DVDs and gone to a friend's house. I could have gone to my office at NYU and watched them on the computer. But I didn't. I didn't take the easy way out, and I had quite a memorable experience because of it.

That's a lot like filmmaking in an industry in which nothing comes easy. When you encounter obstacles, make a decision. It's the stuff you can't predict that forces you to think clearly, quickly, and figure it out. Along the way you too will have amazing new experiences, make great contacts, and "be" a filmmaker.

That's my story.

I hope this book has been filled with stories that inform you and inspire you.

Now take all this information and make it your own.

Make your own films, forge your own path, and tell *your* story.

Swim on!

269

Swim Test:
The Workbook

As you've been reading this book, I hope that you have been contemplating your own projects. Now it's time to pull it all together. This chapter will guide you through exercises to assist you in formulating your ideas, marketing elements, and strategies for festivals and distribution. Here are the topics that will be covered:

1. Creating Your Logline
2. Expanding the Logline into a Short Synopsis
3. Creating Your Tagline
4. Creating Visual Elements
5. Creating the Pitchline
6. Developing Your Festival Plan of Attack
7. Investigating Distribution
8. Designing a Worksheet for Your Short Film's Progress

The order of the elements presented is important. They are building blocks to guide you through to your final evaluation. It is beneficial to do them in sequence rather than jumping around from section to section.

1. Creating Your Logline

What is a logline?

It's a one-sentence description of your project, plain and simple.

You will read or hear the following mantra a thousand times in a thousand different ways from a thousand different people in the industry:

> "You must be able to condense your idea down to one sentence."

The validity of this mantra cannot be stressed enough, even though you'll probably come up with a number of different excuses why you cannot accomplish this task. I've heard a million of them, including:

My plotline is too complicated.

I don't have just one main character.

There are many twists to the storyline.

My film doesn't conform to a standard story or genre.

Open the window and throw all those excuses out of it. Think of your logline as the "seed" of your film from which the story will grow. It is *the* story. It is your starting point. If you don't have a good "seed" that you are comfortable with, it becomes difficult to describe your film to anyone in a clear and succinct manner.

The logline is one of the most critical elements you will create for a short film because it will be used in a number of different and vitally important ways. When you submit a film to a festival, it will be your logline that they use to describe your film. When someone asks you what your film is about, you will respond with your logline. It will be used in your press and marketing materials. A badly written logline weakens the film's impact from the get-go. Take the time to think about your story and develop your logline. Spend some time with it. Live with it and love it. If you're making a short film, your logline better be "short and sweet." With web sites like Withoutabox you "store" all your film's information and that same information is relayed to each submitted festival, so make it solid.

Here's an easy way to get you going:

Start out creating one basic sentence. Do you remember your most dreaded English class in high school? Recall it fondly now, since it will help you to create this logline.

Step 1. It's a _____ (fill in the blank with your genre)

Identify your genre. Stick to one genre, maximum two. Do not say, "It's an action/thriller/comedy." That's too hard for your reader or listener to digest. Pinpoint the genre, which is probably how the term "dramedy" (a dramatic comedy) came into existence. If you're confused about what "type" of film you have, it might be best to think about that before moving on.

Step 2. about a _____ (fill in the blank with your subject)

Is the main character of your film a "45-year-old has-been model" or a "dysfunctional family" or a "group of friends sharing a beach house"? Who are we supposed to pay attention to in your film? Around whom does the story revolve? The subject is your lead-off.

Step 3. who/that _____. (fill in the blank with the "journey" or action)

What is the journey? If your film is 5 minutes or 15 minutes, something happens to the characters, right? So lay it out. Here are some examples:

It's a *comedy* about a *group of different singles sharing a beach house* who *come to blows on the Fourth of July.*

It's a *drama* about a *brother* who *discovers his sister is gay.*

If you were to read any one of these scripts, there is a lot more going on in those films, but it's important to first get to the "seed." But the seed itself is rather boring, don't you think? So once you have your logline written in the above format, now comes the creative part.

Twist it, turn it inside out, and make it visual. One astounding thing I have noticed is that filmmakers make these incredibly creative short films, but then create a logline that is flat and lifeless. It should be enticing. Make someone "want-to-see" it, simply from the logline! Think of the elements (subject/journey) like the tiles on a scrabble board. How can you twist and turn them around to make the story visual and palatable? How many different descriptions can you create from one simple sentence?

Taking one of the above examples, here's how we can breathe more life and a visual quality into it:

Initial logline:

It's a comedy about a group of different singles sharing a beach house who come to blows on the Fourth of July.

Reworked logline:

Slackers and supermodels wind up in an Easthampton share and the fireworks on Fourth of July weekend are not only on the beach.

We've now elaborated on those characters from "a group of different singles" to "slackers and supermodels," which immediately creates a visual identification of the characters and alludes to a conflict without being too specific.

Initial logline:

It's a drama about a brother who discovers his sister is gay.

Reworked logline:

When 16-year-old Todd catches his 18-year-old sister Stephanie making out with her best girlfriend in their parents' basement, does he keep it a secret or use it for blackmail?

Here we elaborate on the potential "fork in the road" journey in addition to giving the characters ages and names, which brings them to life. You should think about leading the logline with your subject, since your reader/listener is then able to quickly grasp who we are supposed to pay attention to.

As with this example, you might also think about posing the logline as a question, such as:

"What happens when a group of slackers and supermodels share a summer house in the Hamptons on Fourth of July weekend?"

Think about action words (verbs) and descriptive words (adjectives) that help the reader/listener visualize your project. Avoid overused words and phrases. If you say you're "edgy," you're not. If we see one more "coming-of-age" story, we'll head for the hills.

You will notice the genre has been dropped from the reworked loglines. It is useful in your initial one-sentence layout, since genre gives clues to tone. A comedy should have a funny logline, for example. A thriller should allude to something unknown. There's no real need to include the genre in the reworked logline, but knowing it helps you to develop the appropriate tone of the logline by keeping it initially in focus.

Helpful Hint
Read the *TV Guide* or the on-screen guide for your cable television provider. Both use loglines to describe the programs. Look for films/programs that seem similar to yours and notice the verbs and adjectives. See when character names are used in the loglines and how they work to establish an immediate character identity.

Exercise #1

Pick up your local newspaper and turn to the movie section. Select three films in release and write a logline for them. Practice makes perfect!

Film title   Logline

_____   _____
_____   _____
_____   _____

Exercise #2

Create a logline for your film idea.
    Begin with the initial format:

It's a _____ (genre)
about a _____ (subject)
who/that _____. (action)

Now rewrite the logline two different ways adding visual descriptive words and twisting it around:

1. _____
   _____
2. _____
   _____

Once you have written your two loglines, say them out loud.

Do they sound natural or awkward? Can you say them in one breath?

If someone asked you what your film was about, could you easily and comfortably speak these loglines?

Use words that you are familiar with and that roll off your tongue. It's not about "writing" as much as it is about planting that visual "seed" with your reader/listener. Keep working on your logline until you are totally happy with it.

2. Expanding the Logline into a Short Synopsis

Whether you submit your film to a festival or to a competition, inevitably you will be asked for a short synopsis. Notice the word "short." There's nothing more detrimental to a short film than a lengthy blow-by-blow plotline synopsis. That's not what it's about. Think of your synopsis as an elaboration of the initial logline. It's your chance to provide a little more information about what happens in the film. You do not have to give away the farm. If your film has a "surprise" ending keep it a secret, just make reference to something unexpected. If you haven't yet given your characters' names, you can do that now. A short synopsis is one paragraph. A paragraph is not one long page without a break. It is the incorporation of your logline plus several additional creative sentences.

I emphasize paragraph length because if someone requests a synopsis, many times they will provide a maximum word count for it, and if you exceed that word count, that means someone else will edit your synopsis. That "someone else" has probably not even seen your film, so do you really want a stranger blindly editing your work? This is an area over which you have control, so create a synopsis that conforms to the word count and presents the best picture of your film. It is still a "tease" to create further interest in your reader.

Using one of the examples previously mentioned:

Sentence 1: Your logline

When 16-year-old Todd catches his 18-year-old sister Stephanie making out with her best girlfriend in their parents' basement, does he keep it a secret or use it for blackmail?

Sentence 2: Elaboration of character(s)

Stephanie and Todd have been battling it out for years, and his adolescent angst has made it even worse.

Sentence 3: Elaboration of plotline
At last Todd has some great dirt on Stephanie and finally has the upper hand.

Sentence 4: The closer
Sibling loyalty and sibling rivalry are put to the test as Todd decides what to do with this juicy information.

Exercise
Here's a starting point for creating your short synopsis:

1. Write your logline. _____
2. Write one sentence that elaborates on a character or characters. _____

3. Write one sentence that discusses some point of action or "the journey." _____

4. Write a closing sentence that makes someone "want-to-see" your film. _____

Now string them together and read it out loud.
Does it make sense?
Is it descriptive?
Does the reader get a sense of "who" and "what" the film is about?

> ### Helpful Hint
> Spend some time in your local video store reading the backs of the DVD cases. Usually there is a short synopsis of the film. See if you can identify the logline and elaboration or notice if the logline has been abandoned and a completely new synopsis is created. Particularly look at films that have a genre similar to yours.

3. Creating Your Tagline

Feature films always use taglines in their marketing campaign, many of which are great at conveying the tone of the film, often using a phrase or play on words. Taglines are generally used on print materials such as one-sheets, postcards, and flyers.

Some taglines are very memorable:

"In space no one can hear you scream"	*Alien*
"Just when you thought it was safe to go back in the water"	*Jaws 2*
"Love means never having to say you're sorry"	*Love Story*

Many taglines are excellent at piquing your interest:

"Just because they serve you doesn't mean that they like you"	*Clerks*
"A lot happens in the middle of nowhere"	*Fargo*
"Watch your back"	*Mean Girls*
"Life is more than the sum of its parts"	*Transamerica*
"He's out to prove he's got nothing to prove"	*Napoleon Dynamite*
"A family on the verge of a breakdown"	*Little Miss Sunshine*

Taglines add a little more punch to your advertising materials. When you think about your tagline, it should be clever. Think about the tone of your film—if you have a comedy, naturally the tagline should be funny. Test it out on other people. Give them your title and your tagline and ask them what kind of image it creates for them.

Helpful Hint
Grab your local newspaper and look at the taglines for current films in release. Notice if they use expressions or quote dialog from the film to lead the reader further into the storyline than the visual image does. Look at the physical placement of the tagline.

Going back to our original two examples, possible taglines could be:
"Flannel vs Fendi"
"To out or not to out"
To help you create your tagline, answer the following questions, thinking back to that first step of the original logline:

1. What is your genre? _____
2. What type of "tone" are you going for in the tagline: _____ (funny, dramatic, mysterious, dark, etc.)
3. What will the crux of the tagline be? _____ (the main character, some element of the story, a vague reference)

Now create two taglines for your film:

1. _____

2. _____

Now that your tagline is written, it's time to create and incorporate the tagline into your visual elements.

4. Creating Visual Elements

Visual elements refer to those materials that you will need for your festival submissions, DVD case, etc. The following hints are based on the premise that you have little or no money and attempt to create what I refer to as "multiuse" items, which means the elements can be used for a variety of purposes, not simply for one particular film festival or screening. You don't want to keep reprinting these items, so make them once and use them forever.

Design your "look."

Consistency of design is very important when you create your visual elements. The look and visual image should carry from postcard to press kit to flyer to DVD case. They establish the film's identity and maintain that identity throughout its life. You don't want one image for the postcard, another for the press kit, etc. This dilutes the impact of the film and detracts from the recognition factor.

The first things you want to think about are the title treatment and/or "logo" of the film, which can be carried from the physical main credits or be a new creation entirely. This is where all those creative friends of yours come in. Film is a collaborative medium. You don't need to do everything yourself, you just need to find someone who will do it well for you. Do you have a friend who's a terrific graphic designer? Come up with a general concept, give them direction, and see what they come up with.

Helpful Hint

Nobody rides the bus for free. That means that nobody does any-thing for you for nothing. Pay them a dollar, sign a contract, and be done with it. You don't want anyone who "does you a favor" to come back to you down the road and ask for money. Even if they are your best friend/boyfriend/girlfriend now, they may not be later, so you want to protect yourself.

The title is an important aspect of your visual elements. It should be prominently placed and in a font and size that are easy to read. Be careful of those strangely italic fonts; if you have to work at reading it, it doesn't work! Is there a physical element of your film that you can "nest" with the title? For example, if the key scene is a birthday party, perhaps you can use a blown-out candle or a half-eaten piece of cake next to the title. This element then becomes your "logo." Think out of the box on this, and come up with something that is visually enticing. Color is also important. Think bright and eye-catching. Go back to that color wheel from art class. What colors go well with, in front of, and behind others?

280

What are some key images or scenes from your film?

_____

List some visuals that can be created from those images or scenes:

_____

Here's one more word about titles. Many feature films tend to stick to the two-word title; it's easy to remember, and thus more adaptable for marketing, and fits nicely on all materials. Do not feel that you have to conform to this with a short film. Independent films are "different," so a title like *Lock, Stock, and Two Smoking Barrels* is a great indie title, but would not necessarily work for a studio feature. Clever and quirky works for indie film; do not try to emulate that *Basic Instinct*, *Fatal Attraction* two-word scenario. Think more about *Welcome to the Dollhouse* or *My Big Fat Greek Wedding*.

The one-sheet

If you want to work in this industry, you will immediately cease and desist from using the term "movie poster." The proper industry title is "one-sheet," and its origins come from advertising and refer to the physical standard size of the shadow box that you see in the theaters. You will normally create a singular one-sheet design that will morph into your press kit, postcard, flyer, DVD case, etc.

You have two basic choices in the one-sheet visuals. You can either be "plain and simple" and use your logo/tagline on a good background or use a digital shot from the film itself. Think about Hollywood feature releases and those films that have used immediately identifiable logos: the dinosaur from *Jurassic* Park or the *Batman* logo. Does this type of look work for your type of film?

If you want to use a photographic image, hopefully during your shoot you took digital photos, so pick one that looks great. Don't drive

SWIMMING UPSTREAM: *A Lifesaving Guide to Short Film Distribution* yourself crazy with this for a short film. In fact, you should *design* a one-sheet, but they are expensive to make, so you may want to just do the design and then go "straight to postcard."

Helpful Hint
Go to a big multiplex movie theater and spend some time wandering around the lobby, looking at all the one-sheets. Do they make you want to see the film? If not, what turns you off about them? Again, pay attention to genre, but remember, you are not a feature, so keep it simple.

Postcards are one of the most economical and multiuse items you can create. They are relatively cheap for a large quantity, and if you design them with the following thoughts in mind, you will be able to make the most out of them.

The "visual" side of the postcard should be clean and easy to read. Be careful of dark backgrounds, and particularly white text on a black background. Make sure your title is prominent on the postcard so the reader knows exactly what film it is. The reverse side of the postcard (that is, the "mailer" side) should be left entirely blank except for your contact information. This way you can make labels for each screening that you have, or use them for personal "notes" to include in a formal envelope mailing, and as your film gets accepted into various film festivals, you can increasingly include that information. When you create labels, it is more aesthetically pleasing to use clear-background labels rather than white ones. They are a little more expensive, but the invisibility factor improves the overall look of the postcard to the recipient.

The postcards can then be used as "reminders" for industry people once you have your screening slot, can be pasted on the front of a folder for a press kit cover, distributed at various functions, etc.

Press kits

You will also need a press kit, and keep in mind that "less is more" here. The basics of a short film press kit should include the following:

1. One page that lists the film, shooting format, running time, log-line, and short synopsis.
2. One page that contains the bios of the director, producer, and writer. You can also include bios of your cast if they help as

a marketing tool. (Please note these should emphasize your professional credentials, not that you were born in a small town in Idaho. They should be written in the third person, identifying the person first by entire name and for the duration by last name or pronoun: "Joe Smith began his career... Smith has made two short films... He hopes to...")

3. Cast and crew listing that should replicate your end credits.
4. Any previous press materials or festival acceptances/awards. Do not include links in this material; reprint the articles and include them.
5. Digital images of the director and from the film itself on a disc.
6. An interesting inclusion for a press kit is a "Director's Statement." It's always great to know what the inspiration was for the film, an experience from the film, or something personal. This statement should be written in the first person. ("When I started thinking about the film...")

A note about the press kit "container" or folder: There are many options for this, but be careful with black glossy stock because it gets smudged and looks "old" very quickly. If you choose a color folder, it should complement the colors in your postcard or logo look. You can use a plain color folder and paste your postcard on the front.

5. Creating the Pitchline

What is a pitchline?

A pitchline is the "meeting" of two other projects and is usually phrased as in "A" meets "B." I like to say that if two films had sex, your film is the "baby," so what are the parents like?

Pitchlines are important for feature films, but much less appropriate for short films. Why? You can't really compare a 20-minute short film with two features that have come out, nor, realistically, can you compare your short film to other short films because most people haven't seen the other short films, so the pitchline becomes much less relevant. However, let's say you have a short film about an awkward teenager. It might be appropriate to use a pitchline such as:

Napoleon Dynamite meets *Welcome to the Dollhouse*

The most important things to remember with a pitchline are:

1. Make sure the comparison films you used were successful! Even if your subject/tone matches a film that wasn't successful, why on earth compare yourself to a film that didn't make money?

2. Do not compare yourself to monumental, classic, or historic films like *Star Wars* or *Casablanca*, since you want to be current with your comparisons (the past five years max), and it's really ridiculous to think of your short film as the next *Star Wars*.

3. Stay medium specific. If you're pitching a film, use two comparison films, not a television series or show. If you MUST compare yourself to another medium, use only one side of the pitchline, the other side should be medium specific, such as *Entourage* meets *Stand by Me*.

4. Your pitchline does not need to be literal. You can cross genres, subjects, etc. The pitchline is like a "recipe" for your film, a little of this and a little of that. Filmmakers get stymied at this point and say, "I can't think of any other films in the universe that are like mine." Be creative and don't be so confined with your concept of what your film is like.

Helpful Hint

Two free web sites for box-office data are boxofficemojo.com and boxofficeguru.com. Peruse these web sites and think about all the films listed, look at the films, and think about your project and what, if anything, they have in common.

Exercise #1

List six films that your film can be compared to and what each film has in common with yours.

1. _____
2. _____
3. _____
4. _____
5. _____
6. _____

Exercise #2

Now pick the two that make the most sense to you and create your pitchline:

It's _____ meets _____

Swim Test: The Workbook

6. Developing Your Festival Plan of Attack

As previously stated, for the short filmmaker, the film festival circuit is the most likely place where a short film will find its initial audience. In the festival chapter of this book, we have covered all the pros/cons and how to figure out the best festivals for submission. Once you have done that, the following exercises and worksheet will help you figure out "the order of things" and keep you organized and on target as you go through the process.

After you have thoroughly researched festivals and have some idea of the ones you are most interested in, answering the following questions will further hone your goals:

Exercises

1. In my "dream world" the festival that will have my short film's world premiere is _____

2. If I get rejected from that festival, my second choice world premiere festival is _____

3. Two places in the world that I've always wanted to visit are _____ and _____

4. The film festivals and dates for those two cities are _____ and _____

5. My top five festivals and their dates are

_____

_____

_____

_____

_____

One of the most overwhelming tasks for a filmmaker is keeping track of everything he/she has done regarding festivals. Deadlines cannot be missed, so you need to create a way to make certain that you know what's happening with your festival submissions so you can move on to other festivals based on acceptance/rejection and new ideas that come to you.

Although we certainly are a digital world, with most correspondence being sent via email or on a disc, create both a digital file and a physical paper folder for each festival you plan to submit to, and make a hard copy of each document, piece of correspondence, the rules and regulations, rejection/acceptance letters to be contained in this folder.

This will save you from unnecessary stress when you're trying to get to that information online or print something and your Internet goes down or your computer crashes. I've received many panicked calls from filmmakers one day prior to the deadline with last-minute questions and concerns, and this will at the very least eliminate that drama. I've also received emails from filmmakers saying, "I spoke to someone, but I don't know who." If you call a festival, ask for the name of the person with whom you are speaking. Make a note of it, this way if you ever have to refer to the conversation, you have some "evidence."

Once you have your game plan solidified, you can use the following worksheet to recap your strategy. The only thing you have to do is remember to fill it in, and keep it current.

Worksheet for Festival Strategy

Date of festival	
Festival name	
Location	
Early submission deadline/fee	
Final submission deadline/fee	
Date submitted	
Method of submission/tracking number	
Method of fee payment	
Accepted or rejected	
Contact name/phone/email	
Materials requested	
Deadline to submit materials	
Materials sent	

7. Investigating Distribution

The life span for your short film is basically 1–2 years, and your focus should be getting that film (and you) as much exposure and visibility possible. I hope the essays in this book have given you a better sense of how your film will work in different arenas so that you can retain the control of being the ultimate decision maker of your film's path.

Your goal at this point is to go on an investigative mission. That mission is to discover where your short film has the best chance of success. It is much easier today to accomplish this mission, since all of the information is available at your fingertips online. Think about which platforms (realistically) are right for your film and detail them.

Internet sites

Site_____ URL _____
Submission rules/notes _____
Submission information _____
Why my film "fits" _____
Perform a similar exercise for each of the platforms listed below.

Domestic broadcast
International broadcast
Compilations
Competitions
Mobile

8. Designing a Worksheet for Your Short Film's Progress

To keep on point with your short film in general, you should create some sort of tracking worksheet that will give you an overview of what you're doing. Listed below are line items that you may choose to include or exclude in this worksheet. Each film is different, but once you have it in the can, you still need to be its parent/guardian and have that overview of its progress in mind all the time.

Helpful Hint
You will meet many people on your filmmaking journey who will give you their business card. On the back of the card, write the date you met them, where you met them, and any follow up, such as "call after festival" or "send screener." Trust me, you will never remember on your own.

Create a worksheet from the elements that work for you.

Physical production information
Running time
Shooting format
Screening format(s)
Film festival budget
Film festival expenses to date (itemized)
Press materials budget
Press materials expenses to date (itemized)
Duplication budget
Duplication expenses to date (itemized)

Contacts
Sales agents approached (with contact information)
Buyers approached (with contact information)
Screeners sent/date sent
Meetings held (details)

Potential revenue sources
Festivals submitted
Festivals accepted
Awards/prizes received
Competitions submitted
Web sites submitted
Broadcast submitted

There you have it. Don't freak out. Don't think it's impossible.
Use all the information and tools presented in this book to help you begin, or continue, your journey as a filmmaker.

Index

Index

293

297

Index

299

302

303

About the Author

Sharon Badal is Short Film Programmer for the Tribeca Film Festival, screening over 1500 submissions annually without losing her mind. She has been with the festival since its inception and has produced special projects for various Tribeca entities since 1999, including the 2005 Sloan Film Summit for the Tribeca Film Institute.

Sharon is a faculty member at New York University's renowned Tisch School of the Arts in the Kanbar Institute of Film and Television, teaching undergraduate courses in what she refers to as "the beginning and the end" of the filmmaking process—*Producing Essentials* and *Film Distribution & Marketing*. In addition, Sharon team-teaches *The Business of Producing* for NYU's prestigious Stern School of Business.

As the self-proclaimed "empress of short film," Sharon has served on the regional jury for the 2005 Student Academy Awards and on the juries for the 2006 Palm Springs International Festival of Short Films and the 2007 Worldwide Short Film Festival in Toronto. She has been invited to speak at numerous industry events and in short film panel discussions.

For the past four years, Sharon has dedicated much of her free time to working for The Leary Firefighters Foundation, founded by actor Denis Leary. In 2007, she worked primarily on The Foundation's New Orleans Firehouse Restoration Project as well as on its annual fundraiser, The BASH for New York's Bravest.

From her humble beginnings at age 14 as an usher in her father's movie theater, Sharon went on to hold executive positions in distribution for United Artists/MGM, Warner Bros., and Orion Pictures and has worked on many live events, including projects for Walt Disney Feature Animation, ShowEast, Cinema Expo International, and the Independent Feature Film Market. She received her B.F.A. in film and television production and her M.A. in cinema studies and business, both from New York University.

She loves Coney Island, searching for alien life, and chocolate in any form. Sharon lives in New York City, and there's no place else she'd rather be.